Ewan McGregor

BRIAN PENDREIGH

ORION

An Orion Paperback
First published in Great Britain by Orion Media in 1998
This paperback edition published in 1999 by
Orion Books Ltd,
Orion House, 5 Upper St Martin's Lane,
London WC2H 9EA

A CIP catalogue record for this book
is available from the British Library.

ISBN 0 75282 595 X

Typeset by Selwood Systems, Midsomer Norton

Printed and bound in by
Clays Ltd, St Ives plc

Contents

For Jenny, Ewen and Catherine

Acknowledgements

AN ENORMOUS THANK-YOU is owed to hundreds of individuals and organisations who helped in the research and preparation of this book. They range from international film companies in California to a little old lady, who my wife met by chance in the street in Crieff and who not only remembered Ewan as a boy, but also his uncle, Denis Lawson. That's Crieff for you. I extend particular thanks both to the people of the town of Crieff, who shared their reminiscences, time and hospitality, and to my wife, Jenny Pendreigh, who acted as my advisor and research assistant, spending days transcribing interview tapes while doing her best to keep the coffee coming and the confectionery rationed. Special thanks also to Ewen McDonald, for his advice and his indexing skills, and to my agent Giles Gordon for his encouragement and his negotiating skills.

This book effectively evolved from an article on Ewan's childhood and teenage years, which I wrote for the *Scotsman* in October 1997, although it might be argued that it really began four years earlier when I visited a Glasgow industrial estate which was serving as a makeshift studio for a low-budget comedy-thriller called *Shallow Grave*. That was my introduction not just to Ewan, but to director Danny Boyle, producer Andrew Macdonald and writer John Hodge, though our paths would cross time and again in the years to come, in Scotland, in Cannes, and in Leicester one snowy winter's day when they unveiled their follow-up movie, something to do with trains.

Ewan was not there, he was too busy having a baby.

In the course of my preliminary work I became the first journalist to conduct a full interview with Carol McGregor, Ewan's mother and personal assistant, to whom I owe a continued debt of gratitude.

A special thank-you to Morrison's Academy for their ongoing co-operation and for the use of photographs and, specifically, to Gordon Wilson and Hector McMillan. Thanks once again to everyone to whom I talked during the research for my *Scotsman* profile, some of whom I have spoken to repeatedly in the course of writing the book – principally Lynn Bains, Malcolm Copland, Vicky Grant, Molly Innes, James Kerr (both of them), Kenneth Rea, the *Strathearn Herald* and last, but by no means least, the Rev. Henry Tait, who plucked the six-year-old Ewan from obscurity and made him the star of the church's Christmas show.

Those early inquiries were the beginning of what was to turn into months of full-time research, made easier by the contributions of some key individuals and organisations, including Jonathan Altaras, Ewan's former agent, who lent his house in France for Ewan's wedding; James Cosmo, who played his father in *Trainspotting, Emma* and the short film *Sleeping with the Fishes*; Colin Gregg, who directed Ewan in *Kavanagh QC* and spent many hours drinking with him and the woman who was to become Mrs Ewan McGregor; Todd Haynes, Ewan's director on *Velvet Goldmine*; Jane Horrocks who co-starred with the actor in two very different projects, an episode of the American TV horror programme *Tales from the Crypt* and the film of her theatre triumph *The Rise and Fall of Little Voice*; veteran entertainer Roy Hudd, whose stories of the old days amused Ewan during the lengthy production of his breakthrough TV series *Lipstick on Your Collar*; Lorna Mitchell at Perth library; Alan Morrison, editor of the *List* magazine; and Peter Mullan, who threatened Ewan's life with a crowbar in *Shallow Grave* and with heroin in *Trainspotting*.

It looked at one stage as if Ewan would authorise the book, but eventually he decided against doing so, leaving many of our mutual acquaintances in a difficult position. Some individuals, including one of Ewan's relatives, chose to speak to me un-attributably. They know who they are. Thanks again.

I am indebted to the following for interviews and services rendered: Nick Allott, Harry Ashmall, BBC Archives, BBC World Service, the British Council, the British Film Institute library, Bill Bryden, Darryl Butcher at Laurie Bellew PR, Edinburgh city library services, Fife College, Figment Films, the General Register Office for Scotland, Donald Florence, Bill Forsyth, George Hall, Gordon House, Kate Iles at Compulsive Viewing, Martyn James, Stratford Johns, Tom Lawrence, Nicholas Jones, Phyllida Law, Lt. Col. S. J. Lindsay of The Black Watch, Lucas-film, Janet McBain at the Scottish Film and Television Archive, McDonald & Rutter, Sandy McEvoy at Eastbourne Borough Council's Film Unit, Maggie MacMillan, John Millar, Arthur Millie at Salisbury Playhouse, the National Library of Scotland, Hilary Norrish, Perth Theatre, Otto Plaschkes, Alyse Pozzo, who runs the Ewan McGregor Internet site at www.geocities.com/~ewanmcgregor, and to whom I am indebted for enabling me to see Ewan's episode in the American cable television programme *Tales from the Crypt* when all other avenues turned into blind alleys, Olivia Pugh at the Society of London Theatre, Scottish Screen, Meriam Soopee and Bob Wiegman.

It is impossible to list every person and organisation that helped along the way, though I would like to thank them all now. Thanks also to the various individuals whom I have interviewed over the years and whose comments now find their way into this volume, and to all the other reporters, interviewers and critics whose work has helped provide me with insight, understanding, comments, facts, leads and, if nothing else, occasional amusement.

Prologue: A Trip to the Cinema

GEORGE LUCAS'S *STAR WARS* may have been just a movie to some. But it was *the* defining moment in the lives of two little Scottish boys, nine-year-old Colin McGregor and his cheeky-faced wee brother Ewan. Little did they know it then, but *Star Wars* would shape their futures and determine the course of their adult lives.

Star Wars is an adventure film set in outer space, with aliens and robots and hi-tech light-sabres, but at heart it is also a gloriously old-fashioned battle between Good and Evil, offering moral certainty in a world of turmoil and increasing moral ambivalence. *Star Wars* opened in the United States in the spring of 1977, but it was not until the end of that year that it was released in London, by which time it was already the highest-grossing film ever. The people of Tayside, where Colin and Ewan McGregor lived, would have to wait another couple of months before the film finally made it to their screens.

Even before its world première, Colin and Ewan had thirsted for information about Princess Leia, Luke Skywalker, Han Solo and Obi-Wan Kenobi. From Rochdale to Rio, kids all over the world were desperate to see *Star Wars* and join in the adventure. But Colin and Ewan had an extra reason to look forward to seeing the movie. Their uncle was in it.

Although Denis Lawson is probably best known for his role as the hotel-keeper, Urquhart, in Bill Forsyth's lyrical comedy-drama *Local Hero*, he was in all three of the original *Star Wars* movies, playing the role of Wedge. His nephews would see him pilot an X-wing fighter plane and do battle with the forces of the evil Galactic Empire, alongside Luke Skywalker.

Uncle Denis, Ewan's mother's brother, had always been a highly exotic element in the life of the McGregor boys. Like his nephews, he had grown up in the Tories' Perthshire heartland (when the Tories still had Scottish heartlands). But now he lived in a galaxy far, far away, called London. Whenever he came back to Perthshire for a visit, he stood out from the locals as surely as Darth Vader would at a Woman's Guild coffee morning. Other local men wore business suits or functional waxed jackets and welly boots. Long-haired Denis dressed in sheepskin waistcoats, beads and sandals. Ewan says that Denis actually handed out flowers in the High Street to bemused passers-by, but it may be that Ewan's memory – or his sense of humour – is playing tricks. One thing was certain however – Denis was different. And Ewan, who already liked nothing better than to attract attention, was excited by that difference.

Ewan was not exactly sure what an actor was, but he did know that actors did not have to be just one person, like everybody else, but got to be a whole series of people in turn – like children in a game. And people – children and grown-ups – would come to see them do it; they would watch and they would applaud. The McGregor family had already seen Denis at Perth Theatre. He had been Simple Simon in *Babes in the Wood* – though Ewan himself was just a babe then – and had been Able in *Robinson Crusoe*. On one occasion Denis even called the boys up on stage. But *Star Wars* was something else entirely; *Star Wars* was a film, and Uncle Denis would be up there, larger than life, splashed right across the cinema screen in glorious Technicolor.

Colin and Ewan lived with their parents, Carol and Jim, in the town of Crieff, 18 miles outside Perth. Its imposing old stone villas, hydropathic hotel and boarding school nestle between the River Earn and the foothills of the Scottish Highlands. Crieff is a quiet little town built on history and tradition, where the siting of a new bus stop is front-page news in the *Strathearn Herald*; the sort of town which, in an age of increasing automation, still employs a human attendant at the public toilets in the town square.

The trip to see *Star Wars* at the Odeon cinema in Perth was to be a grand family outing, a birthday treat for Colin, as well as a celebration of Denis's elevation to the big time. Included in the party were Denis's parents – Ewan's grandparents – who had a jeweller's shop in Crieff High Street, and Denis's granny, Ewan's great-grandmother. The excitement of the big day was such that, even years later, as a full-grown man, Ewan can remember the feeling of anticipation, standing outside school, waiting to be picked up. The short car journey between Crieff and Perth seemed to take forever, but at last they were there, installed in their seats, waiting for the house lights to dim and the big picture to begin. The popcorn and Kia-Ora had been bought, the adverts had run their course and a buzz of excitement ran around the cinema as the opening prologue scrolled upwards and drifted off into the far reaches of space.

Those opening words 'A long time ago in a galaxy far, far away ...' have become part of cinema legend. Although the six-year-old Ewan was too young to follow the written account of the war between the Galactic Empire and the rebels, he was swept up, from the start, in the colour and flow of the film. Like countless millions around the world he was charmed by the comedy of the opening scene between C-3PO, the paranoid android, forever bemoaning his lot, and his little chum R2-D2, who looks like a metal dustbin and communicates in a series of electronic beeps. There was a princess called Leia; heroes called Luke Skywalker and Han Solo; a menagerie of strange space creatures; Darth Vader, a wheezing villain encased in black; and a strange old man by the name of Obi-Wan Kenobi.

Carried along by the action, Colin and Ewan barely had time to wonder when Uncle Denis would appear on screen ... which is just as well, as he does not turn up until the climactic aerial battle, when a squadron of X-wing fighters speed in formation towards the huge Death Star, which looks more like a metal moon than a spacecraft. 'Look at the size of that thing,' gasps Uncle Denis, in pilot's orange overalls and matching visor, behind the controls of one of the aircraft. The action is fast and furious as the aerial combat begins, cutting between Luke Skywalker, Uncle Denis and the other pilots. When Luke is unable to shake an enemy TIE fighter off his tail, Uncle Denis comes to his rescue, blasts his pursuer and saves him. Luke pilots his fighter into the Death Star itself, with the spirit of Obi-Wan Kenobi coolly, oh-so-coolly, urging him to 'use the Force' rather than his electronic targeting device. He fires his torpedoes into the exhaust port and turns the Death Star into a supernova.

Luke Skywalker saves the universe. And all because Uncle Denis had saved Luke Skywalker. It is a pity, then, that Lucasfilm spelt Denis's name wrongly on the credits – sticking an extra 'n' in Denis – and that they felt it necessary to have another actor to rerecord his lines in an American accent, but these were more the sort of details that a mother might worry about rather than his adoring nephews. And his character was one of the few fighter pilots to survive the combat, enabling him to return in the sequels.

'I decided to become an actor,' says Ewan, 'even though I had no idea what that meant.'

He would find out. In due course he would take up the light-sabre, and star in the next generation of *Star Wars* movies. And his brother Colin? He too was inspired by his uncle's example. Colin joined the Royal Air Force.

Two little boys went to the pictures and saw their uncle acting the part of a fighter pilot. One little boy became an actor and the other little boy became a fighter pilot. What follows is the story of one of those two little boys and how he fulfilled his destiny.

1
On Teenage Bedroom Walls

SHIVERING IN A dripping wet tee-shirt, arms crossed and hands tucked into the warmth of his oxters, a crew-cut Ewan McGregor stares down from thousands of teenage bedroom walls – just as posters of another 'twentysomething' actor had decorated walls of previous generations – posters of a young man with a cigarette in his mouth, a look of child-like innocence and bewilderment on his face and the collar of his overcoat turned up against the rain, as he made his way along a cold, wet American boulevard. Ewan McGregor was the new James Dean. He was the epitome of cool; a nihilistic, junkie hero for a junk generation, no matter that the vast majority of Ewan's fans were no more likely to inject themselves with heroin than James Dean's fans were to martyr themselves to the cause of doomed youth by accelerating their cars into the path of an oncoming vehicle.

Ewan had the outward appearance of a rebel. By Crieff standards, he *was* a rebel: the boy who painted his hair red, the boy who dropped out of Morrison's Academy and made a living busking on the London underground. But that was about as far as it went. James Dean really was a rebel without a cause. He lived and died like a character in one of his own movies. Ewan McGregor may have presented Britain with an image of a rebel without a cause, but look at that *Trainspotting* image and you will see, not defeat and bewilderment in Ewan's face, but resilience. At other times his handsome features display a happy, cheeky, boyish confidence and quiet determination.

Ewan McGregor may have seemed like a rebel without a cause, but he did have a cause, a cause on which he remained totally focused. Himself. Or, more specifically, his ambitions as an actor. He enjoyed a pint, or eight, with the rest, but after throwing up in the car park he would clear his head and continue the single-minded pursuit of his goal. Ewan has never so much as tried drugs, even when his role in *Trainspotting* might have given him justification to do so in the name of research. He says, rather sweetly, naïvely, even misguidedly, that he likes his parents too much to upset them by taking drugs. He has never been arrested and maintains he has never done anything criminal. 'I was never hard enough to do anything criminal,' he says, warming the cockles of grannies' hearts everywhere. 'Such a nice laddie.'

James Dean starred in only three films, before his death at the age of 24, the same age Ewan was when he made *Trainspotting*. It was only Ewan's fourth starring role in films. But at this point the careers of the Fifties Rebel and the Nineties Rebel diverge dramatically. James Dean killed himself; Ewan McGregor made movies back to back to back. Most stars make one a year, two at a stretch. Ewan made ten in less than three years.

'I've always been fiercely driven and I'm still driven now, maybe now more than ever, because I can't stop,' he said in 1997, by which time his star was outshining most in the cinematic firmament. 'They keep giving me scripts and I keep fucking doing them. I can't say no.' In another interview, he drew parallels with his childhood hero. 'My dreams were all of old Hollywood, my fantasies about acting were all like being Jimmy Stewart and belonging to a studio and making four movies a year. In a way I'm kind of doing that by knocking out three or four a year anyway. But I've been very lucky to work with some amazing, talented people.' It was as if he feared that the offers of work might suddenly dry up; his backlog of movies still in the release pipeline were some sort of insurance policy against the failure of any individual project, the under-performance of, for example, *A Life Less Ordinary*, the third film from the *Shallow Grave* and *Trainspotting* team, in which his protagonist's life is guided by not one but two interventionist angels. It seems even angels had become subject to inflationary pressure in the half-century since Frank Capra and James Stewart made *It's a Wonderful Life*.

Ewan was a kidnapper in *A Life Less Ordinary*, but his charm shone through, as always. James Dean had charm, but it was a restless, dangerous charm, where Ewan's charm is easy and comfortable. And, even as a kidnapper, there was more than the odd hint of decency. It is the kidnap victim, played by Cameron Diaz, who makes the running in the kidnap demands and forces Ewan's character, Robert, to take part in a bank raid. Robert refuses even to maintain a pretence that they might shoot someone, and ends up getting shot himself.

Roles that include kidnappers and junkies, drinking bouts that end with the star throwing up outside the pub and a tendency to witter on about masturbation and the size of his penis in press interviews cannot disguise the essential small-town decency of Bedford Falls and Crieff. Ewan McGregor shares Jimmy Dean's status as a youthful icon, while refusing to become an ambassador for doomed youth. His is a message of hope, not hopelessness. He shares the decency of that other Jimmy, Jimmy Stewart, that most principled, human and occasionally troubled of film characters, with the gangly walk and much-imitated drawling speech. In Ewan McGregor, Jimmy Dean co-exists with Jimmy Stewart.

Ewan played several sports at school, including rugby; he enjoyed riding horses and he loved to romp around the Knock, the wooded hill behind Crieff Hydro Hotel, pretending to be a soldier on a secret mission and getting up to mischief with fireworks and fir cones and passers-by. But, equally, he appreciated the joys of settling down in front of the television and watching old movies. He would watch three or four a day at weekends or during holidays, if his parents let him. He particularly liked the old Ealing comedies, such as *Kind Hearts and Coronets*, *The Ladykillers* and *Whisky Galore!*; a series that managed to celebrate and undermine the British establishment at one and the same time. His favourite actor, however, at a time when other kids hero-worshipped Sylvester Stallone and

Clint Eastwood, was James Stewart. You might expect a young boy, particularly one who liked horses, to favour Stewart's classic westerns, like *Broken Arrow*, *The Naked Spur* and *The Man from Laramie*, but Ewan was never a great western fan, preferring comedies and dramas. 'If it was black and white and romantic and soppy,' says Ewan, 'it was good enough for me.' Among his favourite James Stewart films were *Harvey*, in which the star played an alcoholic called Elwood P. Dowd, with an imaginary six-foot rabbit as a companion, and *It's a Wonderful Life*, Frank Capra's sentimental tale, with Stewart as family man and general do-gooder George Bailey. It is set in the nondescript little town of Bedford Falls, but it could be set in any community where decent people live decent lives, where everyone knows everyone else and where family values still hold sway. It could be Bedford Falls, it could be Crieff. The altruistic George has fallen on hard times. Faced with financial ruin and disgrace, he contemplates suicide. And ... it is Christmas time. Blub. But a most unlikely angel called Clarence comes along and intervenes.

From an early age Ewan displayed a vivid imagination and a flair for entertaining. He loved role-playing. After the family outing to see Uncle Denis Lawson in *Star Wars*, Ewan and his brother spent days re-enacting the film. Over and over again, they would play out the duel between Darth Vader and Obi-Wan Kenobi, using their own toy light-sabres. They collected *Star Wars* figures and in due course they got the *Star Wars* films on video and watched them again and again, memorising and anticipating lines like 'Watch your back, Luke', 'Fighters above you, coming in' and of course 'May the Force be with you'. But Ewan's favourite character was neither Luke Skywalker nor Wedge. It was Leia, the plucky princess, memorably played by Debbie Reynolds's daughter Carrie Fisher, with a hairstyle that made her look as if she had a circular loaf of bread stuck on each side of her head. Ewan enjoyed a light-sabre duel, but even as a child he demonstrated the sweet, sensitive, some might even say feminine, side of his personality.

Ewan's parents, Jim and Carol, were both teachers. Jim was a PE teacher at the fee-paying Morrison's Academy. Carol taught in the local state high school. They were not especially well-off, certainly not by Crieff standards. But they were eager to do the best for their children and sent them to Morrison's Academy, scrimping and saving to pay the reduced fees charged for children of staff. Colin was a model pupil in the disciplined and demanding environment of the academy. He excelled on the sports field and in the classroom, and was school captain in his final year. Ewan found it difficult to live up to his elder brother's achievements and to family expectations. He left school without even sitting his Highers, the equivalent of England's A-Levels. Colin was the achiever, clearly destined for great things. Ewan was the drop-out.

'I didn't hate school,' he says. 'I just didn't get it.' Colin was the paragon, Ewan was the rebel. 'I just remember not liking many of the teachers,' he says. 'They said I had attitude problems.' There was conflict at school over his lack of effort in subjects which did not interest him and over his hair, a bone of contention for just about every schoolboy in the Sixties and Seventies. To a soundtrack of Billy Idol's 'Rebel Yell', he would spike his hair in the mornings. 'He was always a bit different,' says his mother Carol. 'He always had a kind of style of his own.' One immediate benefit of leaving Morrison's Academy was the freedom to do weird things with his hair, like painting it red or shaving almost all of it off. But it was not just in his appearance that he was different, not just in his appearance that he took a leaf out of his uncle's book. Ewan entertained wild notions of becoming an actor, he did a one-year national certificate course in Fife and went off to seek fame and fortune down south in London. While Colin was at Edinburgh University, reading Agriculture, a good, useful subject for a Perthshire country boy, Ewan was singing at Bank underground station, songs of his own composition ... about how much he missed Scotland.

By this time Ewan also had a place at the prestigious Guildhall School of Music and Drama. He left Guildhall early too, but it was to go straight into the lead role in Dennis Potter's TV mini-series *Lipstick on Your Collar*. That was in 1992 and he has never stopped working since. *Shallow Grave* did not seem a particularly propitious project at the time, but it was acclaimed the best British movie of the year. *Trainspotting*, the same team's adaptation of Irvine Welsh's cult novel, was hailed the best British movie of the decade. It became one of the most successful British films ever at the international box-office and it turned Ewan from a promising young actor into a star and, more than that, an icon, one of the defining images of the age.

After *Trainspotting*, Ewan was the coolest actor on the bedroom wall, but his appeal was by no means restricted to teenagers. James Dean is remembered for his troubled teens in *Rebel Without a Cause* and *East of Eden* and was less successful when called upon to extend his range in the overblown Texan soap opera *Giant*. Ewan has not however been restricted to portraits of contemporary youth. He has been playing costume drama since his schooldays and continued to do so on film and television. He was lucky too that even though the character of Renton in *Trainspotting* is a junkie and a thief, he inevitably retains Ewan's handsome looks, beneath the detox pallor, and Ewan's winning smile. Renton is a junkie, but he is not a loser.

Ewan's looks and his choice of parts helped ensure his appeal extended beyond teenage audiences. While kids went crazy over him in *Trainspotting*, their parents were enjoying his performances in *Brassed Off* and *Emma*. But his biggest fan of all is the camera. The camera loves him and that is the test of a true screen star, as opposed to a good actor. His star quality shines out from beneath a succession of breathtakingly awful haircuts that would have prematurely curtailed the careers of most aspiring actors. And when he cut almost all of it off, in *Trainspotting*, he hit paydirt. Hollywood and international stardom beckoned. He was about to become Scotland's biggest film star since a dinner-suited former milkman sat down at a casino table and announced himself as 'Bond, James Bond' more than 30 years earlier. Ewan was better placed than most British actors to become an A-list Hollywood star. Kenneth Branagh is a better actor, but, even in his twenties, he was too much of a 'luvvy' to capture the young audience. Branagh might make a brilliant Henry V, but he could never have played Mark Renton. Gary Oldman and Richard E. Grant are good actors and they have made some pretty hip movies in their time – Grant was after all Withnail, the ultimate hip character – but they were too intense, too grungy, they lacked Ewan's looks, and they lacked his charm. Daniel Day Lewis is enormously handsome, but again too intense to be truly cool. Renton may have been a junkie, but he retained a romantic innocence and when things went wrong his Mum was there to help. Withnail would not have looked for, nor tolerated, help from Mum.

Ewan remained very close to his real-life family in Perthshire. He was raised to believe in the family. And, at an age when most stars would be playing the field, accepting the sexual favours of young admirers, Ewan married and became a daddy. Crieff was, indeed is, like many other small middle-class Scottish towns that still believe in old-fashioned values. Such communities are not entirely beyond change, but they change slowly. Perhaps even more ingrained in such communities than the importance of the family and the church is the Calvinist work ethic, a philosophy that can be summarised in just three words – work, work and work. Maybe we should enlarge on the philosophy a little – 'work, work, work – and do it now'. Busking, for Ewan, was work. Drumming in a pop group was work. Writing songs was work. He continued to do voice-overs for television commercials even after he became a star. He went on working solidly, going from one film to the next, even when he found the perfect insurance policy, a no-risk project (no risk to him anyway), that would build on the success of *Trainspotting*, a guaranteed international box-office Number One, with two more to follow.

Star Wars, *The Empire Strikes Back* and *Return of the Jedi* were always intended as the middle trilogy of three, but George Lucas was diverted on to other projects after the third film, pushing back the frontiers of electronic effects and providing the ground-breaking, computer-generated dinosaurs for *Jurassic Park*. The years slipped by and every now and then speculation would intensify about another *Star Wars* film. Ewan was shooting the glam-rock drama *Velvet Goldmine*, in Spring 1997, when he got a phone call to say that Lucas's spaceship was finally about to take off once more and inviting him on board as the young Obi-Wan Kenobi, the character originally played by the great Alec Guinness and reprised by little Ewan back home in Crieff after that eventful family outing to the Odeon in Perth almost 20 years earlier. It was Obi-Wan Kenobi that Ewan had dreamed of growing up to become, not Mark Renton, the heroin waster, the icon shivering in the wet tee-shirt. It was a dream come true. The Force was with Ewan.

2
Slaying Goliath

FOR WEEKS THE young cast of eager little amateurs had been beavering away, learning by heart biblical dialogue that would have been a challenge to adult, professional actors. Parents had found time, in between shopping for Christmas presents and writing Christmas cards, to cut and stitch the costumes that would transform their beloved offspring into fearsome Philistine and Israelite soldiers. A muckle great false head had been prepared for the boy who was to play one of the leading roles, that of Goliath, the Philistine giant. He had to appear awesome. After all, Goliath was so confident in his own invincibility that he had committed his people to servitude if any Israelite could defeat him in single combat. But despite all the meticulous preparations, the 1977 Christmas play at Crieff South Church did not go as well as the local minister had hoped.

The church's Christmas production had begun life, some years earlier, as an ordinary nativity play, the likes of which could be found in just about every church and school hall the length and breadth of Scotland and England. The Reverend Henry Tait, however, harboured ambitions beyond a cute wee girl, a shawl around her shoulders and a plastic doll in her lap, attended by three boys wearing dressing gowns, with towels on their heads – and another three in bright turbans and Mummy's clip-on earrings, and carrying oddly-shaped containers empty of the bath salts or liqueurs they had once held. Tait wanted to expand the concept of a Christmas church play far beyond the familiar recipe of kings, shepherds and the Holy Family. He had been inspired by the success of Oberammergau, the tiny Bavarian town that had transformed its local passion play into an international event. He adapted the Bible stories himself, retaining the dialogue and sticking as closely as he could to the original text. Then he solicited the support of Sir William Murray, a local baronet who had set up an ambitious international theatre project on his estate outside Crieff, with Bing Crosby and Bob Hope as patrons. Murray supplied equipment for church productions – though, sadly, that support was not available in 1977, the year that Tait chose the story of Goliath and David.

Over coffee and Christmas mince pies in a packed church hall after the performance, Tait dutifully mixed with proud parents and congratulated them on their children's performances. But inside he felt a certain disappointment, a curious sense of anticlimax. Later in the solitude of his study he expressed his feelings in his private diary. 'The play went well enough,' he wrote, 'but it really is a ragged affair. Perhaps Willie's lights helped before or maybe I only thought they did.' Tait ends the diary entry with a resolution that everyone else must do better next year. 'We have all resolved to get the 1978 production under way in February!!! I will have to be Joseph.'

There was, however, one element with which the demanding amateur producer was well satisfied, one performance that lived up to his high standards, one actor alone among the cast whom he deemed worthy of individual mention in the diary. 'Wee Ewan MacGregor [sic] was outstandingly good, however, as David.' It was Ewan's first review. And an excellent one at that. 'Outstandingly good': those were words with which Ewan would grow comfortably familiar a couple of decades down the road. Tait's review remained strictly confidential until he shared it with me 20 years later. By then he had retired and the big red sandstone church at the bottom of Coldwells Road had closed down, the latest victim of falling church numbers and rationalisation of resources within the Church of Scotland.

Casting a six-year-old in one of the two lead roles might have seemed a terrible gamble for someone whose yardstick was

Oberammergau, but Tait had wanted as small a boy as possible to emphasise the disadvantage David faced against Goliath. He had great faith in Ewan's ability to pull it off and had written the part with him in mind. 'Most children of that age have to be prodded, coaxed, pushed, before they'll do a thing half right,' recalled the silver-haired minister, 'but this child had natural flair and I think I knew where it came from: it was in the family blood. His uncle and his grandmother have got it: she's not an actress, but she is a lady of great presence.'

Christmas should be a time of rejoicing in any township, but a black cloud hung over Crieff and over South Church's production in 1977. The previous month, Sir William Murray had decided he could no longer face the struggle of dealing with his enormous debts while trying to keep alive his dream of a top-class theatre in rural Perthshire. He phoned an actress friend and told her he had had enough and that he was going to shoot himself. She heard the shot, and police found Sir William dead in his office, a shotgun lying beside him. He was 38. It took the innocent, effervescent charm of the young amateur actor, Ewan McGregor, to begin to lay the ghost of the disillusioned theatre impresario and help bring some Christmas cheer to Crieff.

There was no shortage of recruits for the production of *David and Goliath*. Tait wistfully reflected that the Sunday school was very large in those days. 'We had an army of Philistines, dressed in black and white, and we had an army of Israelites. And all the Israelites shouted "Yah" and all the Philistines shouted "Boo". "Yah" was the appropriate thing to shout because "Yah" was the name of God – "Yahweh". I remember the boy who played Goliath. He was a boarder in Morrison's Academy and obviously very much taller than little Ewan McGregor, which was the whole point. I was making a serious Gospel point in the play, because that story was the story of our Lord taking on all the mighty powers of evil, and in the strength of his victory the Israelites chased the Philistines from the field. The words were from the Bible, the words of Goliath and the words of David.'

Tait had confidence in Ewan and of course he discussed the

meaning of the text with his cast – after all their comprehension and appreciation of the story was an essential part of the project – and then he handed them their lines to learn. But there was one major technical problem for Ewan which his producer had overlooked. Ewan was only six years old and he could not read the lines, let alone understand them. 'He handed Ewan the script and Ewan couldn't read it, so he didn't know how this was going to work,' says Ewan's mother Carol. 'There were a lot of lines and he was in a bit of a panic.' Other parents might have simply accepted that their son was too young to play the lead role in such an important local drama production when he had not even mastered the cat on the mat, let alone the fowls of the air, the wild beasts of the earth and his 'thees', 'thous' and 'Yahwehs'. But not Carol McGregor. 'I said that by the time it came to doing it, Ewan would know the lines. And I just read them to him every night and we practised it at home until he knew it virtually word perfect.' And in due course little David not only slew Goliath with his sling-shot, but also slew the audience with his cheeky charm, holding the congregation enthralled on a cold December night. It was a victory for the Lord, but it was also a triumph for Ewan.

It would be wrong, however, to assume that Ewan spent his childhood pursuing his own personal foundation course in show business. *David and Goliath* was an early one-off stage triumph in an otherwise normal childhood. And although Ewan loved James Stewart movies, he was not the type of kid to spend all his time closeted away indoors. From the time he could walk he was just as much outdoors as the next kid. The next kid in this case was Jimmy Kerr, a boy of much the same age, who lived just a couple of houses along from Ewan when they were little more than toddlers. 'We palled about,' says Jimmy Kerr. 'Sometimes we'd fight ... We used to play out here,' he says, outside the house in Sauchie Terrace in which the Kerrs were still living more than 20 years later.

Crieff is an attractive and prosperous town, one of several to claim the title of 'Gateway to the Highlands'. It is dominated by Crieff Hydro, the Victorian establishment that advertises itself as 'Scotland's leading leisure hotel' and occupies expansive grounds on the town's northern outskirts; and by the fee-paying Morrison's Academy, whose buildings occupy several sites spread around the town, in the manner of a university rather than a school. Its neat pupils, dressed in navy blue uniforms, the girls in Morrison tartan skirts, make a striking impression. The streets are lined with imposing Victorian stone villas. Often set in extensive grounds, they whisper 'old money' to passers-by. Every second corner seems occupied by a church. Gleneagles, one of Britain's most exclusive hotels, is just down the road, and Glenalmond public school is also nearby. Crieff sits at the heart of hunting, shooting, fishing country, but Sauchie Terrace is situated only on the very edge of this world of wealth, privilege and history, part of a modern development on the southern outskirts of town, next to the cemetery.

When Ewan was born the McGregors were living in a modest semi-detached bungalow, with a red-tiled roof and harled in the Scottish style. Harling is a roughcast mixture of lime and small stones applied over bricks for extra protection against the severe Scottish weather, and then whitewashed. The houses have tiny rooms, small gardens to the rear and little more than a strip of grass at the front. But Sauchie Terrace was, and still is, a quiet cul-de-sac, enabling children to play outside on the pavement or even the road without fear of being knocked down by passing cars. 'Ewan had a toy tractor and I had a pedal car,' recalls Jimmy Kerr. Kerr grew up to drive cars for fun, and a stock car, complete with painting of Tasmanian devil, sits in the street where Jimmy and Ewan once played. Kerr and his father both work in the motor business, the father as a mechanic, the son as a tyre-fitter. Kerr played in a pedal car as a boy and drove stock cars as an adult. Of course the equation of boyhood games turning into adult occupations is left incomplete by Ewan's choice of a career in acting rather than farming, even though he did do farm work before becoming an actor. There were plenty of opportunities for seasonal work on the lands around Crieff. Ewan, who was always attracted by vehicles, got the chance to drive tractors for real. A man of hidden talents, he can also drive a fork-lift truck.

Ewan followed in the family tradition of going to Morrison's

Academy, beginning with the prep school, where his easygoing attitude, outgoing personality and lively sense of humour made him popular with other boys ... and girls. His father, Jim, was a PE teacher at the school and when he was still a small child the family moved out of Sauchie Terrace and into Academy House, a modern, purpose-built boarding house. It was close to the Hydro, and to the Knock of Crieff, known locally simply as 'The Knock', a wooded hill that rises behind the hotel and affords views, through beech, birch and oak, to the town and the fertile Strathearn valley. Beyond the Knock, Scotland's famous Highlands rise up, their snow-capped mountains reaching up towards the clouds. To Ewan and his friends the Knock was simply an enormous playground. The McGregors subsequently moved to another semi-detached house, tucked away in nearby Murray Drive. It was older and had rather more character than Sauchie Terrace, though by Crieff standards it was still quite modest. It was brick, clad to look like stone, and had three bedrooms. Murray Drive is every bit as quiet as Sauchie Terrace and its location continued to afford Ewan ready access to the Knock.

'If I think about my childhood I think about that,' says Ewan, 'kicking around forests and riding horses and stuff like that, kind of lads' stuff, because in the countryside you kind of live round in packs.' He and his friends built their own little army base using twigs and ferns. David's tactics in defeating Goliath had obviously left a lasting impression on Ewan, for his little force used to sally forth from their base, equipped with Black Widow catapults, and fire fir cones at the haunches of passing horses, making them bolt. They used a slightly different ploy with little old ladies out for a quiet stroll, firing their missiles high into the air so it would seem that the fir cones were simply falling from the trees. Malcolm Copland was with Ewan on many an expedition up the Knock. He does not remember firing fir cones at horses, though he admits they did get into a lot of mischief and does remember one escapade involving fireworks. 'We'd lie them on the road, light them and they would shoot along the road at a group of people ahead ... I suppose fir cones were a far safer option.'

If Ewan and his pals had kept going over the Knock and continued over the neighbouring hills for just a few miles, they would have come across a rare sight. It was not just the fact that the Sma' Glen was playing host to Highland Games – after all Crieff has its own games with such traditional events as tug o' war and tossing the caber – but these games were being staged as part of the action of a feature film. Scotland had never had a film industry of its own, though over the decades it had occasionally contributed locations and stories to the British and American industries, and had more often supplied talented individuals. The list of these would probably be headed by Sean Connery and Deborah Kerr (contrary to popular opinion David Niven was not born in Scotland), but there were distinguished Scots in every field, in front of and behind the cameras. John Grierson, widely regarded as the father of documentary, came from Stirlingshire; Frank Lloyd, a triple Oscar-winner who directed the Charles Laughton–Clark Gable version of *Mutiny on the Bounty*, was born in Cambuslang, just outside Glasgow; director Sandy Mackendrick, a former student of Glasgow Art School, made *Whisky Galore!* on location in the Western Isles, because there was no room to accommodate it at Ealing studios at the time. The little town of Crieff even boasted an Oscar-winner of its own. Writer Neil Paterson was born in Greenock on the west coast, educated in Banff and Edinburgh, but made his home in Crieff and continued to base himself in Perthshire even when the offers from Hollywood came flooding in after he won his Oscar for *Room at the Top* in 1960. As well as winning an Oscar, he had combined writing with football, and captained Dundee United. He continued to live in Crieff until his death in 1995.

Scotland played host to only a handful of feature films in Ewan's childhood years, including a new version of *The Thirty-Nine Steps*, with Robert Powell, Bertrand Tavernier's sci-fi thriller *Death Watch*, with Harvey Keitel, and *The Wicker Man*, which was released as a B-movie but which, many years later, came to be hailed as a cult classic. But the film shooting in the Sma' Glen was not just any old run-of-the-mill film. It would win the Oscar for best picture of 1981. For this was *Chariots of Fire*,

the story of the Scottish athlete and devout Christian Eric
Liddell and his English rival Harold Abrahams. The young
McGregor never visited the set, but the success of *Chariots
of Fire* and the low-budget *Gregory's Girl*, which was shot in
Cumbernauld at much the same time, would, in due course,
indirectly influence his future.

Meanwhile, for the next few years, Ewan was more at home on
the slopes of the Knock than on a film set or a theatre stage.
The Knock was Ewan's playground, his backyard and his escape
when he just wanted to get away for a while. When he ran
away from home, it was to the Knock that he went. Ewan was
always a considerate child and always very close to his mother.
Crieff is the sort of town where if you are going to run away
from home, you would be expected to tell your mother, simply
out of politeness. 'He left home one afternoon, because he was
fed up with everybody,' recalls Carol McGregor. 'So I told him
to take the dog with him and made him a sandwich. I knew he
would go up the Knock and a friend of ours actually met him
when he was up there with the dog, sitting under a tree, looking
fed up. Ewan told him that he'd left home because he was fed
up with everybody. I think he'd just had an argument with his
brother at the time. But he just came back ... They could go
up the Knock quite happily on their own. There was no
problem. He was quite small, but in a small town like Crieff
everybody knows everybody else.'

The fir-cone attacks on horses were nothing more than a lark
and certainly did not reflect any deep animosity towards the
species. Ewan liked horses and regularly went riding when he
was slightly older. He and Malcolm Copland also enjoyed long
cycle rides in the countryside around Crieff. On one occasion
however, when his friends were all away and he had no one
else to play with, he went out on his bicycle and, for some
reason known only to himself, perhaps not even to himself,
went flying down the road towards a busy T-junction, determined to take the corner without braking. If a car had hit him
he might have been killed. As it was he suffered concussion

and spent two days in hospital. For all that Ewan was a well-adjusted, happy child, the episode suggested a reckless streak in his nature. He was never going to be one to play safe.

Crieff was a conservative town, with a small and a large C. Morrison's Academy could hardly be called a progressive school, though it was certainly not hidebound by its traditions to the same extent as certain other established fee-paying schools, such as Fettes College in Edinburgh, where Tony Blair was so unhappy with a regime that included fagging and flogging that he tried to run away. Ewan's contemporaries all attest that he was 'well brought-up' by his schoolteacher parents. Carol's emphasis on tidiness was the subject of a poem by Ewan, called *My Room*, that was published in the school magazine when he was ten. It began:

> My mum complains
> And gives me pains,
> Because my room's untidy.

The writer claims that he always tidies his clothes, but that some mysterious character comes in the middle of the night and messes them up. It represents early, tangible evidence of that trademark cheeky McGregor sense of humour.

Yet his mother was a liberal influence on Ewan. While Jim taught at Morrison's, Carol was teaching at the local state school, Crieff High, and subsequently served as deputy head at Kingspark in Dundee, a school for children with special needs. Despite her job, she always seemed to be on hand to encourage and support her children while firmly believing that they must ultimately live their own lives, make their own decisions and, perhaps, make their own mistakes, to learn through knowledge and experience.

Neither Carol nor Jim was particularly religious, but they wanted their children to attend Sunday school so that they could learn about Christianity and form their own religious views. Both Ewan and his elder brother Colin opted to go to youth fellowship as well. It was a chance to get out with their friends on a Sunday night, not the liveliest night on the Crieff social calendar. By his mid-teens Ewan was seriously committed to Christianity, went to a church camp, and was moved to tears on one occasion by the spirit of Jesus in him. Or so he says. 'I look back on it with slight disgust,' he said later. 'Puberty is a confusing time, and they sank their talons into young flesh and got me.' Their hold was broken suddenly one evening as he sat in the hall listening to a lecture on morality from a man who he knew physically abused his son. But by that time Ewan was no longer reliant on the church to provide him with a platform for his acting talents.

By the early Eighties his uncle, Denis Lawson, had developed a highly successful stage career and the McGregors went down to London to see him in the Rodgers and Hart musical *Pal Joey*, after which Denis returned to his native land to appear in a film that combined the talents of David Puttnam, the English producer of *Chariots of Fire*, and those of Bill Forsyth, the Scot whose films for a short while almost seemed to constitute a Scottish film industry in their own right. Forsyth's debut feature *That Sinking Feeling* (1979) appears in *The Guinness Book of Movie Facts and Feats* as the lowest-budgeted British film ever to get an international cinema release. The cost of dubbing new voices over the original Glaswegian accents was more than the film's entire budget of £6,000. Buoyed by their recent successes, Puttnam and Forsyth teamed up for *Local Hero*, a gentle comedy that cleverly subverts Scottish stereotypes, just as *Whisky Galore!* had done more than 30 years earlier. With a budget of £3 million, they could afford to import a major Hollywood star, Burt Lancaster, for the role of the Texan oil tycoon who plans to build an oil refinery in Scotland, but changes his mind when he is charmed by the beauty of the intended location and its people.

Denis Lawson had one of the major supporting roles, that of inn-keeper Urquhart, who seems to spend most of his time making love to his wife. He has one of the great scenes in the movie when he serves, for dinner, the rabbit his guests had earlier rescued from the roadside. *Local Hero* remains one of the most popular feature films to come out of Scotland, ranking alongside the likes of *Whisky Galore!*, *Chariots of Fire* and *Braveheart*. And Lawson's character can rival any of those in

Quentin Tarantino's *Reservoir Dogs* and *Pulp Fiction* for cool. Ewan of course had long realised just how cool his uncle was. 'I was the only actor he'd ever met, that's for sure,' says Denis. 'And he was inspired to act because I did it, that's true. We've always had a very close relationship ... He started to talk about acting when he was ten and he never wavered. He took it very seriously.'

Local Hero opened in 1983, the same year as *Return of the Jedi*, the third *Star Wars* movie, in which Denis reprised his role of Wedge. Denis also returned to the stage in 1983 in another hit musical *Mr Cinders* and won an Olivier, British theatre's equivalent of the Oscars. Ewan was on stage too that year, in the Morrison's prep school production of Constance Cox's play *The Caliph's Minstrel*. 'How pleasant on a cold day in March to be transported to sunny Baghdad,' said a report in the school magazine. 'As with all "good plays", repentance and a just reward gave us, the audience, that extra feeling of uplift of a job well done,' it noted, pompously. Repentance and just deserts, the very essence of the dour, presbyterian Scottish psyche. Ewan was not the lead in *The Caliph's Minstrel*; he appears only ninth in a cast of twelve, as The Watchman. But by this time he was determined that one day he would emulate his uncle and become a professional actor.

3

In the Footsteps of Rob Roy

AS A BOY Ewan McGregor played war games on the Knock, the hill behind the town of Crieff. A hundred years earlier his great-grandfather had whiled away his free time with his brothers on the other side of the hill, just a couple of miles away. The MacGregors had been in the area for centuries and had established themselves as the most notorious clan in Scotland. In the early 15th century MacGregor lands extended through Argyllshire and Perthshire, but while others formalised their territories by accepting Crown charters, the MacGregors asserted their right to hold their lands through the more traditional method of the sword. The clan chief was captured and executed; it became legal to hunt MacGregors, with bloodhounds, like wild animals; and even the name MacGregor was banned. ('Mac' means 'son of', 'Mc' is simply a contraction.)

It was against this background that we see the emergence of the most famous MacGregor of them all (with the possible recent exception of Ewan) – Rob Roy, immortalised in book and film. The famous outlaw died in 1734, at Balquhidder, just 20 miles from Crieff, but it was not until 40 years later that the name MacGregor became legal again. That was two centuries before Ewan McGregor entered the world, two centuries in which the McGregors remained fairly firmly rooted to the ancestral homelands of Perthshire. Gilmerton sprang up in the early years of the 19th century, at a junction in the new toll road between Crieff and Perth, where the Highland road branches off to the north. For many years Ewan's forebears occupied a little stone cottage on the edge of the village, on land owned by the neighbouring Monzie Castle (pronounced Monee), which was visited by Queen Victoria in 1842.

Ewan's great-grandfather James McGregor, a journeyman mason, married Emily Cramb, a 26-year-old laundry worker, in March 1911, at the little whitewashed Monzie Parish Church, where the baptismal stone font that he carved still stands beneath the stained glass windows. Emily Cramb came from Crieff, which had long been a comparatively major centre of population, capital of the Strathearn area and the local seat of justice. Its location as 'Gateway to the Highlands' made it an ideal site for a tryst of Highland cattlemen and Lowland buyers and during the 18th century its autumn sale was the biggest in Scotland. And just as cowboys had helped develop the notion of the Wild West in America, Scotland's cowboys contributed to Crieff's reputation as an unruly frontier town, far removed from the genteel image it has today. Some mornings as many as 20 wayward Highlanders would dangle from the 'kind gallows of Crieff'. The tryst moved to Falkirk in the 1770s, but the 'kind gallows' still stood at the western end of the town when Sir Walter Scott visited in 1796.

The railways arrived in the middle of the 19th century, bringing trainloads of tourists to the town. The grand Strathearn Hydropathic Establishment was built on the southern slopes of the Knock in the 1860s, and offered guests picturesque countryside and a healthy regime that included Turkish and other baths, using water brought from springs several miles away and declared by a leading academic to be among the purest he had ever examined. Alcohol was banned in the hotel until recent times. Other hotels opened and Crieff acquired another nickname, the 'Montpelier of Scotland', after the French Mediterranean town. 'From every street, a landscape of rare sweetness and beauty is disclosed,' noted *Beauties of Upper Strathearn* in 1854. 'The valley, here widening to 10 or 15 miles, is studded east, south and west, as far as the eye can reach, with mansions and villages, embowered in oak or pine woods.'

Ewan's grandfather, James Peter McGregor, was born in 1916.

By this time his father was 35, but he served during the First World War with the 2nd/6th battalion of the Black Watch, the local regiment, that could trace its history back 200 years to the companies set up to 'watch' the Highlands for smugglers and cattle rustlers like Rob Roy. Quite apart from its military record, the Black Watch is famous for its tartan, the green and blue 'Government tartan' that was so dark that it inspired the name 'Black Watch'. The regiment has worn the tartan since the 18th century and it is now one of the most popular tartans in Scotland, worn by many people with no regimental association, though no one would dream of calling it Government tartan today; the tartan has taken on the name of the regiment that wore it. James was a private in a reserve battalion that did not deploy to the western front, but served primarily as a training unit, providing reinforcements. His unit was stationed at various bases in Scotland, before moving to Norfolk in the spring of 1916, where it remained until it was disbanded in September 1917.

Morrison's Academy opened in 1860, just a few years before the Hydro. It was built, in the Scottish baronial style, using money left by the locally-born stone mason and master builder Thomas Morrison, who built Morrison Street, near Haymarket railway station in Edinburgh. In 1878 the academy provided a 'liberal education' including English, Mathematics and Modern Languages to 120 boys and girls. Its expansion provided work for James McGregor and he faced the stones on the John Smith Building. James Peter, his son and Ewan's grandfather, went to Morrison's Academy as a pupil. He was a talented artist and entertained thoughts of becoming an architect, but had to leave school at 14 to help support the large family James and Emily had had.

James Peter McGregor became a mechanic, rather than an architect, but he also had a number of other jobs, including that of ship's steward. As such, he hardly seemed a suitable match for the daughter of a former consul. John Macindoe may sound like a character newly arrived from Glasgow, but he was born in Valparaiso, the port on the Pacific coast of the long slice of South America that constitutes Chile. It is a country where a very large proportion of the population are of European descent. He was Chilean consul in London for several years, before retiring to Crieff, where he lived in Donavourd, an enormous Victorian villa on the outskirts of town, not far from the Hydro. James Peter McGregor fell in love with Macindoe's daughter Isabella. There would be no dithering by James and Isabella over which branch of the Church they should marry in. They never made it to church at all. They did however make it to Gretna Green, the border village that has played host to thousands of runaway couples down through the years.

Gretna Green had been the traditional destination for runaway couples, at least English runaway couples, since 1754 when a tightening of the marriage laws south of the border made it a requirement that anyone under 21 must have their parents' permission to get married and must marry in church. In Scotland it remained possible for any couple over 16 simply to declare themselves married in the presence of two witnesses. And that was it: they were married. These 'irregular' marriages took place throughout the Borders, indeed throughout Scotland, but nowhere staged as many as Gretna Green, because it was the first place that a couple eloping from England would reach on the Scottish side of the border. The famous blacksmith's shop, setting for innumerable weddings, stood, and indeed still stands, at Headless Cross, where the old coaching road crossed the River Sark, that separates the two countries. Headless Cross is actually at Gretna, rather than Gretna Green, which is the adjacent village, about a mile up the road. But the name Gretna Green perhaps has more of a romantic ring to it. Certainly it has been popularly used to cover the two villages.

Although marriage law was standard throughout Scotland, such was the reputation of the Gretna area, that it became a favourite destination for eloping Scottish couples as well as those from England. James Peter McGregor and Isabella Macindoe declared themselves married at Headless Cross, Gretna, in front of Sarah Armstrong of Gretna Green and Mary Little of Carlisle on 9 November 1936. There was no reference to Gretna or Gretna Green in the wedding notice that appeared in the *Strathearn Herald*, according to which they married in

Carlisle. Before long war was once again raging through Europe. James Peter, who had been working as a grocer, was serving as a lance-corporal in the Royal Army Ordnance Corps when Ewan's father, James Charles Stewart McGregor, was born at Donavourd in October 1942. He was one of five children, all of whom attended Morrison's Academy.

Two years later Paris had been liberated, the Germans were retreating on both the eastern and western fronts, victory was within sight, and Laurence Lawson, a Glasgow watchmaker, and his wife Phyllis were blessed with a daughter, Carol Diane Lawson. They had married just six months earlier at a simple Church of Scotland ceremony in Glasgow, where both families had lived for generations.

Glasgow dates back to medieval times and earlier, but its expansion into Scotland's biggest single centre of population is a relatively recent phenomenon. In 1708 its population was 12,500, in 1831 it was 200,000. More and more people were leaving the countryside to seek work in city factories, but this trend was accelerated by Glasgow's situation, where the River Clyde begins its final lap to the Atlantic Ocean. Ships sailed for America with textiles and iron and leather goods and returned with sugar, mahogany, rum, cotton and, of course, tobacco. Glasgow developed as a great ship-building centre too. Incomers flocked to the city not just from the surrounding counties of Lanarkshire, Renfrewshire and Ayrshire. They came, in their thousands, from the Highlands and over the sea from Ireland.

Edinburgh retained its status as capital of Scotland, but Glasgow became the 'second city of the empire'. The wealth generated by its trade and industry was not evenly shared around however. While the tobacco lords acquired great fortunes, the vast majority of Glasgow's population lived in abject poverty, packed into tenement flats. Sometimes there would be more than 100 people living in a single stair. As late as 1951 most people in Glasgow lived in either a one or two-room flat, not one or two bedrooms – one or two rooms! Fifty per cent of all housing came into this category, compared with only five per cent in London. Many flats had no baths and shared a toilet on the landing with the neighbours. In the 19th century some Glasgow families were living in single-room flats that did not even have windows. Molly Weir, the actress who played one of the teachers in *The Prime of Miss Jean Brodie* and wrote several volumes about growing up in Glasgow in the 1920s, is a distant cousin on Ewan's mother's side of the family.

Laurence Lawson, Ewan's maternal grandfather, was born in Queenshill Street, on the north side of the city. It was a modest address, but far from the notorious overcrowding of the Gorbals and the East End, by no means the worst part of Glasgow. His mother had been an umbrella machinist and his father was an iron moulder, though Laurence was to work with finer metals, learning the trade of watchmaker, clockmaker and jeweller. His bride, Phyllis Neno Stamper, was a young woman with retailing in her veins. Her father made his living as a travelling salesman, selling the latest mod con, an invention that would revolutionise the life of the housewife. No more sweeping and brushing, thanks to Herbert Stamper's vacuum cleaners. Phyllis knew how to make herself popular in a time of austerity and rationing: she sold sweets. When she married Laurence Lawson, the Stampers were living in a tenement flat in one of Glasgow's principal shopping streets, Argyle Street, and Ewan's mother, Carol, was born there.

By the time she was joined by a little brother, three years later, in 1947, the Lawsons had moved to Govan on the south side of the Clyde. A separate town until the early 20th century, it was a predominantly working-class, Protestant area, Rab C. Nesbitt's stamping ground. The Lawsons lived beside the shipyards, not far from Rangers football ground. The new addition to the family was christened Denis Stamper Lawson. Or was he? George Lucas was not the only one who had trouble with the spelling of the name. Maybe Lucas did not get it wrong in the credits for the original *Star Wars* movie after all, for Carol's little brother was registered in the name of Dennis Stamper Lawson. It is the destiny of all those called Denis, and Dennis, to have their names repeatedly misspelt as they go through life. It looks like Dennis has been misspelling his own name for 50 years.

Laurence Lawson was keen to set up in business for himself and eager to provide a better environment in which to bring up Carol and Denis. He brought to an end a long family association when he left the smoke and grime of the second city of the empire and headed for the heathery hills of Perthshire. He set up a repair business in the West High Street in Crieff. He would occupy four different High Street addresses in the course of the next 30 years, during which he developed a solid reputation for his craftsmanship, expertise and generosity. He would often decline payment if all that a timepiece needed was a minor adjustment.

Laurence delighted in exploring the Knock and other walks around the town and enthusiastically entered into the affairs and social life of his adopted home town. He was jeweller to the Crieff freemasons' lodge. And in the days when Crieff had its own town council, he was appointed to maintain the old town clock. Such was the antiquity of the thing that he suggested it would be cheaper for the council to employ a town crier to go around the town shouting out the time. Phyllis ran the business side of their affairs, bought and sold jewellery and even pierced ears. She continued in business after her husband's death in 1981, remaining one of the most colourful characters in the town. 'The most glamorous granny in Crieff,' one local told me, though by this time she was actually a great-granny. The Lawsons were always determined to better themselves, saving up to buy premises of their own, which they did a year before Laurence's death, and sending Carol and Denis to Morrison's Academy.

Carol was a bright pupil. But that was not all. 'She was quite tasty,' says one contemporary. She caught the eye of several boys, including that of Jim McGregor, who is remembered by his peers as a quiet, well-mannered individual ... though he was sergeant-major in the cadet force and leading drummer in the school pipe band, so he could not have been all that quiet. He also had a great aptitude for sport. The boys' and girls' schools were separate in those days, but Jim and Carol would meet up at breaktime and a teenage flirtation developed into a serious romance. They resisted any temptation of rushing into anything and were both too sensible to revive the family tradition of running off to Gretna. They had completed their training and were teaching in Glasgow by the time they got married, in the terrible month of July 1966, a month etched in the nightmares of every Scot. That was the month England won the World Cup.

The wedding in St Michael's Parish Church was front-page news in the *Strathearn Herald*, alongside an item about a farmer who was fined £150 after being found guilty of resetting seven sheep. 'Resetting sheep' is a crime peculiar to rural areas of Scotland. The word 'reset' means to 'receive stolen goods'. Carol made her own silk gown, with lace sleeves, and her 'going away' dress, and she helped make those worn by her bridesmaids. Her veil was held in place by a band of white daisies and she carried a bouquet of pink roses. She was attended by three bridesmaids and by Jim's younger brother Kenneth in a McGregor tartan kilt. After the ceremony, 80 guests were received at the Murraypark Hotel, where Ewan would later work as a waiter. Meticulous in its detail, the newspaper reports that: 'The bride's mother wore a coat of champagne crystal organza over a dress of matching guipure lace with accessories to tone. Her hat of peach French straw was decorated with a silk rose.'

Denis, who was among the ushers, never emulated his sister's academic achievements. He saw his future not in academe, but in the old family trade of salesmanship. He left Morrison's Academy to pursue a career selling carpets in Dundee. 'I was the world's worst carpet salesman and the place closed down shortly after I left,' he says. He decided to try his hand at something different. Both Denis and Carol were keen cinemagoers. The Cinema in Crieff High Street remained open until 1982 – ironically one of the very last films that it showed was *Chariots of Fire*, the Oscar-winner that was shot just up the road in the Sma' Glen. The building subsequently became a book shop, though the elongated shape of the cinema remained clear. It was not the only picture house in town when Denis and Carol were small. There was also the Ritz in Strathearn

Terrace, until it was bought by Morrison's Academy in the late 1950s and renamed Academy Hall.

Denis decided to see if he might fare better as an actor than he had as a carpet salesman. He got into the Royal Scottish Academy of Music and Drama in Glasgow and subsequently spent several years in Scottish rep before heading off to seek fame and fortune in London. He was always blessed with good looks – though there is little family resemblance between him and Ewan. While Ewan has an up-front charm, Denis possesses a quiet, almost understated sexuality. He seemed able to turn his hand to most projects. The rest of the world may know Denis primarily for *Local Hero* and *Star Wars*, but the people of Crieff still talk in awed tones of a mime act he did at Sir William Murray's theatre at Ochtertyre. He met the Dutch actress Thea Ranft in the hippy musical *Hair*, but they eschewed its message of free love and married in London in their early twenties. They appeared in several productions at Perth Theatre together, commuting from Denis's parents' house in Crieff in his Avenger car. The marriage however did not last and Denis has sub-sequently had long-term relationships with Diane Fletcher, who appeared in the *House of Cards* trilogy on television, and Sheila Gish, who was in *Highlander*.

His sister Carol and his new brother-in-law Jim McGregor set up home in Edgemont Street in Langside, one of the more attractive areas of Glasgow, not far from the Pollok estate, which is now the location of the famous Burrell art collection. Their elder son Colin James McGregor was born in Glasgow's Royal Maternity Hospital in February 1969, but they longed to return to Crieff. The following year Jim got the chance to go back to his old school, as a PE teacher, returning in time to teach his younger brother, page boy Kenneth. They bought one of the new houses in Sauchie Terrace and called it Edg-emont, after the street in which they had been living in Glasgow.

Before long there was another baby on the way, one who would get the chance to grow up, not in the big city, the second city of the empire, but amid the hills and glens of Perthshire. The baby was born on the evening of 31 March 1971 in Perth

Royal Infirmary. It was a boy. Jim and Carol chose for him one of the anglicised forms of the Gaelic name Eoghann. They duly named him Ewan Gordon McGregor.

4
Dropping Out

IT WAS AS the emaciated, crewcut junkie philosopher in *Trainspotting* that Ewan McGregor cemented himself in public consciousness, shivering and dripping wet on the poster, disappearing down a lavatory in a surreal pursuit of his opium suppositories, crashed out on bare floorboards in a grotty flat with a hole in the wall, imagining a baby crawling across his ceiling as he goes through the hell of detoxification. Mark Renton was, of course, one of his greatest roles. But Ewan has always been a man of many parts. He showed just how wide his range is when he agreed to follow in the illustrious footsteps of Alec Guinness as the Jedi knight Obi-Wan Kenobi, after George Lucas decided to revive the *Star Wars* series of films. But perhaps the single Ewan McGregor role that is furthest removed from *Trainspotting*'s images of degradation and depravity is one he played in the mid-Eighties, in a pristine white shirt, a stripey tie, a silver-buttoned jacket, a dark tartan kilt and a Glengarry bonnet, complete with flaming red cockade ... and just to complete the look a drum hanging at his waist. This was Ewan McGregor, the little drummer boy, in the pipe band of Morrison's Academy.

Music was one of the few subjects in which Ewan really excelled during his years at secondary school. He played drums in the pipe band and in a pop group, and subsequently he drummed in a ceilidh band, playing Scottish music at weddings and twenty-firsts. Whether in his pipe band uniform of stripey

tie and kilt or his pop group outfit of stripey jeans and bandannas he was already turning female heads. There was a
succession of girlfriends in the handsome youngster's life. 'All
the girls were after him,' laughs his ex Vicky McNally, who
became Mrs Vicky Grant and worked as a bank clerk in the
town. They met at primary school. 'It was just the good looks,
even at that age,' she told me. 'And he was a really likeable
person.' Vicky had to take her turn in the queue and they were
16 before they went out together.

Ewan was an accomplished musician, he sang in the school
choir and he even wrote songs. He sometimes fantasised about
becoming a pop star, despite his real goal to become an actor.
Ewan was involved in school drama, though perhaps not as
much as one might have expected for such an apparently
single-minded individual. No one could accuse him of letting
his ambitions get in the way of having a good time. Others
with their eyes on a career in cinema might have spent their
formative years in regional film theatres imbibing the work of
Tarkovsky and Bergman, but Ewan's cinema trips were not
always for the serious study of film. He was a regular visitor,
along with his school friend Malcolm Copland and their
current girlfriends, to the private cinema below the ballroom
at the Crieff Hydro Hotel, near the McGregor home. 'We would
get up to mischief, I suppose, with the girls in the Hydro,'
recalls Malcolm, who stayed in Crieff and became territory
sales manager for Budweiser. 'They have a cinema up there. It's
not really used very much, which was ideal at the time, because
it was very dark. We'd take the girls for a walk ... into a
dark room. This was probably when we were about 14. It was
unlocked most of the time. We would get chucked out by a
porter eventually, but it was a way of having fun without
disturbing anybody.'

When Ewan moved into secondary at Morrison's Academy
in autumn 1983, it became immediately apparent that he had
a tough task ahead of him. He had to live up to the achievements of other family members, not least his elder brother
Colin, who was going into third year, and was already making
his mark in the classroom and on the sports field. Ewan, too,

played sports at school, including rugby, cricket, athletics, tennis and golf, but it seems he was a jack of all trades and master of none. Colin represented the Scottish Midlands at rugby and had trials for the national team; Ewan reached the heights of the school's fifth XV, though his performance even at this level proved less than impressive. The 1985 *Morrisonian* school magazine reported, 'The departure of last season's scrum-half left a berth difficult to fill: both E. G. McGregor and I. D. McCafferty put much effort into playing in the position, but neither has, as yet, the speed and accuracy of service required.' Fortunately not all his reviews would be so negative.

To make matters worse his father Jim was one of the PE teachers, though Jim's specialties were cricket, swimming and gymnastics, rather than rugby. He was a popular teacher, noted for his cheerful and friendly manner, and occasional 'volcanic eruptions'. Jim tried his best to avoid any potential tensions and conflicts that his presence at the school might cause for his sons by making sure that he was never actually their teacher. When Colin looked the obvious choice to captain the cricket team in 1987, Jim was determined to avoid any possible charge of nepotism. He suggested that he temporarily stand down as first XI coach, and had to be persuaded to continue. There was never any danger that he would find himself in any similar dilemmas regarding Ewan's sporting prowess.

Jim did not want his position on the Morrison's Academy staff to affect Colin and Ewan any more than was necessary. He wanted his influence on Ewan to be that of a father, rather than a schoolteacher, and instilled values in his sons at home, which he hoped would influence their behaviour and outlook at school. 'He was brought up very well and learned to live by the rules,' says Malcolm Copland. 'But that doesn't mean you can't have a laugh,' he adds. 'He showed an awful lot of respect for his parents. Obviously that was very important to him, but I don't think he was goody-goody at school.' Ewan smoked, he swore, he spent a lot of time with the opposite sex and he did not always take school work as seriously as teachers would have liked.

'He was always a funny guy, always a joker,' says Malcolm.

'It was just non-stop joking, him and I, and a few of our other friends, just mucking around all the time.' Ewan's sense of humour made him popular with other pupils. 'I wanted to be in every group, involved in every clique,' Ewan later told one journalist. He attributed this desire to 'deep insecurity and an incredible desire to be loved and wanted, which is also a lot to do with acting: "Please like me! Oh fucking please, everybody like me!"' Not all the teachers shared the view that there was no inconsistency between living by the rules and having a laugh. 'He was always having a laugh and if he was having a laugh in class then obviously the teachers weren't too impressed with that,' says Malcolm. Standard punishments were extra written work and picking up litter in the school grounds.

Ewan maintained links with his alma mater and made a triumphant return to school to conduct an acting workshop in February 1997, by which time he was an international star, but he made a frank declaration in an interview with the *Guardian* later that year that he had disliked many of his teachers – his father's colleagues. He had not forgotten their complaints about his attitude, and now he was prepared to go public with his complaints about theirs. In another interview, with *The Times*, he revealed details of how the relationship with one teacher declined from intimacy into open hostility. 'She was a Jean Brodie type. We'd been quite close, but then she started pushing me in a particular direction. Anyway I started answering back and she kept sending me to the headmaster ... The whole thing became embarrassing.' For some teachers there was just too much laughter around Ewan, and not enough work. And of course they had ready access to his father with their complaints (just as Ewan would later have ready access to the press with his). Ewan could do nothing at school without his father hearing about it. Jim McGregor seemed to be there whenever Ewan put a foot wrong.

Sport was compulsory, but boys were given a choice of which sports they wanted to play and Ewan tried a number, including cross-country running. On one occasion the route he chose for his run just happened to pass his house and he and Malcolm Copland decided it was an opportune moment for a break. A few minutes later, in walked Ewan's dad. 'Him being the games master, it didn't go down too well, skiving when we should have been running,' remembered Malcolm. 'I don't think he was too impressed to start with. But at the end he just laughed it off.' Some people are sporty, while others are academic. Colin was both, Ewan was neither. 'I think he was several years behind in terms of his spelling,' says Malcolm, during an interview in the Murraypark Hotel, a small privately owned hotel just round the corner from where Ewan used to live in Murray Drive. 'He waitered here. His order for haddock was "hadok". It took a bit of getting used to ... He started here first and he got me the job here, so we both did exactly the same. We were a great duo.' English was by no means Ewan's worst subject. Physics and Maths were a real struggle.

Morrison's Academy was geared towards academic success and the pressures on Ewan were intensified by having a father on the teaching staff, a highly intelligent mother who was also a teacher, albeit at another school, and an outstanding elder brother, who would in due course become head boy. Ewan was at least musical, singing in the choir and playing side-drum in the pipe band, but he found it difficult to live up to academic expectations in a school with a long history of tradition and achievement. It celebrated its 125th birthday while Ewan was there. No ordinary school, Morrison's Academy was the sort of place that could expect a visit from the Queen on such an important occasion. There was enormous excitement prior to the big day, 2 July 1985. There were countless rehearsals and sniffer dogs in the grounds. Pupils were ordered to be on their best behaviour and to ensure they were neatly turned out in full school uniform. And every square inch of the school was dusted and polished. Well, almost every square inch. It seems the dogs, the cleaners and the pupils missed one tiny corner. Sure enough, the Duke of Edinburgh managed to spot a bit of old chewing gum on the floor of the memorial hall and duly pointed it out to horrified staff. The choir sang *Non Nobis Domine* for the Queen, and the pipe band played while she watched country dancing and sports in the grounds, including a gymnastics display supervised by Ewan's dad. The royal

couple toured the school, over which fluttered the royal standard. They were clearly in fine form. The Duke told a cookery
class that a perfect rock cake should break a plate when dropped
from a height of two feet. Picking up on the number of black
faces in the ranks, the Queen remarked that the school seemed
to rely on Zambia for all its boarders.

One former classmate says Ewan was 'just ordinary' and lived
in his brother's shadow. Jim McGregor, who normally keeps a
very low public profile, was quoted in a tabloid newspaper as
saying: 'Colin was very good athletically, particularly at rugby,
but Ewan couldn't match him, and I think he always felt they
were being compared.' When Ewan was in fourth year, Colin
was in sixth, the school captain and undoubtedly a hero figure
for many of the younger boys, and not just because of his
prowess at rugby and cricket. Colin was already well on his
way to becoming a fighter pilot. He attended the RAF selection
centre at Biggin Hill for interviews and tests, underwent a 28-
day flying course at Dundee and was subsequently awarded an
RAF cadetship, which entailed the air force sponsoring him
through university and Colin committing himself to the RAF
for 16 years in return.

In an article for the school magazine, Colin wrote: 'Since I
decided to join the RAF, the question I have been asked most
often is "Why?" My answer has been that it has been a long-
time ambition of mine to fly. But, on reflection, it hasn't really
been a long-time ambition – more of a dream that one day I
realised could become reality.' The McGregor family confidence – that can-do attitude – and an undisguised lust for life
are evident throughout the article. Colin goes on to discuss the
thrill of his first solo flight: 'I felt I had really achieved something ... My concentration seemed to have reached a new
height during the flight, perhaps because, had anything gone
wrong, there was no one there to help me.' He recalls a flight
in which he could look down on the skiers in Glen Shee and
another solo flight in which he had to land at Perth and
Glenrothes before returning to Dundee. 'I experienced
immense freedom and at last I felt like a real pilot.' In his own
way Colin was laying down a marker for his younger brother,

setting an example, showing him that dreams can come true.

Both Ewan and Colin were strikingly good-looking: Ewan had an open, fresh face, Colin a more rugged appearance, as befitted an international rugby trialist and would-be military hero. Despite Colin's all-round prowess at school, Ewan was not overshadowed by his brother. 'Ewan had such a persona that he never lived in his shadow,' says Malcolm Copland. 'One was academic, one was sort of . . . wild . . . almost . . . sometimes.' Another contemporary from schooldays, Donald Florence, says: 'Colin was much more reserved than Ewan. I would go as far as saying that Colin was probably the more sensible of the two . . . Ewan was charismatic, he was quite popular with girls, he wasn't exactly a rebel, but he wasn't a goody two-shoes either, very outgoing.'

It was a combination that proved lethal with the girls. 'He was always with the girls, very much a ladies' man, even at a very young age,' says Malcolm. 'They competed against each other a lot of the time.' Vicky Grant was part of the crowd that went under-age drinking at the Rosebank Hotel. On Friday and Saturday nights a crowd of them, including Ewan, Vicky and Malcolm, would meet up at the Meadows or the Crieff Hotel, where pints were just 65 pence each and nips 50 pence, during the nine-thirty to ten-thirty p.m. happy hour, or more often than not, at the Rosebank, a nondescript little hotel in a back street, just along the road from Morrison's Academy. There was no disco, no quizzes or bands, but it was a chance to get together for a chat and a few drinks in a company all much the same age. Ewan undoubtedly knew how to charm the girls even then. He used to write Vicky love letters when he should have been doing school work, and they would meet up and exchange their correspondence at breaktime. 'Going out' meant love letters, breaktime meetings, weekend walks together and, instead of turning up individually at the Rosebank, arriving as a couple. There were kisses of course, but not much more. It was never a serious relationship and lasted only five or six weeks, when they were 16. Then they had a row and split up. 'I never used to smoke when I went out with Ewan,' says Vicky. 'Ewan smoked. And one night down at the tennis –

I was meeting Ewan there later on – I was sitting there having a cigarette with my friends. And he came running up, shouted at me and went away again. So we fell out because I had started to smoke ... I find it very difficult to think of Ewan as being famous. I saw him on Saturday night on the television actually sitting beside Cher and it was like "Oh my God, he's sitting beside Cher," forgetting that he's actually "up there".'

The one area, apart from girls, in which Ewan distinguished himself during his schooldays was the performing arts. He won several music prizes at school, including the McGregor Cup, named after his father, which he received for drumming in the pipe band. Drumming has been a family tradition. Ewan's father, his father's brother, and his mother's brother, Denis Lawson, were all drummers in their day – Denis played a drummer in a pop group in a 1976 BBC *Play for Today* called *Jumping Bean Bag*. When Ewan was still at primary school he used to go round to an older boy's house to have a shot on his drum-kit. 'He was just a wee guy,' remembers Al Niven. 'He would have been about ten. He used to always come down and ring the doorbell and ask if he could play the drum-kit ... He was very confident.' When he was older Ewan got a set of his own. He would hammer away on them at home, as well as drumming in the rather more disciplined atmosphere of the Morrison's Academy pipe band.

Shortly after the Queen's visit to the school, Ewan got the chance to go to the Netherlands for a music festival with the band. Jim McGregor ran the pipe band for several years, stopping shortly before Ewan moved up to secondary school, but he was one of the teachers helping out on the trip. They gave 12 performances in and around the ancient cathedral city of s-Hertogenbosch, where they brought traffic to a standstill in the market place, and in Amsterdam, where they played in the courtyards of the National History Museum and the Scots Kirk, where William of Orange once worshipped. Splendid in their Highland dress, including green, blue and red Morrison tartan kilts, the young bandsmen and women charmed the locals, particularly those old enough to remember the Second World War and the part that Scottish soldiers had played in their liberation. The Scottish National Youth Orchestra was also visiting the Netherlands and the pipe band welcomed them with a rousing rendition of 'Scotland the Brave'. The band also played outside a shop selling Scotch whisky and in two pleasure parks, where they enjoyed free access to the roller-coasters and other daredevil rides in return for their services.

There were other music prizes for Ewan, for French horn and for singing. He was good enough on the horn to win a prize at the Perth Musical Festival and to appear on *A Touch of Music* on Grampian Television, so he was well qualified to play in the colliery brass band in the hit 1996 film *Brassed Off*. Although Ewan took music more seriously than many other subjects, he preferred the practical side to the theory, and even then he did not take it over-seriously. He was not above having competitions with Malcolm Copland to see who could sing the loudest in the school choir. Alternatively they would try to put each other off. 'I'm sure it was putting everyone else off,' says Malcolm. Ewan recalls wiping his nose on his sleeve between each passage of Mozart, during that early Grampian Television appearance, because he thought it looked 'cool'. 'They had to keep cutting to the pianist,' he says. Whenever he took a girlfriend home his father would dig out the video of the spiky-haired young musician and entertain them with it.

David and Goliath had shown that Ewan was perfectly happy getting up on stage in front of an audience and performing. At the end of the 125th anniversary celebrations the school put on a major revue of music, sketches and recitation. It was staged over three nights in July 1986 in Academy Hall, the old Ritz cinema, and involved 250 staff and pupils from Primary One up to Sixth Form. Invariably, interviewees discussing Ewan's schooldays bring up the subject of his solo spot. 'The revue was really the first time I saw the potential that he had,' says Harry Ashmall, who was rector (headmaster) at the time. 'The spotlights were only on him and he had to take the audience through a piece about William the Conqueror.' It was a comic monologue entitled *The Battle of Hastings*, written in 1937 by Marriott Edgar, half-brother of the crime writer Edgar Wallace, and made famous as part of the stage repertoire of

Stanley Holloway, the comedian and actor, whose films include *Brief Encounter* and *The Lavender Hill Mob*. It related the story of the battle as if it were a football match, with great, unrefined dollops of ironic, working-class English humour, minus all the aitches normally found in words such as Harold.

'The kick-off were sharp at two-thirty,' chirruped Ewan, alone on the stage, hundreds of expectant, demanding faces staring up at him from the stalls. He continued:

> And soon as the whistle had went
> Both sides started banging each other
> Till the swineherds could hear them in Kent.

The hall filled with encouraging laughter at the end of each verse. He related the monologue in a working-class English accent, which in itself would seem exotic and amusing to the fine people of Perthshire, and by all accounts *The Battle of Hastings* was the highlight of the show. Many at the school had not seen Ewan's performance in *David and Goliath*, and *The Battle of Hastings* was their first indication of his ability on stage. 'That was quite a long monologue and he learned it and he did it really well,' says his mother, with no attempt at false modesty. 'He was only about nine or ten.' Actually he was 15, but that does not detract from the point that most 15-year-olds would freeze or falter, in front of 450 on-lookers. 'He performed it with the aplomb of a 25-year-old,' says Ashmall.

Although he was not academically inclined, and never mastered such technicalities as spelling, Ewan was undoubtedly comfortable with words, and not just those of others. He had a wonderful imagination, a great sense of humour and the ability to articulate his thoughts and sometimes wacky ideas with a clarity, wit and discipline exceptional in one so young. He contributed a long, ten-verse poem to the 1987 edition of the *Morrisonian*. *Our Mini* by Ewan G. McGregor, 4C, amusingly anticipates his mother buying a car:

> She's waited 20 years now
> For a car she can call 'Mine',
> When Dad said, 'What kind would you like?'
> She said, 'Oh a Mini would be fine.'

The published poem shows that Ewan was at home with words and ideas, in the formal context of the written form. *Our Mini* has a naïve boyish charm and a lively, easy sense of humour. There is something reminiscent of Lewis Carroll or maybe John Lennon in lines like 'It isn't very large inside, In fact it's rather small,' silly and yet absolutely exact, making the point through repetition and the delight of restating the obvious. Quite apart from its debatable elementary literary merit, the poem also underlines Ewan's continuing closeness to his family, particularly his mother. He pokes affectionate, gentle fun at her, suggesting that 'in Fine Fare car park' other drivers better watch their backs, because 'she'll want to make some tracks'; and:

On the Perth road in the morning
The school bus you will pass;
And they will cry, 'There's Ewan's Mum –
She's fairly shifting ass.'

One verse is devoted to Colin and the problems that he might have because of his height – Ewan suggests that when Colin is driving he should sit in the back seat. Ewan enthuses about the front-wheel drive capabilities which will be useful when 'four of us' go skiing to Glencoe. The poem is also a perhaps unconscious admission, and celebration, of the family's lower-middle-class status. Many other pupils at Morrison's Academy came from richer families, the sons and daughters of doctors, lawyers and businessmen; some, as the eagle-eyed monarch had spotted, came from overseas and boarded at the school. But although Morrison's was fee-paying it was not a particularly exclusive or snobbish school, unlike nearby Glenalmond. A large proportion of the pupils were local day pupils. Many came from better-off families, but many did not, and Ewan would not really have stood out as being the poor relation. Far from having any hang-ups about wealth or social status, *Our Mini* shows that he was perfectly at ease with his then station in life. Few images better symbolise the British lower middle classes than the Mini, and the poem ends on a triumphal note, with possibly just the very slightest hint of irony:

> So here is to the Mini,
> That great small British car!
> And here is to my Mother –
> May she drive it long and far!!

Ewan and Colin won the school prize for vocal duet in 1986–87, performing the witty 'Brush Up Your Shakespeare' number from *Kiss Me Kate* at the school's annual musical evening in May 1987; and on another occasion they were joined by Alan Andrews, head of the English department, in a satire on the school choir. Ewan and Colin had also figured prominently with solo spots at the school's Burns Supper in the candlelit Academy Hall in January of that year. Colin began proceedings with the Selkirk Grace and, in broad Scots, Ewan recited *To a Louse*. One of Robert Burns's best-known comic poems, it was conceived when the author spotted a louse on a lady's bonnet in church and began musing on its station in life rather than listening to the minister's sermon, just as Ewan would easily be distracted from his teachers' lessons by some equally fanciful thoughts. Burns observes that while mortal men may regard the lady Jenny as a beauty, the louse simply regards her as dinner.

Ewan found another outlet for his artistic inclinations drumming and singing in a pop group called Scarlet Pride. He wore black and white striped jeans with red bandannas tied round the knees, and dyed his hair red with poster paint. He would occasionally entertain the notion of becoming a pop star. But, whereas acting was a serious and focused ambition, pop stardom was no more than the sort of fancy that floats occasionally through the heads of most teenagers with a modicum of talent for air guitar. Scarlet Pride's music has left very little impression on the consciousness of Crieff. 'It was loud,' says Carol McGregor. 'It was loud, but it was good. They played in town halls and things like that and at the school. They were serious at the time I think, but then they all left school ... He actually played in another group as well. That was a Scottish ceilidh band.' A ceilidh is basically a Scottish party, with traditional music and poetry, though the word is now often applied simply to an evening of Scottish country dancing. 'He was the drummer and the singer in that. There were three of them and one of them was a fantastic accordionist.'

In June 1987 Ewan got the chance to exploit both his looks and acting talent as the romantic lead in a school production of *Sganarelle* by Molière, the 17th-century French dramatist who was a contemporary of Cyrano de Bergerac. It was one of three short one-act farces, along with Tom Stoppard's *After Magritte* and Eugene Labiche's *The Spelling Mistakes*, presented in a single programme in the Academy Hall. Although other pupils appeared in more than one piece, Ewan was only in *Sganarelle*, a romantic farce about fidelity and misunderstandings. A review in the *Morrisonian* acclaimed *Sganarelle* as 'the most readily enjoyable' of the three plays, though not necessarily due to Ewan's participation. 'Perhaps this was because it's the funniest play; perhaps it was the casting (with Donald Florence ... at ease as the cantankerous Gorgibus!); perhaps the characters were such as a young cast can visualise and cope with ... Young Rebecca King made a stunning Celie ("What a spitfire!") and Jennifer MacDonald an admirable contrast as the couthy Nurse ("You educated people are so complicated!"). Despite an excessive wig, Ewan McGregor was a vigorous Leslie [sic], the romantic lead, but it was left to Kenneth Hamilton, surely unexpectedly, to provide most of the laughter with his telling delivery (the diffident "I'd better kill him") and amusing gawkiness.' But Ewan raised more than his fair share of laughs during rehearsals. 'We used to cause each other to corpse quite a bit in rehearsals, just looking at each other,' says Donald Florence, who remained in Crieff, gave up acting and became a policeman. 'When I came on stage or he came on stage we just lost it. It was quite a worry that that was going to happen in the performance, but it was just in rehearsals.' Ewan was quite happy to have a laugh in rehearsals, but he was also taking the exercise very seriously. Donald Florence remembers Ewan telling him that he intended to become a professional actor. 'That's why he was taking part in school plays, for the experience ... It was in my final year and Ewan was just sort of starting to act at that time ... He was certainly very charismatic and very confident, more so than anybody else.' Ewan's charisma and confidence were by no means restricted to the stage. 'I actually taught Ewan to play his first few chords on the guitar,' says Donald Florence. 'And he figured out how to play "Stairway to Heaven". And he was playing it for this girl at a party, a quite pretty American girl. And she was fascinated, or she was pretending she was fascinated, and said "That's really good." I grabbed the guitar and tried a few chords and she said "That's really impressive." When Ewan and I were talking to her later, he asked her what she did and it turned out she was a student at Harvard. We asked her "What do you study?" and she majored in Classical Guitar. We had just made complete prats of ourselves.'

Hector McMillan, head of Business Studies, directed Ewan in *Sganarelle*, having coached him for his rendition of *The Battle of Hastings* the previous year. He maintains that it was not so much Ewan's acting that made him stand out in *Sganarelle* – 'Standing out is not the thing when you're doing a play,' he says – it was his determination off-stage, his interest in the production as a whole and his questioning attitude. 'Lots of people asked me "Did you see then ...?" and I think what I would say is I saw certain talent – there's no denying that; real enjoyment; and he was determined to be an actor, regardless of what the rector said to him about the precariousness of the profession. I think that's the thing that isolated him a little bit, the fact that he was so determined.' Pupils had to audition for the parts. Many actors in school plays are interested purely in their own part, but Ewan wanted to know how the different characters related to each other. He was ready to discuss and even debate not just how a line should be delivered, but where the actor should be standing when he delivered it. But, according to McMillan, he was no prima donna, he was acutely aware of the needs of others and the necessity to fit into an ensemble. School plays are a very different animal from West End productions or feature films: their directors can hardly turn up with an open mind and expect the project to develop its own personality, through the interpretations of the characters by the individual actors. The director has to have a fairly firm grasp of the characters to give to the amateur cast. 'Lots of the children won't have any idea what to do, so you say "Move here and say your line." ' But in the grand tradition of the likes of Dustin Hoffman, Ewan was not prepared to move without fully understanding the big question 'Why?'. Would his character really move? If his character were to move, would it be to that particular spot? It is the big question of motivation. 'He's the kind of boy who would say "I'm not quite sure why I'm moving." And then we would discuss why, and he would understand that and do it, or he might say "I'm not quite sure I would move there." '

Ewan scraped passes in four 'O' grades at the end of his fourth year, whereas a bright pupil might expect to sail through these elementary examinations with anything between six and eight good passes. He had the discipline to take on part-time jobs, washing dishes and waiting tables at the Murraypark, but not to apply himself to subjects in which he had no interest at all and in which he saw no immediate reward and little, if any, future use. 'Colin was more intellectually inclined; Ewan was clever, but in a different way,' says one old friend of the family.

Hector McMillan had not taught Ewan before directing him in *Sganarelle*, but he came to his rescue when Ewan returned to school for his fifth year, and his antipathy towards certain subjects intensified. By this time Colin was off in the big wide world, a university student and RAF cadet, while Ewan remained merely a schoolboy. 'Maths was part of his timetable,' McMillan recalls, 'and that wasn't working out, because Maths wasn't really his thing. And he came to do a little typing course instead of Maths and then very soon after that he left.'

It sounds simple enough, but at Scottish schools bright pupils are expected to do six years, or at least five, not four and a bit. And Morrison's Academy is not just any school. The majority of pupils are expected to go on to university or some other form of further education, not drop out before even sitting their Highers. As well as continuing as a PE teacher, Jim McGregor was now careers master and had grave doubts, to say the least, about Ewan leaving school before the Highers in the hope of becoming an actor. 'It didn't even enter my head that it wouldn't work out,' says Ewan. But Jim knew it was a risky profession, and at this stage Ewan did not have a place on a drama course nor even a job as a stagehand, which might give him some sort of entry to theatre as a career. The rector shared Jim's doubts and he too tried to persuade Ewan to think again. 'He wasn't a stupid boy,' says Harry Ashmall, 'so I tried to encourage him to do his Scottish Highers, then go to drama college ... I suppose in institutions we like to see people with a bit of paper as something to fall back on should the dream not be realised.' Ashmall does not, however, remember Ewan ever being sent to see him because of behavioural problems. 'Ewan is maybe now recollecting it in a slightly more colourful way,' he suggests. He says Ewan never even broke the school's uniform rules and his lasting impression of him is that he was 'nice', not perhaps the adjective that a rising film star, whose big breakthrough has been as a junkie, would choose to describe himself. Ashmall has one more particularly vivid memory of Ewan and that is the effect he had on his two daughters. 'My wife and I were intrigued that they, as young females, regarded Ewan as a kind of handsome film star, long before he was. I would have thought that he appeared less appealing than Colin. Colin was bigger, taller, short hair. Ewan always had that little bit of the artistic about him. But I'm a yesterday's man.'

For the son of the school careers master, the younger brother of last year's school captain, simply to drop out was little short of a scandal in the eyes of many in this tight-knit, twee, little Perthshire town. Even some of Ewan's peers, from whom he might have expected support, were shocked and disapproving. 'I told him he was making quite a big mistake,' says Malcolm Copland. 'I said "You are going off after this dream, you know, and so many people don't make it." And we temporarily fell out, very briefly – I don't think we really fell out any time before that ... I didn't say anything more about it, but still I was a bit dubious. And when he got his first break in *Lipstick* (*Lipstick on Your Collar*) I was the first to phone him and say I made the mistake here, and I don't mind admitting I was wrong.'

Support came from a seemingly unlikely quarter, his school-teacher mum. On the one hand, as a teacher, Carol McGregor fully appreciated the value of academic qualifications; on the other hand her own brother, Denis Lawson, had proven, at very close quarters, that it was quite possible to make a good living as an actor. She had taken Ewan's acting ambitions seriously from a very early age, and believed he would make it as an actor, just as her brother had done. There were long discussions, and sometimes arguments, between Ewan and his parents about his future, and it was Carol who eventually persuaded Jim that staying on at school was not necessarily the best option. 'We actually gave him the option of leaving,' she says, during an interview in the cafe of the Perth Theatre. Ewan would subsequently recall that final discussion with his parents in later press interviews, adding a little colour to more than one account with the memory that it was a dark and stormy night: all the best stories take place on dark and stormy nights of course. 'I think it was quite a surprise to him that we did that,' continues Carol, with no reference to weather conditions whatsoever, 'because he was just in his fifth year and about to do his Highers. My husband and I just decided that what he was doing at school was going to be of no benefit to him later. He knew he was going to be an actor. And I said "If he's not an actor, he'll be something in the theatre." Paper qualifications weren't necessary really at that time and I felt he would be far happier and get on better if he just left and got a job.

'He liked school fine. He wasn't too keen to apply himself to subjects that he didn't like much and wasn't very happy with Physics and Maths and things like that that he had to do. But he wasn't really rebellious or anything, no more than any other teenager. It was kind of difficult in a way when your father teaches at a school as well. And both the boys coped with that really well. School gave him a lot, you know sort of all-round, extra-curricular things. There's a lot of music and a lot of drama work done, and they put shows on all the time. They very much encourage individual talents. The teacher that was in charge of Drama was Hector McMillan and he encouraged Ewan a lot and he was very fond of him ... But when he left he was ready to leave.

'I think there was a period when he was unhappy because he was being pressured by me and by other people into more concentrated study than he preferred to give it. He did up to half-term and then we decided that that would be enough. People were quite surprised that we instigated that, but I felt that that was the best thing for him to do. He left school at the beginning of October and he got a job here within about three days. He knew that the condition that he was allowed to leave was that he got some kind of work ... I knew he would.'

Without Highers Ewan McGregor faced a highly uncertain future, but very soon the curtain was rising on a new chapter in his life as he took his first faltering steps towards becoming a professional actor. 'From a very young age he just said that's what he wanted to be,' says Carol. 'And I never really disputed the fact. I just thought that's what he's going to be ... And I knew he would do it.'

5
A Few from the Fridge

WITHIN DAYS OF leaving Morrison's Academy Ewan entered the world of show business. That same month of October 1987 he made his professional acting debut, trading his school blazer for a turban in *A Passage to India* at Perth Theatre, on the same stage where he had watched his uncle Denis perform. Ewan had been pressing Perth Theatre for months for an opening and it certainly did not hinder his prospects that the director of *A Passage to India*, Joan Knight, was an old friend of his uncle. So what if Ewan appeared twenty-first in the programme's cast list, lumped with a group called 'Servants and others'? Ewan had no lines, but it was a start and he was delighted to have his foot on the first rung of the ladder. Not only was he following in his uncle's footsteps at Perth, one of the finest provincial theatres in Scotland, but in those of actors of the calibre of Donald Sutherland, Gordon Jackson and Alec Guinness, who had appeared in the theatre's production of *Romeo and Juliet* in 1939.

During the play's fortnight-long run, the McGregor family trooped through from Crieff to see Ewan. Friends, accustomed to being entertained by Ewan in Academy Hall, or in the Maths class, welcomed the chance to see him on the big stage. It was not every day that one of their old school chums appeared in professional theatre. 'He came on very briefly,' recalls Malcolm Copland. 'It wasn't much of a part: he just sort of walked on from the back and it was "Which one was he again?" But it was him getting his big break, which was great, and he was thrilled, absolutely thrilled.'

At the beginning of 1988 Ewan appeared in Perth's production of *Pravda*, Howard Brenton and David Hare's satire about Fleet Street, which had won a whole clutch of awards a few years earlier in London when Anthony Hopkins played the megalomaniac newspaper proprietor Lambert Le Roux. This time Ewan did not even get a mention in the programme, which said simply that: 'Reporters, journalists, athletes, showgirls and dog-track men will be played by members of the company.' But proud mum Carol McGregor remembers exactly what he did. 'There were a lot of journalists in it,' she says, 'and he was sort of sitting typing away.' Being a professional actor was a good chat-up line, but it had not gone to Ewan's head. He still hung out with the same friends and continued to live with his Mum and Dad, commuting the 18 miles from Crieff through the village of Gilmerton, home of his ancestors, and through the Perthshire countryside to the bonnie old city on the Tay that had been Scotland's capital in ancient times.

Ewan's primary function at Perth Theatre was not as an actor, but as a stagehand, the labouring class of the theatre world, the people who lug the scenery around. It was a way in. The star of *Pravda* was Martyn James, who had played Capulet to Denis Lawson's Romeo 20 years earlier. He has vivid memories of Ewan, who certainly did not come across as the frank, flamboyant character he would play in interviews ten years later. 'I remember him as being quite quiet,' says James. 'He was studious almost. He was obviously interested in the thing as a whole rather than just treating it as a holiday job. He was watching everybody, you could see him analysing what was going on. Thinking of his connection with Denis, I thought "A-ha, there's somebody who is keen on the business."'

'I did learn a lot watching what the other actors did,' says Ewan. 'That's often the best way to gain experience ... I was a real pain in the ass, because I was so keen, and people there remember me as a nightmare. I wanted to do everything – this, this, this and this – and they would say "Fuck off, Ewan. Shut up".' It was not just on stage that Ewan was watching and learning from the other actors. Their off-stage performances proved a real eye-opener for the boy from Crieff. 'I learned an awful lot about life and about growing, because I hadn't really seen anything before. I met gay people and I met people who were having affairs. I gobbled it all up. It was brilliant.'

After applying for several drama courses, in the autumn of 1988 Ewan enrolled for the year-long theatre arts programme at Fife College, formerly Kirkcaldy College of Technology, where others were taking the first tentative steps on the path to careers in everything from biological science to furniture design and hairdressing. There were 35 on the theatre arts course, mostly teenagers straight from school dreaming of fame and fortune on stage or screen. They had all had to audition for the course and their dreams had been fuelled by their acceptance letters. For most, those dreams would be blown away by the chilly winds of reality that sweep through that bleak, industrial town on the Firth of Forth. Some would make it onto the professional stage, fanning the dying embers of their aspirations through indifferent pantomimes in cold provincial towns; a couple might graduate to television and a living wage from *The Bill*, a soap opera or the occasional serious TV drama; but the law of averages dictated that only one, if any, might go all the way, only one would truly fulfil the dream of becoming a rich and famous movie star.

If one of their number was to make it, make it all the way, which one would it be, the students wondered, as they eyed each other suspiciously on that first morning in the hideous college complex, near the railway station, truly one of the ugliest buildings in Scotland, or rather combinations of buildings – Fife College's St. Brycedale campus consists of two main buildings, a brutal, three-storey, grey-stone block built as a school in the 1920s, and a hideous, yellow-panelled, 1960s tower block. Both are ugly, yet they are ugly in their own very distinct ways. The whole of their ugliness is much greater than the sum of the parts, and yet entirely in keeping with the look of a place which appears unfamiliar with the concept of town planning.

Kirkcaldy, less than 40 miles from Crieff, is a sprawling,

industrial town, 'famous' for linoleum. It spreads out along several miles of coastline where the Firth of Forth begins to widen and the skyline of Edinburgh is a distant vision across the sea, all very different from the affluent little country town in which Ewan had grown up. If things had worked out differently for the then 17-year-old Ewan, he would still have been wearing school uniform and beginning his final year at Morrison's Academy. Now, although he was returning to the classroom, his uniform would be one of blue denim rather than blue blazer. College represented not only an opportunity for the aspiring actor to pursue his dream, but an enormous lifestyle change for a young man leaving home for the first time.

Suddenly he was presented with all the freedoms and temptations student life had to offer. Well, maybe not quite all, this was after all Kirkcaldy in the Eighties, not Berkeley in the Sixties. Nevertheless Ewan got the chance to sample a few of the traditional student temptations. He was a fun guy, he enjoyed a night on the town, in one of the pubs near the halls of residence or at Jackie O's, a bleak, steadfastly provincial nightclub, farther along the front, where the winds from the sea would redden the faces of those queuing for admission. He liked a little something, or even a lot of something, to maintain and enhance the party mood. Sometimes he overindulged, but his drugs of choice were nicotine and alcohol, rather than cannabis, LSD, magic mushrooms or any of the other wilder stimulants traditionally associated with student life. He liked a pint with his new friends, but he never forgot the main reason he was there was to construct a foundation on which he might build an acting career. Some students may have regarded a lecture and a couple of hours' homework as a full day's work, but not Ewan. In common with other students on the theatre arts course he was putting in 12-hour days, in classes and in preparations for student productions. He might be rehearsing one minute and painting scenery the next.

He also found time to fall in love. A ladies' man since primary school, his previous girlfriends had been little more than flirtations, pre-pubescent infatuations, adolescent romances. It was at Kirkcaldy that Ewan experienced the full emotional and sexual power of adult relationships. And, like almost any other teenage virgin, he was understandably nervous about 'doing it'. Boys like to play it cool, pretend they are in total control, but often they are as nervous as their partner, if not more so. Ewan was a good-looking guy, the very picture of cool, with his blue eyes and spiky hair and easy charm. Although his contemporaries did not know it at the time, the whole world now knows that these assets were complemented by, to use Ewan's own words, 'a very large penis'. As the young theatre arts students eyed each other up and down on that first morning, they were assessing not only who they fancied might make the grade as an actor, but also who they fancied. Over the next year they were to know each other very well, much better than students on many of the other courses. They would work, live, eat and quite possibly sleep together. But with whom? There was a nervous excitement in the various possibilities.

Ewan admitted in an interview with *Neon* magazine that he had been scared of sex for a long time. And then? 'Somebody took hold of me and gave me a good one,' he said, with the vulgarity and flippancy that had become the hallmark of a McGregor interview. 'I didn't know quite what it was about ... They seemed to have a good idea. It was great. I felt pretty good about it ... But that'll upset my wife if she reads about that, so I won't talk any more about that.' It might also upset the young lady who 'took hold' of Ewan and gave him 'a good one'. But Ewan would probably not have thought through those implications. Some of his contemporaries from his early days have formed the impression, rightly or wrongly, that he would rather they did not talk about him to the media, yet he feels free to provide his fans with a review of his first partner's performance in bed. 'What you've got to remember,' says one fellow Scot, who has closely followed Ewan's rise to the top, 'is that although Ewan is a big star now, he is also still just a daft wee laddie.'

He might appear innocent, he might even remain largely innocent, unspoilt and genuine in an industry full of hype, hypocrisy and cynicism, but he did not rise to the top purely

by chance and charm. He has always had the drive, the determination and the energy to turn himself into a major star.
Course tutor Lynn Bains reckons his class at Kirkcaldy was an
exceptional one and that Ewan was one of the better students,
but adds that he did not stand out as the best. The course was
designed to give students a comprehensive grounding in the
theatre, a bit of everything, an introduction rather than a
training. Bains describes it as 'a shake-out year', during which
students might discover whether they had what it takes to
become a professional actor or to succeed in some other branch
of theatre, from stage management to make-up. 'For me it was
as much about discouraging people from wanting to be actors
as it was about encouraging them,' she says. 'He was quick, he
was talented, he was bright, but there were a couple of other
talented people in the year.'

Another teacher, Maggie MacMillan, was only 'mildly impressed' by his acting ability. What left a more lasting
impression on her was his determination. 'He didn't particularly stand out from the crowd as an actor, but from the
moment he came here he was very single-minded and determined that he was going to make it in the business. Ewan only
wanted to associate with people who were going to be able to
help him get on and he wouldn't suffer fools gladly. He didn't
have time for people who weren't interested in working hard.'
MacMillan taught make-up, for which Ewan showed considerable enthusiasm, and great imagination in his use of Rice
Krispies and Weetabix. 'I think a lot of them had clubbed
together and maybe bought the odd packet of something like
that and had used them to really horrific effect, because a Rice
Krispie can look like a rather nasty protuberance on the face
... One thing I did notice about him in particular was that he
had a good face to work on. With some students, you think
"Oh dear, can't do much with that face," but he was good.
He had good bones, good structure, nice jaw line, quite a
photogenic face. It's the kind of face that would take
make-up well and easily and could adapt to all different
kinds of things. You find it very difficult to get some people
to look different, but sometimes with him it's like a blank

canvas and you could turn him into all sorts of things just with use of make-up.'

The course included acting classes, voice, movement, dance and mime. For one assessment, other students chose serious dance pieces, but Ewan dressed up as Batman, with a mask and cape, rode onto stage on a child's tricycle and danced around to the theme from the camp Sixties *Batman* television series, much to the amusement of his classmates. It was a very practical course and provided students with a chance to try their hands at all aspects of the theatre by preparing and staging productions of their own in the Adam Smith Theatre, a 19th-century grey-stone hall virtually next door to the hideous college complex, named after the famous economist and philosopher, who was born in the town. 'You would rehearse your lines and then you would come off stage and paint scenery, or go and get props,' says Bains. 'Everybody was doing everything all the time. It was not like drama school: there were no spoiled people . . . I remember Ewan always smiling. Even when he had to do jobs that weren't glamorous, not exciting, he just got on with it.'

The theatre arts class was very much a self-contained unit. Unlike many other students, they were not with different groups for different subjects, they were together all the time. 'They were a tight bunch,' recalls Tom Lawrence, who was warden at the halls of residence, three floors of spartan, white-washed rooms, curiously reminiscent of prison cells, each equipped with a bed, wardrobe, table and wash-hand basin, set in a circular building on a hill above Kirkcaldy Harbour at the east end of town. 'They went out about eight o'clock in the morning and they were generally out all day, and they came in at half past five for tea, and then maybe went back to rehearsals and they would be out until maybe nine . . . Lynn Bains was the tutor in charge and she ran it like the army. She really made them work and as such they came back in exhausted.' Molly Innes, the student that some considered the single most talented in that year, says: 'It was really hard work. Lynn Bains was a superb teacher, but there was also a lot of stress, because we would work really long hours and it was really hard going, because that's the way that Lynn wanted the course to be – a real challenge.'

During the year it became increasingly apparent which students might have the raw talent to make it in the acting profession. There was no doubt that Ewan was in that group and he was growing in confidence all the time. He was happy. 'I realised this was exactly what I wanted to do, that I hadn't been mistaken all this time.' And he was in love, with one of the other students, an attractive, well-spoken English girl called Hannah Titley, who was also in the halls of residence. Ewan and Hannah were very much an item within the self-contained theatre arts crowd. They would go out with the rest of the gang, to the pub or to Jackie O's, but they were very clearly with each other. At weekends Ewan would take Hannah back to Crieff in the old green Volkswagen Beetle he acquired after passing his driving test and on which he lavished almost as much loving care and attention as he did on Hannah. She was intent on a career in stage management and Ewan was happy to help her behind the scenes. 'Hannah was very good at telling people what to do, in the nicest possible way,' says an ex-classmate. 'They were a very serious couple, almost from day one. It was such a major romance we all thought they might even be a marriage case. Hannah looked and acted older than her years and that seemed to rub off on Ewan. They were both a good laugh as well, but, perhaps because they were a very definite couple, they seemed more mature than the rest of us.' Another contemporary remembers, 'He did have male friends on the course, but he was most particularly friendly with Hannah. He spent a lot of time with her, but he was there to work and he was really determined to get on.'

It was no great surprise when Ewan and Molly Innes were chosen for the leading roles in a send-up of Arthur Miller's *A View from the Bridge* called *A Few from the Fridge*. It was part of a student drama festival, which gave the class the chance to perform away from home on unfamiliar stages to unfamiliar audiences. 'They were wonderful,' says Bains. 'The play was most bizarre. I have no idea what it was really about and I wrote it. He just jumped in and he was hysterical. We played the Tron [Glasgow] and we played the Traverse [Edinburgh] and the audience just loved it.' Innes says: 'We had to eat this spaghetti, because in the play they're always going on about spaghetti. One day somebody hadn't come in with the spaghetti. There was nothing to eat and Ewan just said "Oh, it looks like Props have fucked up." He wasn't afraid to say things like that, he was so calm on stage, he would let the audience in [on the joke], without saying "Oh, we're on stage and something has gone wrong." '

The main dramatic production that year was *The Prime of Miss Jean Brodie*. Bains would have liked to have cast Ewan as the romantic lead, the art teacher Teddy Lloyd, opposite Innes's Jean Brodie. But, bearing in mind the limitations of some of the other student actors, she decided to give him the less glamorous and arguably more difficult role of Teddy's rather dull rival, the music teacher Mr Lowther, the character played by Gordon Jackson in the film version, which of course had featured Ewan's distant cousin Molly Weir. Molly Innes subsequently established herself as one of Scotland's leading young actresses and has appeared in, amongst other things, *The Bill*. 'I always thought Ewan was good,' she says, 'but there were a lot of good people on that course ... He had a bit of everything. He was a good actor and he had the looks and I suppose also there was his accent, what I mean is his voice being East Coast, being Perth. It's a pleasant Scottish accent that people like to hear. You do hear the West Coast lilt more often and I think it just came at the right time, with Irvine Welsh's stuff coming out ... I never felt that he was insecure about anything; I always felt that he kind of knew that he was going to get there.'

Lynn Bains says: 'I don't want to use the word "sparkle", but he had that quality that made you want to watch him ... He was just good, inventive, and I think he was quite mischievous as an actor. I remember that look in his eye that you still see when he's playing pranks on telly. But I do remember how hard he worked, and during the course of the year we discovered that this was the first time he had really bloomed. This was when he was finally doing what he had dreamed of doing; everything was realised and we were very lucky to have him at that time and I think he felt he was very lucky to be there. He surprised himself I think in terms of all of these long hours and mucking in. When I went to *Trainspotting* [the Edinburgh première], one of the things he said to me was it was the hardest year of his life, even Guildhall wasn't hard compared to Kirkcaldy, because we didn't just focus on the acting, but he seemed to just relish everything ... In a course like that, which is different from the real drama school, you get to know people extremely well and you have such an influence at that time, for that short period of time. When Ewan began to be successful I just remember being very proud.'

Bains had not seen Ewan for quite some time before the *Trainspotting* première and was slightly nervous about the prospect. Ewan was now a major star. 'It's that thing about – Do you dismiss the people from your past, or do you stay what you were?' she says. Ewan gave a short introduction to the film and then made his way up the aisle to leave. Bains walked up the other aisle, determined to speak to him before he disappeared into the night. 'He saw me, and it was worth the whole damn career, the joy of the hug ... And then we met again at the party and he took me over to his parents and his gran, whom I had met during *The Prime of Miss Jean Brodie* and introduced me to his agent and all that stuff ... Drama teachers have fantasies like everybody else and I suppose one fantasy is to see somebody in *Star Wars*.' But *Star Wars* represented the far distant top rung of the ladder of fame and fortune. Perth was the first rung. Kirkcaldy was the second. But that second rung was a greasy one on which many a would-be actor lost his footing. 'A number of them auditioned for drama schools at the end of it,' says Lynn Bains, 'a number of them changed their minds about what they were going to do, a number of them really couldn't have gone on: they just didn't have it.'

Ewan applied to RADA, the Royal Academy of Dramatic Art. He recalls that he forked out about £100 in train fares and application fees to go for the interview and audition in London, only to have the RADA assessor tell him, without even watching him perform, that he would have 'a good few years' of auditioning ahead of him before he got anywhere. Ewan admits to being 'arrogant' in his belief in himself, but he was not so arrogant as to assume a place at RADA was a foregone conclusion. He also describes himself as 'driven' and he was not prepared to hang around for 'a good few years' for RADA to consider him. He also applied to the Guildhall School of Music and Drama, another prestigious London college. 'When he came back I said "How did you get on?"' Lynn Bains recalls, 'and he said "I think I did OK" and "I got a little help from my uncle." And I thought "What are uncles doing helping?" and then he said it was Denis Lawson. I didn't actually know his uncle was Denis Lawson.'

Seven hundred applicants were considered for the Guildhall course. There was an exhausting series of auditions in London, over three days, at which Ewan had to read Shakespeare and be a piece of elastic ... without using his arms. Eventually 700 were whittled down to 24. Ewan was one of them. He was climbing the ladder. And yet the confidence that he had built up at Kirkcaldy would be all but destroyed in the very different, rarefied, luvvy atmosphere of Guildhall.

6

'I just tried to become a piece of elastic'

FOR TEN YEARS Ewan McGregor was convinced that he was going to be an actor. He impressed everyone with his confidence. Then he went to Guildhall School of Music and Drama. And for the first and only time he began to doubt whether he really had what it took to make it. The prevailing ethos at Kirkcaldy had been the one pioneered by Judy Garland and Mickey Rooney in what seemed like countless Hollywood teen musicals in the days before anyone talked about teens: a case of 'Let's do the show right here in the barn' and everyone knuckling down and learning their lines while painting scenery, working in the firm belief that it would be 'alright on the night'. Guildhall's philosophy was built not on the work of Garland and Rooney, but that of Stanislavsky, the Russian pioneer of what was to become 'Method' acting, and Brecht, the German architect of theatre's alienation theory. Guildhall certainly alienated Ewan. Instead of just getting on with it, the students were encouraged to uncover those mental blocks which might prevent them from getting on with it. Instead of having to paint the scenery, they had to become the scenery, maybe even the paint itself.

Bear in mind Ewan was accepted into Guildhall, not on the strength of his achievements at Kirkcaldy, not on his performance as a slightly awkward music teacher in *The Prime of Miss Jean Brodie*, but on his ability to 'become' a piece of elastic. 'I'm not a cerebral actor,' he said later, 'so I didn't think "How

can I portray elastic?" I just tried to become a piece of elastic.'
That may have been good enough for the audition, but such a
crude approach fell far short of what was required on the
course, where character motivation and history obviously
become much more important. How old was the elastic? Who
owned it? What had it been used for in the past? Why did it
want to stretch? One of Guildhall's guiding lights was the
Russian theatre director Konstantin Stanislavsky who rejected
the rhetorical, romantic traditions of 19th-century theatre. He
forced his actors to continue to wear their costumes and go on
acting 'in character' even when they were off-stage. His ideas
led to the development of the 'Method' approach to acting in
America, adopted by stars such as Marlon Brando and Robert
De Niro, but not by Ewan McGregor.

The Method maintained that if students could not become
the paint, then obviously there must be some deep-seated
reason why not, some childhood trauma. Such a mental block
would be nothing to be ashamed of, but rather a subject for
discussion, analysis and deconstruction. At the beginning of
the first term each student was invited to strip in front of their
classmates, not physically (Ewan would not have had a problem
with that), but emotionally. Ewan was one of the youngest in
the class. Eighteen was the minimum age and many of the
others had been to university before going to Guildhall. Each
in turn had to relate the story of his or her life so far. Many
actors do come from broken homes or emotionally unstable
backgrounds. They feel a need to attract attention to themselves. Maybe they feel a need to *be* someone or something
else. Ewan's classmates related their tales of trauma and heart-
ache while Ewan thought about growing up in a cosy, middle-
class little town in Perthshire, with his mum and dad and
big brother, and he thought about his respectable, fee-paying
school, with its neat uniforms and sprawling grounds and royal
visitors.

The only story he could come up with, buried deep in his
subconscious, was the rather unenthralling tale of losing a Fry's
Chocolate Cream on a river bank when he was two years old.
Compared with the stories that others had to offer, however,

the early loss of a bar of chocolate, even one as delicious as a Fry's Chocolate Cream, simply was not good enough. 'Fuck it, I'm never going to make it,' Ewan thought. 'I'm obviously not of the right stock.' When it came to Trauma, Ewan was a D-minus. 'I didn't suffer enough,' he said later. But fortunately Guildhall was going to be in a position over the next three years to provide him with a first-class course in Trauma: Guildhall *was* that trauma.

The Guildhall school was founded in 1880 and is run by the Corporation of London, the local authority for the City of London. It describes itself as 'a conservatoire whose purpose is to provide and develop the highest attainable quality of creative education, training and research in musical and theatrical performance'. It is housed in modern, red-brick premises adjoining the Barbican Centre, home of the London Symphony Orchestra and London base of the Royal Shakespeare Company. Violinists and other musicians can look out from the comfort and solitude of their Guildhall practice rooms onto an artificial lake in a clearing in the concrete jungle. The *Time Out Guide to London* however calls the Barbican a 'grim cultural stalag'. It is tucked away to the north of London Wall, beyond the normal tourist trails and well away from the theatres and other cultural attractions of the city centre. The arts centre is just part of a much bigger development built in the Cripplegate district that was heavily bombed in the Second World War, a sprawling mix of performance venues, public buildings, cinemas and high and low-rise flats bearing names like Shakespeare Tower and Ben Jonson House. Buildings are linked by paths and covered walkways. 'A phenomenally ugly and highly expensive ghetto,' says *England: The Rough Guide*. The Barbican stands as an experiment in architecture that did not quite work, with Londoners forever complaining about the difficulty they have finding their way into the concert hall and out of the blocks of flats. Despite this attempt to blend living, learning and performing, Guildhall and the real world would seem to exist in parallel universes and an air of unreality permeates the whole area.

London, not just Barbican, was a whole new world for Ewan. After the gentle pace of growing up in Crieff, he enjoyed the hustle and bustle of the metropolis, the energy of the streets and vigour of the pubs, and the freedom of being a long, long way from home. He grew his hair and wore an earring in his left ear, giving him a slightly piratical look. He did however remain extremely close to his parents, he suffered bouts of home-sickness and his freedom was restricted by lack of money. Money was going to be a worry throughout his time at Guild-hall. Despite his parents' concerns about him dropping out of school before doing his Highers, they subsequently supported him as best they could and he later recalled that they 'sold things so that I could go'. If nothing else, Ewan is thankful to his time at Guildhall for giving him an introduction to life in one of the major capitals of the world. This was no film star's introduction, via the comfort of the Dorchester and the shaded glass windows of a chauffeur-driven limousine. Ewan lived in some rough areas during his early days in London. There was 'a dodgy place' in Snaresbrook, up beyond Wanstead, and another on the Kingsmead estate in Hackney. 'Apparently it's the big dangerous one,' he enthuses, 'but I didn't see any trouble there. Well, I saw two guys drive a car into a wall and then get out, look at each other over the roof and fall about laughing ... I liked it there. It was weird.'

While Kingsmead offered a crash course in street theatre, Guildhall provided a very formal, classical training, with a strong emphasis on Shakespeare and Chekhov, and traditional, highly disciplined and stylised theatre forms such as Italy's *commedia dell'arte* and Japan's Noh theatre, with their costumes, masks and strict rules. The Guildhall drama course also includes dancing, games and animal studies. Either way, it was a million miles away from the raw realism of film and television acting. The school began to undermine Ewan's self-confidence, he began to start doubting himself and to feel self-conscious. 'Luckily I managed to get through that on my own,' he says.

Kenneth Rea, one of his teachers, insists that such loss of confidence was all part of the school's deliberate master plan. 'That's a natural process,' he says. 'One of the first things I say to actors, on the first day, is "Remember where you are today, remember who you are, because once we start working on you, it's going to erode your confidence, it's going to erode your sense of identity; once you start learning to speak standard English, it's going to threaten your very identity, so you must remember the point [at which] you began, because that's the point that you leave; that's all you take away with you." By the nature of a challenging training, a lot of it will take away somebody's confidence. But we hope that it puts the confidence back, so by the time they leave they have a training and a vocabulary that is able to last them all their working life. They can grow and build on that.' One can imagine how Ewan felt when faced with this introduction. He had to work hard at Kirkcaldy, but no one there threatened him with a loss of identity.

'The earliest memory,' says Rea, 'is of a student who was very open and had a lot of charm, and so there was a good potential, and that's the kind of student we look for at Guildhall. We don't look for people who speak beautifully polished English necessarily, or are ready-made polished actors. We look for raw talent, something that is there that can be developed. There was a good generosity of spirit and that quality is attractive in an actor ... He was outgoing, sociable and a little bit shy initially.' It is, according to Rea, a challenging course, and many students fail to fulfil their potential. But, despite Ewan's crisis of self-confidence, he excelled at improvisation from the start and Rea recalls a gradual improvement and growth as an actor over the first two years of the course. 'He was very diligent, very hard-working, and he worked with great sincerity and integrity,' he says.

Ewan's crisis of self-confidence at the Guildhall was coupled with serious financial problems. He resumed his 'career' in pop music, busking at Bank tube station with fellow student Zubin Varla, who later played Judas Iscariot in the West End production of *Jesus Christ Superstar* and performed with the Royal Shakespeare Company. On Sundays they played in a vegetarian restaurant in Clapham under the name of Mano et Mano. Ewan wrote songs about missing Scotland, with the same wry sense of humour that had characterised his poetry. He recalled a verse during an interview with *Neon* film magazine:

You don't need to worry, babe
I'm not in any pain.
But just the thing that stops me going mad
Is me slowly going insane.

Attempting to find any rhythm in that third line must surely have caused him as much discomfort as anything he encountered on his Guildhall course.

His relationship with Hannah Titley continued after he started at Guildhall. She was studying theatre management at Queen Margaret College in Edinburgh. But they were 400 miles apart and Ewan did not have the resources to nip back to Scotland every other weekend, so the romance, which had been so intense when they lived in the same halls of residence in Kirkcaldy, began to falter. It was inevitable that they went their separate ways, and Ewan began to see other girls in London. He and Hannah remained good friends, but the first great romance of his life was over.

Ewan was so hard up at the end of his second year that Guildhall nominated him for a Laurence Olivier bursary, a scheme designed to ensure that promising drama school students can make it through their final year, when the demands of the course and student productions make it much more difficult to take on part-time work or go busking to earn extra money. Each year Britain's main drama schools nominate one or two students for the awards, which are made on the basis of a combination of the nominee's potential as an actor and his or her financial circumstances. Bursaries do not necessarily go to the best nominee, nor do they simply go to the most needy. Recipients have to prove that they are in financial need, and they also have to convince the judges they have the talent to justify the investment of scarce resources. The awards are regarded as highly prestigious within the theatre world, and previous winners include the successful stage actor Michael Sheen, who subsequently played Henry V for the RSC. A panel, chaired by Nick Allott of the theatre production company Cameron Mackintosh Ltd, watched each of the 25 nominees audition on the stage of the St Martin's Theatre, long-time home of *The Mousetrap*, and interviewed them afterwards at the headquarters of the Society of West End Theatre in Covent Garden. Ewan missed out on the two main grants of £1,500, which were awarded to former sheet metal worker Joe Duttine, who went from drama school into the BBC's *Between the Lines*, and Sarah Knight, whose parents were in the process of selling their house to help her. But Ewan was one of two students who were specially commended and received £500 awards. 'We were all insistent that Ewan should get something,' says Allott. 'He had very similar qualities to Michael Sheen, who got it the year before. They had the same kind of Jonathan Pryce edge to them. There was nothing safe, secure, about their performances. You never took your eyes off them for a second.'

Guildhall, unlike Kirkcaldy, does not aim at simply pushing its students through a series of stage productions. The emphasis in the first two years is very much on tuition rather than public performance. Endless hours were taken up with lessons in voice, speech and movement. The class studied theatre history and analysed plays, rather than actually performing them. Ewan got his chance on stage in front of an audience at the end of his second year. It was a big moment for him, probably the biggest in his career so far. Mum, Dad, and Uncle Denis, who had not seen any of his work at Kirkcaldy, all came along to see him as Orlando, the hero of Shakespeare's comedy *As You Like It*. Orlando is a man of action, a man of letters and a man of romance, taking on a wrestling champion, writing verses for his sweetheart Rosalind and pinning them on trees, as once Ewan had written love letters to Vicky McNally and handed them over at school breaktime. Ewan would not only be performing at the Guildhall itself, but going off on tour to Germany and Turkey. He had been bombarded with 'technical stuff' during his first two years at college. He had become very self-conscious about technique and was terrified of Shakespeare, but suddenly he discovered he could feel the rhythm of the language and it became easier. One can almost hear Alec Guinness intoning in his ear: 'Feel the force, Ewan, feel the force.'

'Obviously getting into the Guildhall was a great achieve-

ment,' says Carol McGregor, 'but you are in there with everybody else who is good at it. When I saw him do that [*As You
Like It*], that's when I knew that I really didn't have to worry
about him. I knew then that he'd be fine, because I thought he
was absolutely brilliant in it.' His performance made a similar
impression on Dad, and on the man whom Ewan had gone to
see in *Star Wars* at the Perth Odeon, the man who was his
role model and inspiration down through the years, who had
coached him before his Guildhall audition, Denis Lawson.

Ewan's next big performance came when final-year students
put on a show of song, dance, drama and short monologues
for an audience composed largely of casting directors and theatrical agents. It was make-or-break time for the class of '92. A
good agent could make the difference between life on the dole
and ... well, it might even mean stepping right into the lead
in some prestigious film or television drama series. Jonathan
Altaras was, and is, one of London's leading agents. There
were several students he already knew and in whom he had a
particular interest. Ewan was not one of them. 'He'd never been
someone that everyone said was going to be *the* person from
that year,' says Altaras. Ewan turned his back on Shakespeare
for the agents' night and opted instead for a scene from
Withnail and I, the cult 1987 film starring Richard E. Grant and
Paul McGann as two degenerate unemployed actors. 'It wasn't
very wonderful,' says Altaras, and you suspect he is maybe
being polite. After that, Ewan felt his evening deteriorate.

He had written a monologue for himself about a legless oil-
rig worker. He wheeled himself onto the stage in his wheelchair
... and did something that the old, confident Ewan would
never have done, not in *David and Goliath*, not in *Sganarelle*,
not in *A Few from the Fridge*. He dried up. He sat there on stage
in his wheelchair desperately trying to remember his lines. And
in the silence he conveyed real pain and fear to the audience.
'It was a really dark speech,' says Ewan. 'The whole thing had
one moment of light relief in it, one little joke, and that's what
I missed.' He sat there in silence and all he could think to do
was awkwardly rub his stumps. He felt it was a disaster. But for
once in his life he was completely wrong.

Suddenly the hard-bitten, seen-it-all, cynical agents were mesmerised. 'You could feel everybody's spines around you tingling a bit,' says Altaras, 'and that was what did it ... It does happen like that at those evenings: suddenly someone strikes a chord. I mean they just find a piece that is perfect for them. And I'll tell you the thing about Ewan was that you could absolutely see he was "of the moment" ... In the crassest sort of way, as an agent, you're selling merchandise in the market place and it was just that you quite obviously knew that somehow the market place was ready, he was exactly what everybody was looking for in terms of sexiness, in terms of charisma, in terms of everything. There are obviously hugely different fashions at different times. Sometimes it's upper-class girls, sometimes it's something else; in the Seventies it was the whole Phil Davis punk thing, but somehow you just knew that in this moment there was an absolute demand for a series of sexy young actors.'

Jonathan Altaras was not the only agent interested in Ewan. He had offers from a dozen different agents, before plumping for Altaras. Altaras was discussing his new signing with a showbiz friend, who suggested that he should put him up for *Lipstick on Your Collar*, a six-part drama series set at the time of the Suez crisis in 1956. It had been written by Dennis Potter, one of the biggest names in British television, and was due to begin shooting shortly for Channel 4. They needed two young actors for leading roles as National Servicemen – one was a gormless Welshman who was into Chekhov and the other was a cooler, more laid-back character who was into rock and roll. As one of London's top agents, Altaras simply phoned the producers, told them he had 'this fantastic boy' who might be ideal for the series, and an audition was arranged immediately. It was all very quick. 'We must have been having a drinks party of some sort in the evening,' says Altaras, 'and we'd heard in the afternoon that he'd got it. I asked him to come up to my office in the middle of this drinks party and I explained to him that he'd got it, and I explained to him what the money was. I know that he'd been living in fairly bad circumstances in London. I know he had no money at all, he was living at the

YMCA in Tottenham Court Road, I think. I said "It will be £26,000" or something, "Is that alright?" And his little face lit up. And the first thing he said was "Can I phone my mother?" Which was sweet.'

His casting in *Lipstick on Your Collar* was no fluke. If he had not made his television debut in *Lipstick* he would probably have starred opposite John Hurt and a talented young actress by the name of Tara Fitzgerald in the BBC production of Luigi Pirandello's play *Six Characters in Search of an Author*. It presents the life stories of six characters who claim to be the unused creations of an author's imagination. Director Bill Bryden says that every year there seems to be one 'hot young thing' from drama school. 'They tend to be the first choice for everything and Ewan was in that position then.' He recalls that Ewan read with Fitzgerald and was excellent, but had to drop out of the reckoning after getting the lead in *Lipstick*. His role went to Steven Mackintosh, who would later co-star with Ewan in *Blue Juice*. It was a distinguished cast, the other three characters being played by Brian Cox, Susan Fleetwood and Patricia Hayes, though it did not have the sort of impact that *Lipstick* did.

Ewan never completed his three years at Guildhall, never appeared in its final productions, but not because he dropped out, as he had at Morrison's Academy. He was allowed to leave early and still graduate. While his classmates were staging their own productions in the Guildhall's 65-seat studio theatre, Ewan would be performing his own graduation show elsewhere. He would be appearing in *Lipstick on Your Collar* in front of an audience of millions. The rise to stardom had begun.

Kenneth Rea insists that Ewan deserves his 'notoriety', but warns that he may lose touch with his audience by doing too much film and television to the exclusion of theatre. It is arguable whether commedia dell'arte and Noh theatre connect more effectively with young people than *Trainspotting*, with its drugs and nihilistic outlook and hip soundtrack. There seems no doubt that losing touch with reality is indeed a danger for everyone involved in the acting profession.

7
The Elvis Presley Connection

EWAN MCGREGOR WAS always something of an exhibitionist. When he was just a little boy in Crieff he liked nothing better than grabbing the attention of the adults and showing off. One of his favourite routines was miming along to Elvis Presley records. He would wiggle his legs and hips, hunch his shoulders and adopt expressions he thought appropriate to the passions of songs like 'Hound Dog' and 'Don't Be Cruel'. 'I would spend a great deal of my time being Elvis Presley, because he was the best thing,' says Ewan. 'I don't remember ever not knowing about him.' An early photograph, taken when Ewan was at primary school, shows him in his navy blue blazer with white trim, school scarf hanging loose around his neck, with a pencil held up to his mouth in imitation of a microphone.

As a young man Ewan was a keen fan of Oasis, as a teenager he was into the Irish rockers U2, but as a small boy it was Elvis, Elvis, Elvis. His mother well remembers his obsession with the American superstar. 'He loved Elvis Presley at one time,' she says. 'He had a greatest hits LP that was always on.' That Elvis record has left a vivid impression in her memory. 'He's on the cover,' she adds, 'with a sort of gold lamé suit.' Ewan's fascination with the American superstar developed from infant impersonations into a dream of pop stardom that would help pass the long, dull hours in school, when he would rather be elsewhere. It was a fantasy in which a lyric hummed inside his head could transport him from the boredom of the maths class to a swinging rock and roll party in his mind. And then one day it happened. Just how he always imagined it...

The huge wood-panelled room is enveloped in silence as figures bend in concentration over the papers on their desks. Ewan looks up dejectedly at the old-fashioned wall-clock, whose Roman numerals indicate that it is not yet quarter past two. With a click and a judder, the big hand records the passing of another single, solitary, painfully slow minute. Mr Church, or rather Major Church, a brisk, no-nonsense military man, spots Ewan clock-watching. 'Not good enough,' says Church and he launches into a tirade about Ewan not working hard enough on his translations. He is only on the fifth page. 'Sorry, sir,' says Ewan. He opens his Russian–English dictionary but his heart is not in it. With a gleam in his eye, he looks once more at the clock. The hands begin to spin and the silence of the room is punctured by the thick, insistent thump of a bass rhythm. Suddenly Ewan leaps to his feet, his arms spread at his side, and blasts out, or pretends to blast out, the opening line of 'Don't Be Cruel', a hit for Elvis 14 years before Ewan was born.

Ewan wiggles his hips, spins, and points to Major Church, in the unlikely hope that he is about to pick up where Ewan has left off. And he does. Or seems to. Maybe he takes over only in Ewan's head. But he seems to sing the next section of the song, before pointing back at Ewan. Ewan leaps up onto his desk and resumes his impersonation. A couple of locks of his greased-back hair have now fallen untidily forward over his brow. He looks spookily like the young Elvis Presley and moves with the loose-limbed fluidity that was Elvis's trademark. As Ewan mimes the song he tosses around a white guitar. His grey jacket, white shirt and tie have been replaced by the famous sparkling gold lamé suit.

But this is no ordinary schoolboy fantasy. This is Ewan at work. He had found a job in which he was paid for doing the impersonation he had perfected as a child. And not just any job. He was playing the lead in the latest mini-series from Dennis Potter, quite possibly the most eminent and most controversial dramatist in the history of British television.

Dennis Potter was born into a mining family in Gloucestershire in 1935. He won a scholarship to grammar school and, after National Service, studied politics, philosophy and economics at Oxford. He joined the BBC as a general trainee and worked as a feature writer at the *Daily Herald*, during which time he discovered he had psoriatic anthropathy, a hereditary disease whose symptoms include swollen joints, blistered skin and hallucinations. A virtual invalid in his mid-twenties, he became the *Herald*'s television critic, though he did manage to stand for Parliament as a Labour candidate in a Tory stronghold. After the *Herald* mutated into the *Sun*, Potter resigned and began writing plays for the medium that was now supplying screen entertainment directly into the nation's living rooms, often drawing on his own life for inspiration and subject matter.

Controversy attended his work from the outset. In 1965 the BBC postponed the transmission of *Vote, Vote, Vote for Nigel Barton*, a portrait of an idealistic young Labour candidate standing in a Tory stronghold and coming face to face with the cynicism and corruption of the British political system. But that was nothing compared with later works. *Son of Man* caused a furore with its portrayal of a very human, fallible Christ. The BBC rode out the storm of public and press complaints over *Son of Man*, but banned *Brimstone and Treacle* in 1976 because of a scene in which a comatose girl is raped by a satanic attacker ... and gets better.

Potter was not always controversial, showing discipline in his dramatisations of other writers' work, including Thomas Hardy's *The Mayor of Casterbridge* (1978) and F. Scott Fitzgerald's *Tender is the Night* (1985). And even his detractors had to admit that Potter was one of the most exciting and innovative individuals in British television. He used adults to play children in *Blue Remembered Hills* (1979). And although the series *Pennies from Heaven*, the previous year, had its fair share of sex scenes, its primary importance lay in the way in which Bob Hoskins's character, a sheet-music salesman, punctuated the drama by appearing to burst into song. Of course characters had been bursting into song in traditional musicals for years, for no logical reason other than the conventions of the form. But Potter recognised the surrealism of such conventions and turned them on their head. Hoskins's character does not actually burst into song, *à la* Julie Andrews, but mimes to the original hits of the period, the Thirties, and the songs provide an ironic commentary on the drama itself. The idea was much copied and the series was turned into a Hollywood film in 1981 with Steve Martin in the Hoskins role. Potter moved on to the music of the Forties in *The Singing Detective*, in which Michael Gambon's central character suffered from the same skin disease as Potter. *Lipstick on Your Collar* completed his musical trilogy.

Ewan was one of three newcomers. along with Giles Thomas and Louise Germaine, who took top billing above a highly distinguished cast that included Peter Jeffrey, Clive Francis, Nicholas Jones, Nicholas Farrell, Roy Hudd and Bernard Hill. Ewan plays a National Serviceman, a private with the fiercely proletarian name of Mick Hopper. He is serving as a Russian language clerk in the War Office in 1956 when the Suez crisis breaks out. Again Potter was drawing on personal experience. Not only had he been a Russian language clerk in the War Office shortly before the Suez crisis, but he had already used the exact same scenario for a single play called *Lay Down Your Arms* in 1970. Potter himself dismissed similarities as 'a coincidence of the place and the time', adding that the two works were 'about utterly different things'.

Lipstick on Your Collar is about Suez, it is about empire, but specifically it is about the end of empire. It is about change, the emergence of youth culture, sexual and amorous awakenings, and it is about rock and roll. For Ewan, *Lipstick on Your Collar* was a chance to act out and get paid for those pop star fantasies of his childhood. Ewan got a chance to turn fantasy into reality and we, the audience, are treated to a series of elaborately choreographed song and dance numbers, but they remain, in terms of the drama, fantasies inside Hopper's head, a means of whiling away the days until his demob.

The camp, comic and surreal feel of the series is established in the highly stylised credit sequence when three girls pop up from a row of records on a giant, cartoon, golden juke-box, dance around an embarrassed, wide-eyed private (Giles Thomas) and, to the sound of Connie Francis's title song, strip him of his uniform, leaving him cowering in his regulation white underwear, like a refugee from a Carry On film. Each episode opens in a cinema, where a newsreel is playing. In the opening instalment schoolchildren are advised to pull their jackets over their heads in the event of an atomic attack, while a red-lipped, arch-eyebrowed, blonde usherette (Louise Germaine) chews gum and looks bored, immediately bringing to mind Diana Dors and a cheap and ephemeral Fifties concept of beauty.

The action then cuts to the War Office, an enormous parade-ground of a room that was constructed at London's Twick-enham Studios, not far from the international rugby ground, with portraits of the Queen and Churchill on the wall and desks dotted about like islands in a sea. They are occupied by men of varying ages, all in civilian clothes, but all smartly turned out in just slightly varying degrees of conservatism. Ewan is pictured in the foreground, his hair slicked back and shining with Brylcreem, studying a newspaper and writing notes. 'Bum holes,' says one of the older men, Major Hedges (Clive Francis), whose bright red braces are the only apparent challenge to the office dress code. But it would not be his braces that were worrying Mary Whitehouse and the moral majority. 'Bum holes,' he repeats in case she had still been settling into her armchair with her cuppa first time round. He continues by inviting them to picture 'row upon row of bare arses', setting a familiarly profane tone and sending Mrs W. scurrying off for her complaints book.

The other officers ignore Hedges, and he asks if he has become a bore. In the first of innumerable close-ups Ewan is heard to confirm, in his thoughts, that he, at least, is bored. His line is pared right down to 'Boring, it's boring' from a much longer version in the script, which overdosed on sarcasm and bit-terness. It is obvious from the start that here is an actor who does not need a lot of words in order to speak to the viewer. There is a hint of a smile on his lips, even a smirk, suggesting a latent mischief and perhaps a kindred spirit with Hedges.

The camera loves this young, handsome face, despite the odd youthful pimple barely masked by make-up, and it will turn its gaze to it again and again in the course of the series, like some besotted schoolgirl, looking for a smile or a laugh or just simply looking.

Ewan sits back in his chair and surveys the room with a certain bored detachment until his eyes alight on Major Church (Nicholas Farrell), at which point his eyebrows jump up, then his shoulders, then his whole body and his demeanour becomes one of alertness. Church asks if he is keen. 'Yes, sir,' replies Ewan briskly. Church returns to his work. The room is silent but for the scratch of fountain pens. Ewan's face breaks into a smile and he sings 'Oh yes, I'm the great pretender', miming to the Platters hit. Hedges breaks into the fantasy with a spirited chorus of 'Ooo, ooo'. Ewan's eyes register surprise, before his smile returns, to both his lips and his eyes. Ewan sings only two lines, though the song continues on the soundtrack, with a declaration that the singer is adrift in a world of his own. It is a brief foretaste of things to come.

Ewan's character, Mick Hopper, has apparently been translating a report from *Red Star* about the need for an improved performance from Soviet soldiers ... at football. No wonder Hopper is bored. He draws musical notes on a sheet of paper and as he draws them they are heard on the soundtrack and he launches into the Crew Cuts' song 'Earth Angel', imagining the others in the office providing a chorus of 'boo-abba', while continuing with their various desk tasks of stamping documents and measuring maps. Hopper rests his head on his hand and conjures up the vision of a beautiful, young blonde, dressed only in a fig leaf, sitting on the desk of the thuggish Corporal Berry (Douglas Henshall). Light sparkles in Ewan's blue eyes, which widen when she removes her sparse foliage and passes it to him. The song and dance routines become even more animated with Thurston Harris's bouncy 'Little Bitty Pretty One', with the officers humming, clapping and dancing, closing in menacingly on Hopper, while maintaining their stiff military bearing throughout. In an outrageous and wonderful display of camp, Hedges strokes Hopper's chin and squeezes his cheek and Majors Church and Carter (Nicholas Jones, the stuffy advocate from *Kavanagh QC*) bark 'woo-oo-oo-oo-oo-oo-oo' at each other, before the threesome adopt Ewan as a plaything to be thrown from one to the next, mussing his hair and squeezing his bum.

Older members of the cast spotted Ewan's talent more or less immediately. 'I remember watching the rushes with Dennis Potter,' says Roy Hudd, 'and I said "Good Christ, you can't take your eyes off that boy." It didn't matter who was on screen with him. He really had got something. He was absolutely brilliant. I don't know if it was his acting or if it was his personality. It was in the War Office with actors like Peter Jeffrey and Clive Francis, but you really couldn't look at anybody else … I think it hit me more with the rushes than watching him do the scene.' Nicholas Jones says: 'He's just right for the cinema. He's got great eyes – dreadful complexion he had then – but you could tell he was just really easy and relaxed and there was something very engaging about him … I actually told him, "You're going to be a …" I don't know if I used the word "star" actually, but I said something like that. I probably did use it.'

Ewan had been auditioned for his dancing as well as his acting, but the older actors had not. His colleagues in the War Office were established dramatic actors, effortlessly convincing as fuddy-duddy army officers. Somehow they had also to be turned into a dance troupe capable of carrying off big show-piece musical numbers. Two weeks were allocated to work on the dance numbers at the start of the project. Choreographer Quinny Sacks would have known exactly what to expect from professional dancers, but she realised she was going to have to make allowances for this cast and take a different approach, allowing for their own natural, individual ways of moving. In any case she did not want to be too rigid in her directions and wanted the actors to express the personalities of their characters in the way they danced. 'Lip-synching is very, very hard,' says Sacks, 'and the only way of getting it right is by hard work.'

Lipstick on Your Collar was going to be a long shoot. Feature films can be shot in as little as four or five weeks. *Lipstick* was going to take five months, beginning production in March 1992 and stretching out until August. It was not a single two-hour drama, it was going to end up as six one-hour instalments. Each of them cost just under £1 million, which was expensive by British television standards, but the budget was pushed up by the period setting, the design costs and the production numbers, which ultimately would involve belly-dancers and even a pantomime camel. It was an early rise to be on set, in costume and make-up, and ready to shoot, by about nine in the morning, but there were no awkward locations or night shoots, so actors could go home to their own beds.

Song and dance was a refreshing new experience for mature actors more used to serious drama and they threw themselves into it with gusto. Ewan, who had always been a great music fan, spent days listening to Fifties records – they constituted his principal research, but he was not the only one who immersed himself in the music of the period: most of the cast went home from Twickenham with Sony Walkmans over their ears. They would practice their dance steps not just on set, but in the dressing room as well. And when it came to filming, they were not simply miming, but belting out the songs full-blast. 'We learned the words and we sang along to the singers, but obviously you don't record that,' recalls Nicholas Jones. 'And, yes, it was fun to do. I don't remember anybody having a "voice" in particular.'

Private Mick Hopper appears to be well established as the principal character by the time Private Francis Francis, the soldier seen in the credits, reports for duty mid-way through the first episode. Francis reports to Hopper, who he seems to think is the senior officer, reporting in an accent that suggests he has come to London direct from the valleys. He is incorrectly dressed, in uniform, complete with ammo pouches and steel helmet. And he is late. He had asked directions to Whitehall, and found a likely building, but it was full of 'pictures' – he positively sings that word, breaking down the syllables as only the Welsh can do. The building turns out to have been the National Gallery. The humour that has been bubbling away finally explodes in the gormless character of Francis Francis, who would indeed fit easily into the Carry On films or *Dad's Army*, conjuring up, as he does, vivid memories of Corporal Jones bobbing around saying 'Permission to speak, sir,' and generally making a fool of himself.

While Ewan delivers a highly internalised performance as Mick Hopper, Giles Thomas acts like a Welsh rabbit caught in the headlights of a car, eyes popping, body jerking. It is not simply pantomime, but a 'character' performance that underlines Ewan's restraint as an actor and Hopper's easy charm as a character. Asked for an example of his Russian, Private Francis quotes Pushkin. 'I remember a wonderful moment', he declares with all the literary passion that the line demands, and he explains to Major Church that it refers to a meeting with an 'enchantingly lovely young lady'. Church informs him that he will be needing military words, not 'mush'. Some critics felt Thomas overplayed his character's awkwardness and that his characterisation allowed little scope for empathy or even sympathy. 'The difference between Ewan and Giles,' says Nicholas Jones, 'is that Giles was looking very hard for a character and it probably held him up, whereas Ewan would just open himself up ... It's a difficult thing to be open on camera. But he's able to come out on camera and he doesn't hide.'

Francis has a 'wonderful moment' of his own at the end of the first episode at his Aunt Vickie's house, where he is lodging and where he meets the cinema usherette Sylvia, only to discover subsequently that she is the wife of Corporal Berry and that he beats her. Meanwhile Harold Atterbow (Roy Hudd), the organist from her cinema, lurks outside, his designs on Sylvia somewhat less idealised than those of Private Francis. Hudd was playing very much against type as the leering, lascivious organist. The 1986 edition of *Halliwell's Television Companion* describes Hudd as 'cheery, cheeky ... an eager-to-please all-rounder'. Hudd had started off as a stand-up comic. He discovered that Ewan had the same 'warped' sense of humour and between takes would amuse him with stories about the old variety theatre days and life on the road.

Ewan seemed relaxed and comfortable sharing a set with such an array of British dramatic talent, though he was also understandably excited. The Elvis impression was no problem for Ewan. 'Doing him for *Lipstick* was extraordinarily easy because I'd spent most of my childhood pretending to be Elvis Presley. I just suddenly felt like Elvis. It was great.' But other pop stars were more of a challenge. 'I was really terrified when I did Gene Vincent because there were all these people from a 1950s club who came along to be extras and they kept shouting "Nah, nah, that's not right". It was bad enough having to do all this lip-synching for the cameras and acting at the same time, never mind getting crits from everyone in the audience.'

Some young actors, making such a breakthrough and being encouraged to believe that they had enormous star potential, might let it go to their heads; they might want to play it cool and start acting out the role of hotshot-in-waiting. But Ewan remained the same unaffected, genuinely nice Scottish kid he had been when he first came to London three years earlier. He arranged for his parents to come south and see him at work. They impressed other cast members with their sensible attitude. Roy Hudd is convinced he met Ewan's sister. When it is pointed out that Ewan does not have a sister, Hudd affects some surprise. 'He hasn't got a sister? Well, it must have been some bird he was trailing about then and calling his sister.'

Dennis Potter was on set for much of the time. Ewan recalls him as 'a genius, full of good advice for a young actor.' Potter had previously directed *Blackeyes* (1989), which was intended as an attack on sexual exploitation, but wound up getting him labelled 'Dirty Den' by the tabloids, and also the Channel 4 film *Secret Friends*. He would have liked to have directed *Lipstick* too, but Channel 4 said no, and Renny Rye was installed as director. Nevertheless Potter was producer as well as writer. He rewrote parts of the script as production proceeded, lived up to his tabloid nickname by expanding the role of the naked blonde girl, who was originally in only one number, and offered advice to the cast on how they should be playing their parts. 'Renny Rye banned him from the set,' says Roy Hudd, 'because he was always changing lines and things. So he used to lurk round the back and he would suggest a few to you just before you were going to do the scene, but not so that Renny would know. I think Renny Rye was quite impressed that I came out with ad libs that he thought were brilliant.'

Hopper is a much more wordly character than Francis. During a Garden of Eden fantasy he imagines an Eve (the naked blonde girl again) with a serpent whose head is a penis. He shocks Francis by telling him the Russian letters they are translating have been used as toilet paper by Soviet soldiers and retrieved from their latrines by corporals like Berry. And, to the sound of Fats Domino's 'Blueberry Hill', he imagines the office overflowing with paper covered in shit. Hopper is intent on becoming a drummer when his National Service is concluded in six and half weeks. 'Everything's changing,' he tells Francis. 'For the worse,' Francis replies. While the officers are outraged at Nasser's plans to nationalise the Suez Canal, Hopper's main concern is that it will delay his return to civilian life.

He reads Prime Minister Anthony Eden's speech in the *Daily Mirror* and imagines it delivered by his commanding officer Lt. Col. Harry Bernwood (Peter Jeffrey) in the House of Commons, with the other officers on his side of the house, and Francis, Berry and himself on the opposition benches. 'So I say to Nasser, take heed,' intones Bernwood solemnly. 'You may imagine you can do what you will but . . .' Ewan looks thoughtful, worried and then smiles as Bernwood breaks into song and adds 'don't step on my blue suede shoes'. Fantasy is heaped upon fantasy, with Ewan jiving around in blue jeans and aforementioned footwear. Hopper is more excited by the arrival of rock and roll than the loss of the Suez Canal. 'He's a character who is not so much rebellious as in tune with the times,' says Ewan, 'and especially rock and roll music. He can see all the changes about to happen, and meanwhile he's stuck in the War Office doing his National Service, translating Russian into English, surrounded by people who don't want to change and are doing everything to avoid it.' Hopper plays in the dance band at the Hammersmith Palais on Sunday afternoons, but is sacked when he tries to liven up an insipid version of *Try a Little Tenderness* with a vigorous and prolonged drum solo. In his first acting job after drama school, not only did Ewan get the chance to star in a Dennis Potter drama series and impersonate Elvis, he also got to play the drums in front of a bigger audience than he ever reached during his short-lived career as drummer with Scarlet Pride.

Francis meets Sylvia at the Palais, though she is late having been selling sexual favours to Atterbow. Meanwhile Hopper becomes infatuated with Lisa (Kymberley Huffman), the niece of an American officer at the War Office. He takes her to *The Seagull*, but it quickly becomes apparent that he does not share her passion for Chekhov. Rejected by Sylvia, Atterbow attempts to run her and Francis down with his car, but accidentally knocks down and kills her husband instead as he comes out of the pub at the end of the street. Francis steals up to Sylvia's room in the night and they make love, though he realises he is not *in* love. Hopper is attracted to her when he delivers Bernwood's letter of condolence and he imagines them duetting on the song 'Love is Strange' by none other than Mickey and Sylvia.

Francis falls into the grave at Berry's funeral, meets Lisa on the way to the hospital and discovers they share an interest in Russian literature. Hopper renews his acquaintance with Sylvia and they leave the funeral together. Back at the War Office, Bernwood, who has been falling apart under the strain of the crisis and the collapse of the established world order, warns a new recruit about the high casualty rate in his unit – one clerk dead, one seriously injured and a third with only a day or two left. Ewan smiles in amusement and then wipes the smile from his face, leaving it expressionless, and inviting the viewer to enter his thoughts. It is the same technique Greta Garbo employed at the end of *Queen Christina* when she sailed off into exile, having lost her throne and her lover. Garbo was acclaimed for her restraint, her cool exterior, with only her eyes hinting at the turmoil within, but she subsequently insisted that there was no performance involved at all and that she was thinking of absolutely nothing. Such an approach allows the viewers to see exactly what emotion they want to see in a face. And what they see is determined by the context. The audience sees Ewan, but hears Sylvia, saying she could do with some company. Hopper's thoughts return to Sylvia's flat after the funeral, and the audience assumes Ewan's look is one of wistful remembrance. This is clever film technique, far removed from the theatre arts Ewan had learned at Kirkcaldy and Guildhall.

Hopper and Sylvia do not talk of Pushkin and Chekhov, but about music, about songs that are not about mum and dad, the empire and knowing your place. Francis tells Lisa he has been in love with the idea of love, but has learned the error of his ways. Hopper and Sylvia have sex. They have sex up against the wall in her flat to the sound of 'Lotta Lovin'' by Gene Vincent, and, as the record plays, Hopper imagines serving up cups of condoms, in the War Office, instead of tea.

Potter was among those who spotted Ewan's talent early on. It took Ewan a while to get to know him, though the distinguished playwright subsequently took on the role of mentor to the young actor. 'He'd talk to me and warn me about what might happen after this came out, and about my responsibility to my talent,' said Ewan. Near the end of the shoot, at the scenes in the graveyard, Potter took Ewan aside and reiterated his warning not to simply accept whatever was offered. Every few minutes Potter had to excuse himself. He would go off and be sick behind a gravestone, before returning and picking up where he had left off, as if nothing had happened. He had only a short time to live, but it was long enough to see *Lipstick* completed. 'I think *Lipstick* is the one that people are going to approach more easily and enjoy more readily than most of my other stuff,' he said. The critics were not so sure. Several papers dismissed the characters as stereotypes. The *Mail on Sunday* pointed out that the musical numbers no longer had the element of surprise that they had had in previous productions. And in *The Times* Lynne Truss complained that the character of Hopper was simply too shallow to arouse much interest. 'All he ever did was stare into the middle distance and smirk at visions of a naked woman,' she said, before adding that Ewan was 'good in the part'.

The War Office characters are stereotypes, but that rather misses the point, which is that they are meant to be stereotypes, whose stereotypical view of the world is being undermined by the values of a generation composed largely of youths who would rather stare into the middle distance and smirk at visions of naked women than discuss Pushkin and Chekhov. *Lipstick* is a slightly uneven work. Splitting its focus between two young male characters is ambitious, but robs it of any possibility of a single towering performance such as those of Bob Hoskins and Michael Gambon in Potter's earlier musicals. The musical numbers remain enormously enjoyable, but there is a feeling that Potter is to some extent hitching a free ride on other people's songs. What had started as an innovation had now become a formula; paint your musical by numbers.

At its best *Lipstick* is tremendously funny, managing to combine the humour of *Dad's Army*, with its stereotypes, with that of *Monty Python's Flying Circus*, subverting stereotypes by placing them in the most absurd and humiliating situations. It is true however that over six hours it is difficult to work up much enthusiasm for any of the characters. The officers are pompous old farts, Private Francis Francis is a drip and Corporal Berry is a thug. Harold Atterbow is an abomination, and yet, for a price, Sylvia is prepared to help him cover up the true story of what happened the night her husband died. Despite Ewan's charisma, Hopper remains a shallow character, almost more of an observer, an everyman, than a genuine character, and yet he is the most normal character of the lot. What is perhaps most surprising, given Potter's track record, is *Lipstick*'s sense of optimism, as the four young characters appear to find their perfect match in a fairytale happy ending.

Ewan said: 'The scripts were amazing, brilliant to read … You didn't have to figure out the meaning or how to say a line, it was all set out in front of you … It seems like comedy at first, but there's as much meaning in it as you want to take from it. Although it's set in the Fifties, a lot of what he's saying is relevant today.'

With mounting expectation he awaited nine o'clock on Sunday 21 February 1993, wondering what new offers the transmission of the first episode might bring, but by that time he was already making preparations for the lead role in another big television series. More than 5.5 million viewers tuned in to

Ewan gets a taste of costume drama in a school production of Molière's *Sganarelle*. This was not his first acting role however. In a church play, aged six, the local vicar remarked in his diary that, 'wee Ewan McGregor was outstandingly good...'

Little drummer boy. Following the family tradition, Ewan joined the school pipe band, complete with kilt and Glengarry bonnet.

Playing the French horn at school provided a valuable grounding for his part in *Brassed Off*.

With his mates mid-1980s. Bleary-eyed Ewan McGregor (front) is determined to get his close-up.

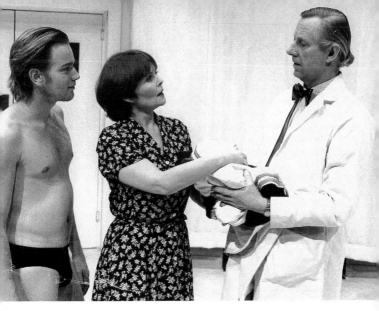

The Salisbury Playhouse, early 1993, appearing as Nicholas Beckett in Joe Orton's *What The Butler Saw* with Isla Blair and Jeremy Child.

Uncle Denis (left), with Peter Riegert, in Bill Forsyth's classic 1983 film *Local Hero*. After the heady days of *Star Wars*, Denis Lawson was offered a wonderful role as the hotel owner in a small Scottish seaside town approached by a huge American oil firm who wanted to buy up the entire village and build a refinery on the land.

Mick Hopper in *Lipstick on Your Collar* was the dream part. Written by celebrated TV writer Dennis Potter and co-starring a host of veteran actors, McGregor could not have landed a better first starring role. His childhood obsession with everything Elvis paid off when he was required to give an impression of the King during one fantasy sequence, delivering a wonderfully confident performance.

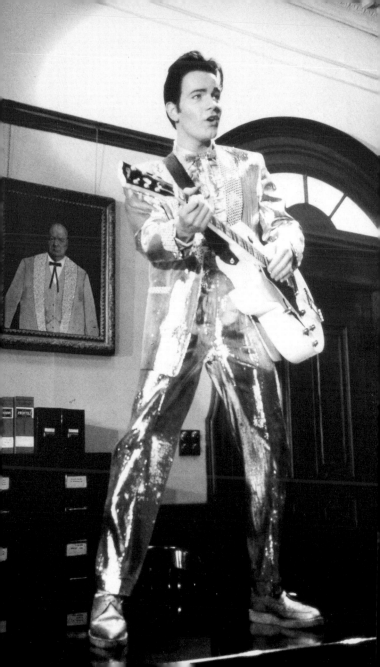

Landing the role of amoral journalist Alex Law in *Shallow Grave* was the first step along the road to the big break in *Trainspotting*. Danny Boyle directed, John Hodge scripted, and Andrew Macdonald produced: the same trio who created *Trainspotting*.

Some light refreshment for Sick Boy (Jonny Lee Miller), Renton (Ewan McGregor), Tommy (Kevin McKidd) and Spud (Ewen Bremner) before they face the challenge of 'the great outdoors' in *Trainspotting*.

#5

RENTON

Trainspotting

DUE TO ARRIVE:
23:02:96
From the makers of
Shallow Grave

18

From the worst toilet in Scotland to a thousand bedroom walls, *Trainspotting's* abiding imagery transformed Ewan's character Renton into an icon for the 1990s.

the first instalment, which is good for Channel 4, though
audiences subsequently dipped below 4 million. The six episodes were packaged and released on a double video by Polygram. On the box they put a picture of Ewan from one of the
musical fantasies, mouth open, head back, hair falling over his
forehead, a white guitar in his hand. And of course he is wearing
a gold lamé suit.

There is one little footnote to Ewan's association with Potter.
The playwright died the following year, his last two plays
Karaoke and *Cold Lazarus* were subsequently made by the BBC
and Channel 4, in co-operation, and Ewan paid his respects to
the great man by agreeing to do a walk-on appearance in the
former. He passes Albert Finney and Roy Hudd, who play two
of the main characters, outside a hospital, he has only a couple
of throwaway lines, overheard in passing, and is billed in the
credits simply as 'young man'.

8
Robin Williams, French Affairs and Radio Days

EWAN'S FIRST FILM was a $20 million international feature shot in Britain, California and Africa and starring one of Hollywood's most bankable movie stars. Robin Williams had started off as a stand-up comic, and, after an uncertain beginning in movies, he was now on the crest of a wave of box-office smashes that had included *Good Morning, Vietnam*, *Dead Poets' Society* and *Mrs Doubtfire*. He frequently mixed his distinctive madcap humour with the pathos that underlies so much serious comedy and he helped revive Disney's cartoon features by providing the voice and the comic inspiration for the genie in *Aladdin*. The new film would be produced by David Puttnam, the Oscar-winning producer of *Chariots of Fire*, and directed by Bill Forsyth, the acclaimed Scottish writer and director of *Local Hero*. Ewan could not have found a more promising project for his first appearance on the big screen than *Being Human*.

He spent a month on location in Morocco, in the winter of 1992, playing Alvarez, one of a group of survivors from a Portuguese shipwreck in the 16th century or thereabouts. Two of their number are caught trying to run off with bread and water. Robin Williams's character, Hector, declines to act as hangman on the grounds that he is no use with ropes and Alvarez, a young man with tousled hair and a neatly sculpted beard volunteers in his place. 'I'll do it,' he says. The downside of Ewan's film debut is that he does not have much to say. He has a grand total of seven words, seven different words, eleven in all, for he gets to repeat his second line. The following morning one of the condemned men appeals to Hector to stop anyone from eating them. 'That was a joke,' says Alvarez in a pronounced west of Scotland accent, stronger than Ewan's usual Perthshire lilt. 'That was a joke.' And off he runs along the beach with the prisoners and escort towards the cross which will serve as scaffold. Ewan does not even have a close-up.

Few British cinemagoers got the chance to see Robin Williams, let alone spot Ewan McGregor. With the range of talents involved the project could have been a triumph, but it turned into a disaster. It is perhaps lucky that Ewan had such a small part and escaped unscathed. It was Forsyth's most ambitious film, his own personal comment on the state of 'being human'. Williams was presented with one of the biggest challenges in his film career, playing five different characters called Hector, in five different episodes, set in different times and places, from prehistoric Scotland to modern-day California. Down through the centuries Hector meets, re-meets, leaves and loses a succession of friends, lovers and children. Shooting began in Sutherland, in the north of Scotland, in September 1992, followed by studio work at Pinewood in the south of England and the African leg in November. The shipwreck episode was meant to begin with the survivors on a raft at sea. They reach land and discover they are on the edge of a jungle. It was intended to shoot in Kenya, but insurance problems forced a late switch to Morocco. Instead of jungle there was just sand, Atlantic breakers smashed the raft and the whole episode had to be rethought and rewritten as they shot.

Ewan has said he thought he was going to be 'raping and pillaging as a hairy Highlander' in the Scottish segment, in which Hector the Caveman watches helplessly as his wife and children are abducted by raiders, including a fearsome Celtic priest played by Ewan's future *Trainspotting* co-star Robert Carlyle. But Bill Forsyth maintains that he cast Ewan specifically for the role of Alvarez. Forsyth had given Ewan's uncle, Denis Lawson, one of his best roles, as Urquhart the inn-keeper in *Local Hero*. Forsyth knew that Ewan was Denis's nephew, but says he was not influenced by the family connection and cast him after Ewan made a favourable impression when they met to discuss the project.

The final segment takes place in the United States, production was completed by spring 1993 and within four weeks there was a preliminary version of the film that reportedly ran to 2 hours and 40 minutes. Williams delivers a very effective, poignant series of characters. But the film has little humour, compared with previous films from both Williams and Forsyth, and the overall mood is one of pessimism and loneliness. Test screenings were disastrous. One elderly woman asked Forsyth if he had anything to do with the film. When he confirmed that he did, she suggested he should 'dig a hole and bury it'. There then followed a lengthy battle between Forsyth and Warner Brothers over the final shape of the film. It was reported that the studio prepared and tested an 85-minute version, which presumably eliminated at least one of the five episodes. Episodes three and four, in which Ewan appears, both end with Hector leaving a woman, so it would have made sense to drop one of them.

'There was no such cut,' Forsyth told me. He was reluctant to discuss what was obviously a very painful experience. But his comments now contradict those he made to Allan Hunter for an excellent article in *Sight and Sound* in 1994 when he said: 'The same number of people who thought the movie was slow at 2 hours 40 minutes thought it was slow at 85 minutes.' It seems quite possible that Ewan's debut might have ended up on the cutting-room floor. Various narrative voice-over ideas were discussed and two versions recorded by Williams. In the end Warner Brothers simply washed their hands of the whole project and handed it back to Forsyth. He worked on another voice-over idea with the Scottish playwright Liz Lochhead, which was recorded by the actress Theresa Russell, with Williams chipping in occasionally.

The film is undeniably downbeat and undoubtedly flawed. But it has much to commend it, including the very sense of melancholy that proved such a turn-off at the box-office and Williams's rich characterisations; not however the voice-over narrative, which may just be the worst voice-over ever, with

Russell waffling over the credits, like a drunk in a New York bar, about this being 'the story of a story' and how the story said to itself 'How shall I begin?'. Nor can the film be commended for Ewan's performance. There is nothing wrong with it particularly. He is like the substitute in a football match who comes on in injury time and never gets a kick of the ball. Ewan volunteers his services so quickly and enthusiastically that you wonder if he was worried that Forsyth might rewrite that scene too if he delayed for even a moment. Despite Ewan's prolonged presence in Morocco, Forsyth maintains his role was never bigger, that it was cut at neither script nor edit stage. The film finally opened in the United States in May 1994 and grossed only $1.5 million, which is incredible considering *Aladdin* and *Mrs Doubtfire* had recently grossed way over $100 million each. It received a belated European première at the Edinburgh Film Festival in August 1994, but never received a full cinema release in Britain.

However, Ewan did reach an international audience with a starring role in *Tragic Prelude*, though you will not find it listed in any Ewan McGregor filmography: this was a one-hour radio play he did for the BBC's World Service in 1992. A drama about the nature of political terrorism, it was written by Alfonso Sastre, one of Spain's foremost modern playwrights. Director Hilary Norrish did not think it was a particularly good play, but the World Service was promoting Spanish drama at the time and it fitted the bill. She opted for a cast of Scottish voices, including those of John Hannah, who subsequently made such an impact in *Four Weddings and a Funeral*, and David O'Hara, one of William Wallace's lieutenants in *Braveheart*. Ewan was cast as the pivotal character Oscar, a young political activist who becomes disillusioned – understandably so, given that it seems he has accidentally killed his own brother.

He was still working on *Lipstick on Your Collar* when *Tragic Prelude* was recorded in the bowels of Bush House in London in May 1992. *Lipstick* had a production schedule of five months, whereas *Tragic Prelude* was recorded in just three days. It was easy enough to fit it in and provided an early indication of how readily Ewan can switch between roles. His casting in

Tragic Prelude had nothing to do with *Lipstick* and the buzz that that was creating in the industry. Norrish had seen Ewan the previous year as Orlando in the Guildhall production of *As You Like It* and made a mental note to use him. Although *Tragic Prelude* was a very different sort of play from *As You Like It*, she believed he had the talent to move comfortably from comedy to drama, from stage to radio. She maintains radio drama is 'really a question of courage and confidence and working quite fast'. And although he was the new boy on the block, he had the courage and confidence to pull it off.

Norrish still bumps into Ewan at parties and social occasions in London. 'What is wonderful about him is his generosity and the way he doesn't stand on ceremony about his successive work. He remembers his radio work. He enjoyed doing it, he was pleased to have done it and was quite grateful, I think, at the time. And he remembers – that's not always the case.' Norrish was right however – the play is not very good. It comes across more like a political debate than a story. Ewan tries hard, perhaps a little too hard at times, but the characters never seem real – hardly surprising given that they speak in broad Scots accents but have names like Julio and Pablo, a touch of sur-realism of which Monty Python might well have felt proud.

Ewan was back at Bush House after Norrish recommended him to her colleague Gordon House. He needed a young Scot for a small, but important role in an adaptation of the Tom Stoppard play *The Real Thing*. Ewan was required only for a read-through and a half-day of recording, for which he received the standard fee of £200, give or take the odd pence or two. But it was work and the play did reunite him with his *Lipstick* co-star Clive Francis.

Francis is Henry, a successful playwright; Ewan is Brodie, a Scottish soldier who goes AWOL, meets Henry's wife Annie (Emily Richard) on a train and sets fire to a wreath at the Cenotaph during a demonstration against nuclear missiles. Brodie spends most of the play in prison, where he writes a play based on his own experiences. Henry does his best to knock it into some sort of usable form. Brodie is much talked about, but only appears at the end of the play when he gets the chance to watch Henry's version on video. Ewan got to deliver a few choice lines in a muscular Scottish accent. 'I lived it and I put my guts into it and you came along and wrote it clever,' he complains to Henry.

There was a small role for a young actress and it too went to someone who would later make a name for herself in films. Henry's daughter Debbie is played by Emily Woof. She had already attracted considerable attention with her one-woman show *Sex* at the Edinburgh Festival and went on to appear in *The Full Monty, Photographing Fairies, The Woodlanders* and *Velvet Goldmine*, with Ewan. Woof had some difficulties in adapting to radio, whereas Ewan took to it quite readily. Director Gordon House, who claims to have given Jeremy Irons and Charles Dance their first breaks in radio, says Ewan had 'enormous ... not arrogance, but confidence.' It is the adjective that comes up time and time again.

'You have to learn in radio to present the whole picture just with the voice,' says House. 'It sounds simple, but it can be quite difficult for an actor if they have done a lot of stage training ... Radio is desperate when people start overacting. The general note is less is more: you give as little as possible, but that little should be as rich as possible ... He would have to learn, in a very short time, to give the performance he would want to give on stage, but make it work in a totally different and more naturalistic medium. Radio and film are actually very similar in some ways. The raise of an eyebrow in film is the same as the little turn of the voice in radio.' After the read-through Ewan was not required again until the final scene, but he came back early to watch the other actors. Ewan had left drama school and played the lead in an important television series, he clearly had talent and confidence, but he was still pursuing his studies.

Ewan's speedy rise from drama school to international film stardom has seemed like a dream come true, with none of the depressing knock-backs that every actor, at least every other actor, must expect. The only real period of unemployment and uncertainty came after the conclusion of filming on *Lipstick* in August 1992. It was anathema to the ambitious, workaholic young actor, who became uncharacteristically depressed and convinced himself that he would never work again. He says he was out of work for four months, but he was shooting *Being Human* in November and the following month was in rehearsals for a three-week run of Joe Orton's *What the Butler Saw* at the Salisbury Playhouse, with Isla Blair and Jeremy Child.

It was to be his only professional stage appearance, excluding his walk-on roles at Perth Theatre, before the offers of starring roles in feature films started rolling in. But it did set the pattern for many later screen performances in providing him with an early opportunity to get his kit off.

What the Butler Saw was the last play written by Joe Orton before he was battered to death by his deranged lover Kenneth Halliwell in 1967, the relationship at the heart of the 1987 film *Prick Up Your Ears* with Gary Oldman as Orton and Alfred Molina as Halliwell. Orton's career was extremely brief. His first play *Entertaining Mr Sloane* was staged for the first time in 1964. It was daring stuff, a grotesque black comedy, in which a landlady and her brother both have sexual designs on the young murderer whom they are harbouring. Despite, or maybe even because of, its scenes of undress, *What the Butler Saw* seemed relatively tame after the darkness of *Entertaining Mr Sloane* and *Loot*, employing the form of the bedroom farce, with its multiplicity of misunderstandings and widespread loss of clothes. It was booed off the stage when first performed two years after Orton's death, but had been favourably reassessed in the years before the Salisbury Playhouse production, with critics acknowledging that it worked not just on the level of a farce, but also as an examination of notions of sanity and normality and a critique of psychiatry, authority and ultimately society itself.

What the Butler Saw replaces the farce's traditional bedroom setting with that of a psychiatric clinic. Dr Prentice attempts to seduce his new secretary Geraldine Barclay on the psychiatric couch, only to be interrupted by the arrival of his wife and the mental health commissioner Dr Rance. The wife is sex-mad, the mental health commissioner a complete fruitcake and the secretary is the sanest, most principled and chaste of the lot of them. Ewan played messenger boy Nicholas Beckett. Not only did he have to appear on stage naked, but also dress up as a woman. Orton had written the play not long after the Profumo scandal, when it was revealed that a British government minister had shared the favours of a call girl with a Soviet diplomat. The scandal contributed to the public's increasing readiness to question the establishment and the rights, values and propriety of those in authority.

The Salisbury production boasted a strong cast, headed by Ewan's fellow Scot Isla Blair, star of television's *The Advocates* and seen in *The Darling Buds of May* shortly before her Salisbury appearance. She was Mrs Prentice and Jeremy Child, whose extensive screen credits ranged from *Father Dear Father* to *The Jewel in the Crown*, was her husband. Roger Sloman, star of Mike Leigh's *Nuts in May* was Dr Rance. Although *What the Butler Saw* was booked for only three weeks, the cast had six weeks in which to rehearse it, spread across the Christmas and New Year holidays.

The Salisbury Playhouse had a reputation for solid, rather unadventurous productions, and the choice of *What the Butler Saw* was considered rather daring for it, even a quarter of a century after it was written. Salisbury is a staid, affluent, medieval city, much larger than Crieff, but similar in terms of historic pedigree and traditional values to the town in which Ewan had grown up. There were gasps from Salisbury's sensitive theatregoers when Ewan ran on stage naked. But the nudity did not stop the play attracting packed houses. 'It can't be easy making your stage debut without clothes but Ewan McGregor does it like a future star,' wrote Peter Blacklock, critic of the *Salisbury Journal*. 'And his clothed acting confirms his quality,' he added, as if a creditable performance in the nude may be only a flash in the pan, requiring confirmation when subjected to the more rigorous disciplines of acting with clothes on.

Ewan was prepared to do anything in character and had no problems taking his clothes off in front of an audience. 'I loved prancing around the stage stark naked ...' he says. 'That was great and you couldn't even be arrested. But I wouldn't do it as Ewan McGregor. If someone said "Take off your clothes,

Ewan", I would tell them not to be daft.' Ewan was only 21
and youthfully good looking. His long hair was swept back for
the part. But between neck and waist, he was no Adonis. It
would be pushing it to call him porky, but too many pints had
left their mark and he had the beginnings of a beer belly ...
not that it was his stomach that caught the audience's eye. Any
concerns that Ewan had with the play were of a very different
nature. Having renewed his acquaintance with the theatre,
Ewan was now coming to the conclusion that he preferred film
and television and the intimacy of the camera. 'It practically
reads your thoughts,' he says. 'I love filming. It's an amazing
process, with so many people involved to achieve the end-
product. What puzzles me about theatre is that all you're doing
is so much larger than on camera, but you're projecting to the
back of the circle, what on earth do the people in the front
row of the stalls think you're doing? I don't understand that
balance.'

Blacklock reassured his readers that the play was extremely
funny and no more disturbing than a Sunday school outing,
which rather suggests it completely failed at any level other
than that of straightforward farce. Reviewing it for the *Guardian*, Mick Martin suggested the production was a 'customised
version, with the potential bleakness and blackness of Orton's
vision diluted to taste'. He argued that it relied on the mechanics of the farce for success, while skating over the more
contentious and disturbing elements of the piece. 'As a result
Nicholas Beckett (Ewan McGregor) becomes arguably less sin-
ister and manipulative a presence in the play than he might
be.' That of course would be no reflection on Ewan's acting,
but rather the approach of the director Penny Ciniewicz. In a
largely positive review in *The Times* Jeremy Kingston was critical
of 'local lapses in tone' and an 'uncertain' performance from
Jeremy Child, but thought 'the oversexed pageboy (was) amusingly played by Ewan McGregor, particularly when wobbling
on high heels.'

Julien Sorel in *Scarlet and Black* was undoubtedly a plum role.
Unlike Mick Hopper in *Lipstick on Your Collar*, Sorel does not
have to share the limelight with any other characters. *Scarlet*

and Black is Sorel's story. Other characters move in and out of it as they enter or leave his life. It was a prestigious, three-part dramatisation of a classic French novel. The BBC had an outstanding reputation for period drama and were sufficiently confident to commit £4 million to the project. It would film largely on location in France and it would offer three months' well-paid work to whoever was lucky enough to land the lead role. There was just one problem for Ewan. 'He was not at all what the brief asked for,' says none other than his own agent Jonathan Altaras.

Julien Sorel is a slender, rather serious and determinedly bookish protagonist in Stendhal's original novel *Le Rouge et le Noir*. His story is set against the backdrop of political uncertainty and the debate between royalists and liberals that culminated in the abdication of King Charles X in favour of a 'citizen king' just months before the book's publication in 1830. Julien's origins are humble – his father runs the saw mill in a small provincial town – but he proves himself an extremely able Latin scholar and is engaged as tutor to the children of the local mayor, from which position he works his way into the heart of Parisian society and undertakes a secret mission for the king. He serves in both the army (scarlet) and the church (black). Julien is not afraid to use sex to advance himself, but *Le Rouge et le Noir* is hardly a romp like *Tom Jones*. It affords a commentary on the political and class structure of contemporary French society and was belatedly acclaimed for the psychological depth and complexity of its protagonist. The casting of Julien was absolutely vital. Director Ben Bolt, son of playwright Robert Bolt, said: 'The first thing that struck me on reading the book was that if we couldn't get the right Julien, it wasn't worth making the film at all.'

'They wanted sort of dark and smouldering and rather intellectual,' says Altaras. 'And, with respect to Ewan, he's not any of those things ... The intellectual bit, that's not what he gives over. Nor in fact is there anything period about him at all: he's very contemporary.' But it was Altaras's job to persuade others that Ewan was right for parts, not wrong for them, even if that is what he himself felt. And it was such a choice part that Ewan simply had to try for it. Bolt was impressed with Ewan as an actor, though Ewan certainly did not fit his preconceptions of the character. In an interview with the *Radio Times* Ewan said: 'The first time I went to see Ben, I got the impression I wasn't what he was looking for. The second time I was determined to make him change his mind.' Ewan saw Julien as an 'extra-ordinarily proud, angry, arrogant and brave' individual. 'He is driven by this obsessive desire to succeed, yet he never purposely does anyone any harm.' The interviewer Chris Middleton asked if there were similarities between Julien and Ewan. 'I am very ambitious I suppose. I always wanted to be an actor and I took no notice of people who tried to put me off. It was the same with getting this part.' Over five years Altaras cannot remember putting Ewan forward for any role that he did not get. 'Directors, in the nicest possible way, always fall in love with him. We sent him to things that he was so not what the brief was asking for, almost with a sinking heart, because you just thought it's so unfair, because people who are absolutely what the brief is looking for are not going to get it ... It's one of the things that's unexplainable, particularly to actors who want the whole business to be more fair and rational than it is. There are some people that directors love instantly on meeting. They find them exciting and charming and charismatic. And there are others, however good they are as actors, that directors are not excited by.' Ewan persuaded the programme-makers that all he needed to do was dye his hair and he would be Julien.

Ewan himself had a crisis of confidence shortly before starting rehearsals for *Scarlet and Black*. 'I suddenly felt crushed by the weight of responsibility inherent in the part,' he says, 'and genuinely doubted I was up to it. I was scared, but the final straw was when a fellow actor told me that, bar Hamlet, this had to be the best part for a young actor.' So what did Ewan do? Who did he turn to? He went home to his mummy and returned with renewed confidence in himself. 'Suddenly everything just fell into place.' Channel 4 had just finished broadcasting *Lipstick on Your Collar* when *Scarlet and Black* began shooting in April 1993, with a cast that included, as Julien's lovers, Alice Krige, the South African actress who had a small part in *Chariots of Fire* and would later play the Borg Queen in *Star Trek: First Contact*, and a young Rachel Weisz, who went on to develop a big-screen career that included Bernardo Bertolucci's *Stealing Beauty* and *Chain Reaction* with Keanu Reeves. Playing Julien's mentor and protector Father Pirard was Stratford Johns, another South African, who had made a name for himself as Inspector Barlow in *Z-Cars* and the spin-off *Softly, Softly* in the Sixties.

'I hadn't actually heard anything about him at all,' says Johns. 'I met him in France on the set. He was very quiet, a very diffident young man, very professional.' There was not much time to rehearse, but Johns and Ewan rehearsed scenes privately together; Ewan would already be totally familiar with his lines . . . whether they be in English or in Latin. He might not have shown much aptitude for books and study at Morrison's Academy, but he proved that he could turn his mind to it if it was to further his acting career. At a society dinner another character taunts Julien and attempts to show off by quoting Horace, but falters half-way through. Julien takes up where he left off, faultlessly continuing the passage. 'He was brilliant in that,' says Johns. He reckons there were no more than two takes, such was the poise with which Ewan delivered his lines in Latin. 'I was quite surprised to hear that he hadn't had a great deal of experience, except for the fact that he was obviously very young.'

Much of the filming took place in or near the locations in the novel, including Besançon, birthplace of Victor Hugo; though Paris was an amalgam of Besançon, Lyon and Dijon, and the series also used several English stately homes and Shepperton Studios. A considerable invasion force crossed the Channel, supplemented by local troops. The French public were curious to see the man chosen to play Stendhal's hero and seemed suitably impressed, whether Ewan was wearing the sombre black coat of a cleric or the scarlet, black and silver uniform of a dashing young hussar. 'Everyone was interested in how we would present Julien Sorel,' says producer Rosalind Wolfes. 'I think they wanted to see that we had caught the spirit. When they saw Ewan at work they approved; the women certainly did.' A fake altar was erected in the cathedral at Besançon, much of the old quarter of Lyon was cordoned off and television aerials and bus shelters were removed to accommodate the demands of the period. Bolt and Wolfes were presented with copies of the Marseillaise at a reception in Lons-le-Saunier. And in the little town of Mouthier Haute-Pierre, the local mayor supplied free sparkling wine in the expectation that *Scarlet and Black* would boost tourism.

Ewan turned tourist himself when filming finished. During the shoot, he had become romantically involved with a French woman off-screen, as well as on. He fell in love with a French member of the production team, six years his senior, and at the end of three hard months of filming, they took off together on her BMW motorbike. They spent five weeks touring the French countryside. 'She was completely in charge,' says Ewan, 'a real role reversal. We toured around wearing our bandannas and Ray-Ban sunglasses. It was like a French version of *Easy Rider*.' Two years later Ewan married Eve Mavrakis, a French film production designer, who was also several years older than Ewan. Journalists writing profiles of Ewan understandably assumed it was Eve with whom he spent that idyllic summer of easy riding, but he did not meet Eve until the following year. Ewan clearly had a thing about older French women and Eve was following in another's footsteps, or rather tyre tracks. It was as well that Ewan enjoyed himself that summer, before *Scarlet and Black* was broadcast and the critics got stuck in.

With his long, dark hair parted in the centre, Ewan looks very young in his first scene, lifted straight from the novel, in which Julien's father finds him sitting in the rafters of the saw mill, reading a book, when he should be working, though the words traditionally translated as 'lazy scamp' have become 'bone idle little shit' in the BBC version. Stendhal's style however was plain and colloquial and the translation is consistent with his tone. Monsieur and Madame de Renal want to hire Julien as a tutor, but he is concerned that he will be no more than a servant. He goes to church and kneels before Christ on the cross, asking for guidance. When he looks up

Christ has turned into Napoleon (Christopher Fulford), for it is Napoleon that Julien really worships. 'The sword is no more the way to power, my son,' says Napoleon. 'That lies now in the hands of the priests ... If a man must play the hypocrite to find his path to destiny, then so be it.' This is the theme of the piece in a nutshell, but one fears the audience may have been so surprised to see Napoleon suddenly evicting Jesus from his usual spot that they may well have missed what he was saying.

Extremely ambitious, Julien becomes not only tutor to Monsieur de Renal's children, but lover to his hitherto virtuous wife (Krige), having been advised by Napoleon that he should treat his relationship with her as a duel. Their first sex act lasts a matter of seconds, but fortunately Julien's performance seems to improve. He is however forced to leave the household and enrol in Pirar's seminary at Besançon to stifle rumours about their relationship. When Pirar is forced out for political reasons, Julien also leaves, and resumes his relationship with Madame de Renal. On one occasion he is forced to flee out of her bedroom window, jump down the last dozen rungs of the ladder and run off naked across the French countryside. 'One day I was naked the whole time,' he says. 'We had to film a sequence in four different places, so I was driven about town wearing just a dressing gown ... I quite enjoyed it all.' Ewan may have dyed his hair, but the nude scenes underlined the fact that he was a long way from fulfilling the criterion of slimness.

Julien goes to work as private secretary in Paris for the powerful Marquis de la Mole (T. P. McKenna) and becomes the lover of his daughter Mathilde (Weisz). Krige and Weisz both had nude bedroom scenes with Ewan. In one interview he took the standard tack of maintaining that there is nothing erotic about love scenes on camera, comparing them to 'dance steps', but in another, he said: 'Anyone who says you feel nothing because it's all technical is lying. In fact, the camera crew adds a certain frisson to the proceedings.' Julien embarks on the relationship with Mathilde as a challenge, but Mathilde becomes pregnant and Julien realises he is in love. The Marquis consents to allow them to marry, after Julien has spent three months in the

military, which allows Ewan to display the horsemanship he
learned as a boy in Crieff. But Madame de Renal writes to the
Marquis claiming to have been seduced and abandoned by
Julien. The Marquis forbids the union and Julien shoots
Madame de Renal in church. She survives, but Julien is charged
with attempted murder and faces the death penalty.

Julien remains a pawn in the power games of those around
him. The jury is rigged to return a 'not guilty' verdict, even
though a repentant Julien tells the court he deserves to die.
Having said that, he adds that the judgment will not arise from
a spirit of justice, but from the dead heart of corruption, 'a
sentence on a peasant, who in the eyes of you, our masters,
committed only one crime, that of attempting to rise against
the lowliness of his station'. Ewan delivers a measured speech,
full of controlled anger and, one fears, with the rather too
deliberate technique of the professional orator or actor, ensur-
ing all the pauses and looks are in all the right places. But the
speech will have no effect on those in court. Political allegiances
shift at the last moment and the verdict is 'guilty'. Even then,
Pirar brings him an offer of a reprieve in exchange for his
support of the Jesuits, but Julien is no longer prepared to
compromise his integrity. He is executed and Mathilde is left
cradling his decapitated head in her lap.

Ewan seems extremely stiff and earnest at times, but then
his character is stiff and earnest and he is landed with some
awkward, highly literary lines to deliver. 'I pledge to you eternal
secrecy,' he assures Mathilde. 'All that has transpired will be
consigned forthwith to the sea of forgetfulness.' Stendhal was
renowned for the plainness of his writing, but Stephen Lowe's
script fails to update it with any great consistency. It also fails
to either cut through or illuminate the dense political context
of the novel, which obviously meant much more to a French
audience in the 1830s than to a British one in the 1990s.
Allegiances are forever shifting between the various factions
within the church and the secular royalist and liberal camps.
What is complex on the page simply becomes confusing on
the screen. Even on repeated viewings, it is impossible to work
out where everyone stands at any given moment. There are

political allusions aplenty, but it is as if we are simply hearing snatches of a conversation, and listeners would have to turn to the novel to make sense of them.

Scarlet and Black did not fare well with the critics and Ewan received his fair share of abuse. 'Julien isn't the slight, pallid figure of the novel, but a Chippendale in a frock coat', wrote one. And another referred to 'McGregor's baffled performance' and branded him 'a bargain-basement Daniel Day Lewis'. Cosmo Landesman in the *Sunday Times* wrote: 'Ewan McGregor is simply too soft and too sweet. He's meant to be a young man in the grip of a demonic form of ambition, and yet he struts around looking like a young David Essex.' The public showed no more enthusiasm than the critics. The first episode attracted 7.69 million viewers, but it had a prime spot on BBC 1 at nine o'clock on Sunday evenings and research showed that a high proportion of viewers had switched off or changed channels before the end. By the third week *Scarlet and Black*'s audience had fallen to 5.8 million, which *Broadcast* magazine noted was fewer than the poorest of the Screen One telefilms which had been shown in the same slot. *Scarlet and Black* was not just a disappointment, it was little short of a disaster and the BBC did not even bother to release it on video.

Ewan makes for a handsome Julien, but his performance lacks depth for one very good reason for which he can hardly be blamed. What should be his defining moments as a character are taken away from him and handed over to Christopher Fulford's ghost of Napoleon. Instead of Julien agonising with his inner demons, he can simply turn to Napoleon for a chat. 'Ah, there you are, me old mate. Remind me, what's the bottom line on this hypocrisy business again?' Napoleon is a crude dramatic attempt to bring Julien's thoughts to life, but his presence upsets the balance of the drama and ends up over-shadowing Julien. At every great dramatic moment, there's Napoleon, on the roof of the seminary, in the middle of a waterfall, up on Jesus's cross in church, ever ready to tell Julien what to do, like Jiminy Cricket in *Pinocchio* or Humphrey Bogart in *Play it Again, Sam*, with Julien as a French, period version of Woody Allen, stumbling through life, never able to make his

mind up for himself. Fulford's world-weary, conspiratorial
Napoleon might actually have stepped straight from the pages
of a Raymond Chandler novel, but for the funny hat. It is not
entirely Ewan's fault if his performance lacks depth, but he
must be held responsible for any shortfall in terms of height.
His résumé had him listed as six foot. But if Ewan is six foot,
then most of the other young men in the series must have
been six foot two or three, for there are several scenes in which
they tower over him.

Another critic said: 'I don't think *Scarlet and Black* did him
any particular favours ... I don't think he's very comfortable
in period pieces.' This is not the voice of a cynical newspaper
commentator, but of Ewan's agent Jonathan Altaras. 'I per-
sonally don't think he ought to do them very willingly. I think
he's very contemporary. I think you cast Ewan as near Ewan as
possible, and then you get this wonderful charisma coming
through. I don't think you cast someone who's obviously very
contemporary in period – Lana Turner in *The Three Musketeers*
is always Lana Turner – and no way do you put Ewan McGregor
in *Scarlet and Black*, because he is Ewan McGregor.'

By the time *Scarlet and Black* was broadcast in October and
November 1993, Ewan was already working on his next project.
He was back in his native Scotland, on a contemporary drama,
a feature film that would key into his natural sense of mischief.
Its success would ensure that there was no lasting damage from
an uncomfortable period of service in the colours of the French
military and church. By the time it was released, Ewan's
awkward double act with Napoleon was just the ghost of a
memory.

9
A Low-Budget Scottish Thriller

WITHIN 18 MONTHS of leaving Guildhall Ewan McGregor had played the lead in two prestigious television drama series. *Lipstick on Your Collar* raised his profile within the industry and he was occasionally recognised in the street or in a bar, but it was surprising how quickly the public forgot just exactly who he was. He was simply someone they had seen in the corner of the living room sometime or other, as likely as not just by chance. Many actors face long periods of uncertainty, unemployment and enforced rest; Ewan had a constant stream of offers. Nevertheless he felt a slight sense of deflation, of anticlimax, after *Lipstick on Your Collar* was broadcast.

One night he was a star, the next morning he was no more than a vaguely familiar pretty face. Television remains an ephemeral medium. His uncle, Denis Lawson, had appeared in a string of television dramas and hit plays, but it was with *Local Hero* and the *Star Wars* films that he had made his mark on the public consciousness. Cinema is to television what books are to newspapers. Cinema offered Ewan the promise of genuine stardom, but more than that, it meant people would be queuing up and paying money to see his work, night after night, maybe even week after week, watching him without going to make the tea, or phoning Aunty Mary half-way through, or switching over to see what was playing in cinema two. Later they would rent the film on video, maybe. And after that, it would be shown on television. Again and again. Who knows, maybe they would still be showing it in 50 years time. Films offer immortality. After the false start of *Being Human*, Ewan was looking for another chance to make his mark in the bigger picture.

Shallow Grave provided Ewan with that chance, though only after director Danny Boyle fell out with one of Ewan's 'co-stars' from *Being Human*. Robert Carlyle was another emerging Scottish actor, though he was ten years older than Ewan. He was already 28 by the time he appeared as the soft-spoken Glaswegian builder Stevie in *Riff Raff*, directed by Ken Loach, a survivor of the Sixties school of English social realism. Carlyle showed his versatility as a psychopathic serial killer in *Cracker* and his commitment to his art by living rough on the streets of London before playing homeless in Antonia Bird's TV drama *Safe*. In due course Ewan McGregor and Robert Carlyle would appear together in *Trainspotting* and establish themselves as joint heirs to Sean Connery's throne as Scotland's pre-eminent film star.

But in many ways Carlyle could not be more different from Ewan – working-class, the product of a broken home; an intense, private individual who does not seek popularity either in his professional or private life. It was Carlyle's refusal to compromise that opened the door to Ewan getting the role of Alex Law, one of the three young professionals who share a decidedly des-res flat in *Shallow Grave* and who are driven to deceit, betrayal and murder by the discovery of a suitcase full of money. Carlyle thought Alex should be working-class and wanted to play him with his own strong working-class accent. 'I didn't think middle-class people would be driven that far for the money,' he says. 'If you put it in a working-class perspective, when people have got nothing, then there's a chance they might take that kind of risk.' Carlyle turned down the role, just as he would subsequently turn down parts in *Braveheart* and *Rob Roy* that would have raised his profile considerably. Boyle and Macdonald respected the actor's integrity. Instead of making *Shallow Grave* Carlyle and the members of his Raindog Theatre Company appeared in a short called *The Last Ten Minutes*, made by Macdonald's Figment Films company, written by Macdonald's partner John Hodge, and shown as a curtain-raiser to *Shallow Grave*, Carlyle was always more likely to follow a hit by making a short, a BBC 2 drama or a political film with Ken Loach than by grasping the chance to appear in something as starry as *Star Wars*.

But in order to make such career choices you need to have the hits in the first place and there was no guarantee of course that *Shallow Grave* would have the public queuing to get in to see it. *Being Human* had a $20 million budget, an acclaimed director, one of the biggest stars in the world and it disappeared without trace. *Shallow Grave* had a budget of £1 million, no big-name stars and a first-time director. Few would have predicted that the project would even get that far when John Hodge met Andrew Macdonald for the first time at the Edinburgh Film Festival in 1991.

Hodge was not a professional writer. He was a junior hospital doctor, though he was never a typical one. With his Glasgow accent and his hair sheared to the bone, he looked like someone you might expect to see on a hospital trolley, wearing a football scarf rather than a white coat. He had vague notions of becoming a scriptwriter and had scribbled down the outline of a blackly comic thriller on napkins, envelopes and other scraps of paper in his spare time. He was influenced not by British and Scottish traditions of film-making, but by the successful independent American film-makers who were emerging: people like David Lynch and the Coen Brothers. Joel and Ethan Coen had made their debut a few years earlier with *Blood Simple* in which a husband hires a man to kill his wife and her lover, but nothing goes to plan. It was a story of deceit, betrayal and murder, made with a £1 million budget and lots of style and imagination. Lynch and the Coens made films on relatively low budgets, with small casts of apparently ordinary characters who often find themselves in bizarre situations. Most films can be reduced to a simple premise: 'What if ...?' What if you found an ear just lying around? You set up your premise and you allow your little band of characters to react to it in their own distinctive and often conflicting ways.

Hodge needed characters and he needed a premise. When he

was a student he had shared a flat in Jeffrey Street in Edinburgh's Old Town and he thought the friendships and tensions of such a situation might provide the characters and the framework for his story. 'In any town, anywhere in the world, there are probably three people sharing a flat,' he says, 'but I realised this wasn't particularly interesting to a cinema audience looking for weekend entertainment. I knew it had to have a harder story than just their tensions over how to share the phone bill.' His first draft contained most of the elements that ended up in the film in which a journalist, an accountant and, predictably, a doctor interview various applicants for the vacant room in their flat. They choose one, who promptly dies on them, leaving a suitcase of money under his bed. This proves a much more dramatic device than a disputed phone bill. He also leaves them with the sort of question of how far people will compromise their principles for money that had so intrigued audiences in *Indecent Proposal*. Do the flatmates phone the police? Or do they keep the money, which of course necessitates getting rid of the body in the hole that gives the film its title? Of course if they phoned the police there would be no film. The case full of money is the engine that drives *Shallow Grave* at a furious pace as suspicion festers and greed strengthens its grip on each of the characters.

Hodge was living and working in Edinburgh and he thought all he needed to do was go along to the local film festival, select a film-maker from the assembled ranks, and in due course the film would be made. At festival time the Filmhouse is full of wheelers and dealers, visionaries and dreamers, chancers, freeloaders and losers, making grand plans for films that never materialise. Thousands of scripts are written; few are filmed; but Hodge was unaware of the statistical unlikelihood of getting his ideas on screen. He knew more about the workings of the human body than the film industry. If he had known statistics of the film business he might never have started writing *Shallow Grave*.

1991 was the year of *Barton Fink*, *Jungle Fever* and *Dr Reitzer's Fragment*, the work respectively of the Coen Brothers, Spike Lee and Andrew Macdonald. *Dr Reitzer's Fragment* was a 30-minute

16mm short, about the reconstruction of an old film by archivist Dr Reitzer from the fragment of the title. Hodge's sister Grace had worked as sound editor on it and it was she who set up the meeting with Macdonald. Hodge provides an amusing account of that first encounter in his introduction to the published screenplays of *Shallow Grave* and *Trainspotting*, recalling how Macdonald introduced himself as a film producer. 'This was a lie,' writes Hodge.

While Ewan was at Morrison's Academy, Macdonald was at school just along the road, at the rather more up-market Glenalmond College, and he had the silver tongue and smiling confidence – some would say arrogance – that top public schools often instil in their charges. His grandfather was Emeric Pressburger, one half of the Powell and Pressburger team that made some of British cinema's most imaginative and highly regarded films, including *The Life and Death of Colonel Blimp*, *A Matter of Life and Death* and *The Red Shoes*. He had indeed followed his grandfather into cinema, but not as a producer, not yet. He was a 'runner', the film industry version of a message boy, on *Revolution*, the English film industry's ill-fated attempt at a big-budget historical epic. Although he did have a spell in Hollywood, it was as a personal assistant and script reader – he worked as the director's assistant on the film *Shag* with Bridget Fonda. Macdonald was born in Glasgow, but there was little opportunity to work in his native land. *Venus Peter*, the story of a boy growing up in a fishing village in the Forties, was the first feature film to shoot in Scotland for three years when it went before the cameras in the autumn of 1988. Macdonald was an assistant director on *Venus Peter* and locations assistant on *The Big Man*, which shot in Glasgow and Lanarkshire the following year with Liam Neeson and Billy Connolly. Macdonald was not a fan of the few films that were coming out of Scotland. 'There's either the bloody hard man films or there's the twee Bill Forsyth thing,' he told me at the time. He wanted to do something different. 'It's a different generation,' he said. In the meantime he served as location manager on *The Long Day Closes* and TV's

The Advocates and *Taggart* and made documentaries and
shorts with his younger brother Kevin.

John Hodge wrote in the early hours of the morning, in
between treating patients, handing each new draft to Macdonald for comment and guidance. Hodge was the creative one
and Macdonald the business brain. 'From the start we were
looking at our market,' says Macdonald, 'and also writing for a
film that would not cost more than £1 million.' The fact that
there were only three main characters, one primary location
and few special effects kept costs down. 'It was a *Blood Simple*
or *Reservoir Dogs* audience, and I became a complete addict of
facts on how independent American films were made, down to
the tiniest detail of budgets and shooting schedules.' *Shallow
Grave* began to take on a very definite shape, not only in terms
of script but also budget requirements and the whole approach
to making it. The creative triumvirate behind it was completed
with the addition of a director, not Danny Boyle, but Kevin
Macdonald. A year, and a lot of work, after that first meeting
between John Hodge and Andrew Macdonald, the trio went
back to the Edinburgh Film Festival and made a short in which
they sought advice on the project from various luminaries.
They secured development funding of several thousand pounds
from the meagre coffers of the Scottish Film Production Fund,
whose chairman Allan Shiach hailed it as one of the most
exciting projects he had seen for a very long time, and he
should know a decent thriller when he sees it, for as Allan Scott
he had written the haunting *Don't Look Now*, in which Donald
Sutherland discovers too late that the vision he thought was
his dead daughter is a homicidal dwarf.

If Andrew Macdonald was not a film producer, he certainly
had the makings of one. He had charm coupled with absolute
determination – which led him to present a copy of the script
to the chauffeur of David Aukin, who was in charge of Channel
4's film arm. 'We found ourselves in the offices of Channel 4,'
Hodge wrote in the introduction to his scripts, 'facing two
responsible adults, who liked the script but wanted to know
just who did we think we were. I would have immediately
confessed to our status as bona fide no-hopers but Macdonald

intervened and revealed why he is a producer and I am not. I sat in awed silence while he calmly described his background in "film" and "television": the formative experiences at Pinewood and Shepperton (back in the days when there was a British film industry, of course), the Hollywood years, the loss of faith in the studio system, the return to small-scale, low-budget short film-making, the directorial dabbling, and the limitless commercial and artistic vision ... It was a marvellous performance.'

Channel 4 were impressed by the script, and by Macdonald, Andrew that is, not Kevin. Channel 4 were prepared to accept Andrew Macdonald as producer, but they wanted someone with more experience behind the camera. In return they would put up 85 per cent of the £1 million budget. Andrew Macdonald is not only confident, he exudes efficiency, he possesses a can-do, will-do mentality, and his easy charm has a steely, totally ruthless edge. Kevin would get to make a film alright, but it would not be *Shallow Grave*. Instead he would get to make a film about the making of *Shallow Grave*. Andrew Macdonald set about looking for a director with more experience, but not too much. He wanted someone with talent, but someone over whom he could still exert considerable influence. He found what he was looking for in Danny Boyle, a Mancunian who had an impressive track record in theatre. Boyle had worked with the Joint Stock and Royal Court Theatres and the Royal Shakespeare Company, before deciding he wanted to reach a wider audience. In television he had worked on *Inspector Morse* and *Mr Wroe's Virgins*, a spicy period mix of sex and religion, with Jonathan Pryce as Mr Wroe and an amazing cast of up-and-coming actresses – Kerry Fox, Lia Williams, Kathy Burke and a young Minnie Driver. Macdonald interviewed numerous possible directors, but Boyle was the one who most readily understood the characters, the script and the intended tone. He was the one who mentioned *Blood Simple*. It was the right film to mention.

Channel 4 gave the go-ahead in early 1993 and Boyle signed up in March, bringing with him several key personnel from *Mr Wroe's Virgins*, editor Masahiro Hirakubo, director of photography Brian Tufano and the New Zealand actress Kerry Fox, who had also starred in Jane Campion's *An Angel at My Table*. She would play the doctor, Juliet Miller. Chris Eccleston, who had played the dimwitted petty crook Derek Bentley, who hangs for a murder committed by his partner in *Let Him Have It*, was to be the introverted accountant David Stephens. When Carlyle dropped out, Ewan completed the film's on-screen triumvirate as the cocky, wisecracking journalist Alex Law. He was available at the right time, he was sent by his agents for a normal casting session and he hit it off with the film-makers, simple as that.

Fox and, especially, Eccleston can be extremely intense actors, the sort of people who might make Bobby Carlyle seem laid-back. In order to break the ice and establish a rapport between his principals, Boyle had them move into a flat together. For a week they ate together, watched films together, slept in adjoining rooms, and basically lived together as flatmates. 'They were right on top of each other all the time,' says Boyle, 'and all their habits and bad habits were exposed to everybody straight away.' After stealing a few minutes to go over his lines with Stratford Johns on *Scarlet and Black*, Ewan was impressed by the luxury of having time to get to know his fellow actors and discuss their characters in *Shallow Grave*. 'That rehearsal period was brilliant from the word go,' he says. 'We used to get up, have breakfast and do scenes in our pyjamas. In a rehearsal room, you'd set up chairs and tables, and pretend there was a wall here and a door there; but we were in a real flat, so there *was* a wall there. It allowed us to get used to each other at the same time as getting used to our characters.'

At the beginning of the film David's voice-over announces that it could be any city. 'They're all the same,' he says. It is an uncharacteristically stupid line and fortunately not one that the film itself believes. What David, or rather John Hodge, is trying to say is that the story could take place in any city. *Shallow Grave* was shot mainly in Glasgow but, although no city is ever named in the film, its makers went to enormous lengths to model the set of the flat, in which most of the action takes place, on the distinctive and incredibly spacious apartments in Edinburgh New Town. Exteriors were shot in

Edinburgh and the head office of the *Scotsman* newspaper is seen quite clearly early in the film. Glasgow offered a ready pool of technicians and £150,000 from a new city film fund if Macdonald shot there, so the flat was constructed in a disused warehouse in Anniesland, Glasgow.

At 90 ft by 150 ft, it was reckoned to be the biggest indoor film set ever constructed in Scotland. It was slightly larger than a real New Town flat – huge, high-ceilinged rooms, full of character, painted in bold combinations of rich colours like lilac and baby blue, jade and yellow, with enormous hand-painted canvases of the dramatic Edinburgh skyline visible through the windows. The hall is like a vast theatre stage, in which you hardly even notice Alex's drum-kit. The set cost about £50,000 to construct, but that would be only a fraction of what a real four-bedroom flat would cost in Edinburgh New Town. 'What we always wanted was that it should be a flat worth dying for,' says Boyle. 'A flat that stirs up feelings of slight envy about these people's lives, and so you want to join in with them and be with them in a way. This flat shouldn't just be a place where they sleep – the whole world is in there. The characters have to go to work to earn money, but apart from that they appear to have no other life – only the flat and each other ... It's a cocoon really that they have made for themselves.'

Shallow Grave shot over six weeks beginning at the end of September 1993 and finishing on Guy Fawkes Day. It was a relaxed shoot, for the actors at least. Kerry Fox worried that her character was under-developed compared with the others, but even she was finding it fun to do after the stresses of *An Angel at My Table*. She told me at the time how she would get totally immersed in her characters and how they left something of themselves in her, changing her as a person. In *An Angel at My Table* she had played the painfully shy writer Janet Frame, who was mis-diagnosed as schizophrenic and spent years in a mental home. Afterwards Fox found herself crippled by an inability to talk to other people. But on *Shallow Grave* she felt like a 16-year-old again, with hardly a care in the world.

Fox was the star of the film. It was she who got top billing, followed by Chris Eccleston. Ewan was third on the credits. He hardly appears in *Digging Your Own Grave*, Kevin Macdonald's film of the film. To visiting journalists he was simply 'the third flatmate', the one from television, though *Scarlet and Black* did start going out shortly before *Shallow Grave* finished shooting, Ewan appeared on the cover of the *Radio Times*, copies were jokingly posted around the set like 'Wanted' posters and Ewan became the butt of a few jokes about his elevation to the status of 'cover boy'. His mum came to see him and wound up with a small role in the film – Ewan could hardly get himself into his previous movie, let alone his relatives. Carol is one of the succession of people who come about the vacancy in the flat. She describes her appearance as 'ten seconds', though it is closer to a tenth of a second. There is just about enough of it to freeze-frame her on the video and no more.

Bobby Carlyle's idea of research is living rough on the streets of London, Ewan's is listening to comedy records. 'Alex was openly aggressive,' Ewan says. 'The only time you ever see him speaking to people he's being rude ... I had to find a way not to feel uncomfortable about being aggressive to people.' So he went off and listened to Billy Connolly. Much as Kerry Fox had found the character of Janet Frame rubbing off on her, Ewan began to find Alex Law rubbing off on him. 'I'd suddenly be humiliating people at parties. It was quite worrying,' he says. Ewan also spent some time in the newsroom of the Glasgow *Evening Times* to familiarise himself with the routines of reporters and he was surprised by how much of their time is spent on the phone. There were no nude frolics in this one, but Ewan did feel naked acting a contemporary character in his own accent on screen for the first time. 'I've got nothing to hide behind – no cravats, no English accent,' he said.

It is Alex who suggests that the flatmates keep the suitcase full of money and dispose of the corpse after the new flatmate Hugo (Keith Allen) overdoses on drugs. It is Alex who makes the running. Alex and Juliet go on a spending spree, with Alex ending up dressed in a sparkly little dress, wearing make-up and dangling earrings. But David, with the cool mind of an accountant, worries at such extravagant behaviour. Increasingly paranoid, he retreats to the loft to guard the money. And he has good reason to be paranoid; not only is the friendship between the flatmates beginning to fracture, but the police are starting to sniff around, in the shape of Ken Stott and writer John Hodge, who delivers a wonderful cameo as the straight, silent one, a characterisation that appears to have been modelled on Ron Mael, the stony-faced keyboards player in the Seventies pop group Sparks.

A couple of Hugo's former associates Andy (Peter Mullan) and Tim (Leonard O'Malley) are also on the scent, leaving a trail of blood and mayhem in their wake. They break in and attack Alex and Juliet, unaware that it is not just the money that awaits them in the loft. Boyle gave the actors the freedom to work on the detail of the eventual attack for themselves, and between them Ewan and Mullan came up with the idea of Mullan sticking a plastic bag over Ewan's head. 'I was getting really worried that he was going to hyperventilate,' says Mullan, 'but Ewan, being the good actor that he is, really wanted to go for it. So about take four or something we had to stop because he really was starting to hyperventilate ... the bag was over his head and he was genuinely having breathing difficulties.' In common with other cast and crew Mullan remembers Ewan as 'an all-round nice guy'. Mullan also had to clobber Ewan with a rubber 'iron bar'. 'He told me to really go for it and, given that I was going to be hitting a padding, I did. But I missed and it cracked him right on the knee ... When he screamed he really screamed ... But he was absolutely "brand new" about it; there was no sort of "Watch what you're doing", there was no kind of huffs or anything. He took it for exactly what it was, which was a mistake on both our parts, and he was honestly, absolutely "brand new" about it, whereas other actors might have been more ...' He lets the sentence drift away unfinished, but the implication is quite clearly that one might not expect all actors to display quite the same degree of newness.

Ewan believed that, despite his character's greed and cynicism, Alex had his more endearing side, that he was 'a lovable bastard', and that his finer qualities were reflected in his passion for Juliet. His most attractive feature, however, is the sheer quality of his nastiness, not so much the wittiness of his put-downs as the sheer exuberance of their delivery. 'So tell me, Cameron,' he says to one nervous young applicant for the vacancy in the household, 'just tell me, because I'd like to know: what on earth could make you think that we'd want to share a flat like this with someone like you?' He continues to lambast poor Cameron (Colin McCredie), suggesting, firmly, but matter-of-factly, that Cameron possesses none of the qual-ities for which they are looking – 'things like presence, cha-risma, style and charm.' He is outrageous in the way that a three-year-old child might be, renewing his attack on the hapless Cameron when they meet at a dance. You cannot help laughing, and yet you are not unhappy when the worm turns and thumps Alex when he goes to the loo.

It was a relaxed shoot for the actors because *Shallow Grave*, despite the darkness of its humour, is still essentially a comedy – an updating of Ealing's blacker moments for the 1990s. And Danny Boyle took the pressure off the actors because he was so relaxed and so well-organised on set. It was not quite so relaxed for the production team. Kevin Macdonald's delightfully patient, drily humorous film about the film manages to expose the chinks in his brother's charm, capturing moments of anguish over out-of-focus footage and over the realisation that they are running out of film because they ordered 18 rolls instead of 18 boxes. Kevin gently probes the sudden replace-ment of the first assistant director. 'Compatibility,' says Andrew. 'Things like that.' Kevin's camera lingers. 'It happens,' says Andrew awkwardly. In the age-old tradition of little brothers, Kevin follows Andrew around and niggles away at him until Andrew finally tells him he has had enough.

Macdonald had hoped *Shallow Grave* would be accepted into the official festival at Cannes in May 1994. When it was rejected he decided to première it in the Cannes 'market place'. Cannes is really several festivals rolled into one, with official screenings, quasi-official screenings and a huge market, just like any other market, where traders try to sell the rights to hundreds of films ranging from Asian arthouse movies to *Marco Polo: Oriental*

Sex Journey. Can-do-will-do Macdonald hired a cinema in the backstreets and played his film to an invited audience of film buyers, executives and journalists. The viewers included a large contingent of Scots, who had had little in the way of native cinema to enjoy over the years. Their presence and the news that Polygram had already bought British and American rights contributed to the buzz of anticipation that Macdonald had carefully nurtured.

It was obvious from the outset that Boyle had brought with him a fresh approach to cinema. Other directors might have zoomed in on the flat where the action would take place. Not Boyle. He treated the audience to a breakneck tour of Edinburgh New Town, to the breakneck accompaniment of Leftfield's techno bagpipe music, before drawing up outside the flat. Then it is straight into the story. Poor Cameron has 'come about the room', but it seems more like a court martial, in front of the surreal tribunal of Eccleston, Fox and McGregor. Eccleston is the bespectacled accountant, the quiet one, the one who likes to be on time and to have everything in perfect order. Fox is the slightly manic one, whose fleshy features can look extra-ordinarily ugly or deliciously sensual – there is more than a hint of sexual cruelty in her face as she grinds her high heel into Alex's chest when he falls over at a dance. And Alex – Ewan McGregor – laughs in drunken, masochistic delight as she does so. But it cuts both ways. His enthusiastic smile and twinkling eyes reflect the delight he takes in torturing his own victims. 'And Cameron,' he shouts down the stairwell as a final parting gesture, 'I mean this – good luck'; and the three existing flatmates collapse in smug, self-satisfied laughter.

The film is driven by its 'What if' premise. What if three flatmates find a corpse and a suitcase full of money? It does not bother with details, like where the money came from, who the characters are who are trying to track it down or how they eventually trace it. It is more concerned with the tension that the money creates, the shifting allegiances, the growing suspicion, the incipient violence that explodes with the arrival of Andy and Tim at the flat. Alex, the cocky one, is forced to reveal the whereabouts of the money. David, the quiet one, kills them. One corpse has become three. The accountant, who felt he could not bring himself to dispose of the original body, has become a killer. Alex and Juliet are safe from Andy and Tim, but not from David. His ordered life of balance sheets has been reduced to a primeval battle to survive in the attic. He drills holes in the floor through which he can spy on Alex and Juliet and through which light pours like miniature searchlights cutting through a night sky, catching a giant in their beams – an example of the enormous visual flair that Danny Boyle exhibits throughout the film.

Juliet is the object of Alex's infatuation, but it is David who becomes her rather wary lover. Alex meanwhile is sent by his editor to report upon the discovery of the corpses. Alex and Juliet are safe from Andy and Tim, but not from David, nor from each other. David attempts to leave with the money. Alex tries to phone the police. Juliet tries to persuade David to take her with him and blocks the door. Aware of her plans for a solo trip to Brazil, he punches her in the face, and it is as if he has punched the audience, flinching in the darkness of the cinema in Cannes. The killing of Andy and Tim had been off-screen; now, suddenly, the film is shifting from witty and cynical comedy into the realms of graphic violence and vicious horror. Alex is prompted to come to Juliet's rescue. David stabs Alex in the shoulder, and in turn is stabbed through the neck by Juliet. But, instead of tending Alex's wound, Juliet hammers the knife farther into his shoulder with her shoe, driving it through his flesh and into the floor. She escapes with the suitcase, only to discover that it is full of copies of Alex's front-page story about the discovery of the corpses. Police arrive in the flat, Andy Williams's delightfully jolly 'Happy Heart' plays on the sound-track, Alex smiles through his pain, and blood drips from his wound, through the floorboards and onto the money he has hidden beneath them.

The buzz continued long after the screening as critics and executives attempted to get their breath back, analysing the film over a few litres of overpriced wine in the restaurants and cafes around the Croissette. *Variety* called it 'a tar-black comedy that zings along on a wave of visual and scripting inventiveness'. Most of the reviews were positive, though the film did have its detractors. Kevin Macdonald was on hand to catch the raw, unconsidered opinion of Richard Mowe of *Scotland on Sunday* as he came out of the screening. 'It's dire,' he declared. 'It's awful. I've never seen such a load of old garbage.'

While *Shallow Grave* was creating a stir in Cannes, another Ewan McGregor film was broadcast with hardly any publicity on Channel 4, though it contains one of the best performances of his career. *Family Style* was a ten-minute short made under the auspices of the Lloyd Bank Film Challenge scheme to encourage new writers, and Matthew Cooper, who wrote it, was an unemployed teenager from Leeds. Ewan plays Jimmie, a young man devastated by the death of his elder brother in a car crash. A cliched shot of speeded-up clouds over a bleak, monochrome landscape seems to symbolise the film-maker's frenetic attempts to cram too much into ten minutes, hinting at a post-industrial family saga to rival *Wuthering Heights* and ending up with something that looks more like a trailer than a complete work in its own right, but it does enable Ewan to display a wide range of emotions in a very short space of time.

The film opens with a close-up of Ewan in a black leather jacket at the graveside. The combination of the long, flowing hair and the pain that marks his features gives him a strongly Byronic air, but the subsequent performance of restless intensity and incipient violence brings to mind no one more so than James Dean. Jimmie rips posters from his wall, he breaks down in tears, he tries to find comfort in a bottle of Jack Daniels and by playing his guitar. He discovers that his girlfriend Julie (Amelia Curtis) is pregnant and his father (Ian Redford) is about to sell some of their land. Jimmie explodes into violence and viciously beats him up. He heads off down the road with a bag over his shoulder, only to change his mind and come back. *Family Style* took only a few days to shoot in February, but Ewan put as much into it as any other film, impressing all those around him, with his ability to suddenly move in and out of character, switching between Scottish and Yorkshire accents in the process. 'I've never had a showreel as such,' he says. 'But I was so proud of the film that I showed it to a lot of people. It's been really useful to me.'

Shallow Grave received its British première in August, appropriately at the Edinburgh Film Festival, where Andrew Macdonald and John Hodge had met three years before. People either loved it or hated it. It was certainly very different from anything that had come out of Scotland before. In no way reliant on Scottish stereotypes of kilts and hardmen, it could indeed have been set anywhere. At the Dinard festival in France it won the best film award and its three stars shared the best actor award. It was finally released in Britain in January 1995, more than a year after filming. Unusually, and perhaps a little annoyingly, for Ewan, though he would probably never admit it, media attention tended to focus on the trio behind the camera rather than those in front of it. *Empire* carried a small picture of the actors and a large one of the film-makers, with individual interviews with the latter trio. Macdonald, Hodge and Boyle had made themselves available for interviews from Cannes onwards, while the actors were elsewhere. While *Shallow Grave* undoubtedly boosted Ewan's career, it did more to make stars of Macdonald, Hodge and Boyle than McGregor, Fox and Eccleston.

The debate over the film's merits continued, with Caroline Westbrook calling it 'the best British thriller for years' in *Empire* magazine and Philip Kemp writing in *Sight and Sound* that 'anyone who feared the British cinema was becoming mired in tasteful period adaptations and the twitteries of the idle rich should take heart from *Shallow Grave*,' while elsewhere in the same edition writer Ronan Bennett complained of 'the freezing and cruel emptiness at the film's heart'. But there is a long tradition of extracting humour from cruelty, from the man who slips on a banana skin through to Kevin Kline tormenting Michael Palin by eating his pet fish in *A Fish Called Wanda* and Michael Douglas and Kathleen Turner as an estranged couple who end up killing each other in *The War of the Roses*. Boyle told Bennett that at one point they actually considered calling the film *Cruel*.

One detractor was Robert Carlyle. 'I've no regrets about

turning it down,' he said. 'The film was an exercise in style geared to an English audience.' But Carlyle had misread it all along. The characters' comfortable lifestyle and elegant surroundings are a vital ingredient in the plot. They mean that the characters do not have the excuse of being poor to justify their behaviour. In its own way *Shallow Grave* is as political as a Ken Loach movie, for it is a comment upon, and an indictment of, the Thatcher ethos of money, more money and naked greed. But the political comment is incidental. First and foremost *Shallow Grave* is entertainment. Some critics suggested there was no character with whom the audience could identify. But ultimately they might identify or at least sympathise with any or all of them – Juliet, who thinks she is walking off with the money but ends up with nothing; David, who clearly has been driven off his rocker and ends up dead; and Ewan's Alex, who shows that when it comes to the bit his heart is in the right place after all, and who ends up with the cash.

It was his most accomplished performance so far, after the discomfort of *Scarlet and Black*. There was a danger that Alex would prove so obnoxious in the early part of the film that he would alienate the audience – and there is no doubt he alienated some – but yet again McGregor's legendary boyish charm is sufficient to carry a large proportion of the audience with him, to have them reserve judgment on his character. *Shallow Grave* is brilliantly written and directed, but it still needed three very fine actors to carry it off. McGregor more than holds his own with two of the finest young film actors around and their collective contribution was acknowledged in many of the reviews, as well as in the award at Dinard. *Shallow Grave* provided Ewan with a critical and commercial hit to launch his film career. It exceeded all expectations at the box office. It was far and away the highest-grossing indigenous film of the year in Britain. It grossed more than £5 million in Britain in 1995 and about £13 million worldwide.

Ironically, given the source of its inspiration, the one territory where *Shallow Grave* failed to make much impression was North America. It languished behind Hugh Grant's *The Englishman Who Went Up a Hill But Came Down a Mountain* and *Priest*, with

Robert Carlyle. Ewan told *Premiere* magazine that he wanted to work with a director who used film as art. 'But if I was offered the lead in an adventure movie in the States,' he added, 'I'd be the first one to jump on a plane. I'd love to run about a jungle with a gun.' North America was a challenge to which Ewan would return in due course.

10
How Oxford Changed Ewan's Life

WHEN EWAN WENT along to meet director Colin Gregg for a casting session early in 1994 he could have had little idea how dramatically the meeting would change his entire life. He joined a distinguished cast that included John Thaw, Geraldine James, Alison Steadman and *Lipstick* veteran Nicholas Jones in 'Nothing But the Truth', the pilot episode of what was to become one of the most successful drama series of its time – *Kavanagh QC*. Ewan was becoming increasingly accustomed to such exalted acting company. He plays David Armstrong, a soft-spoken young student accused of rape – and by the time the production went on location to Oxford for the courtroom scenes his main requirement was simply to sit in the dock and look nervous while Thaw and James engaged in a verbal duel to decide his fate. If David Armstrong looks tired and emotional that may not be entirely due to the quality of Ewan's acting. 'My vivid recollection of the shoot with Ewan McGregor was actually the social side,' says Gregg. 'He liked his margaritas.' It was the social side that was to prove so significant for Ewan.

Gregg and Ewan were part of a younger set, whose drinking sessions were 'just a little bit more' than you would normally expect on location. After a long day's shooting, they would drink in a wine bar till midnight, continue to imbibe back at the hotel till three o'clock or so and would be up and ready to start work just a few hours later. 'I don't think we had much more than two hours sleep any night,' says Gregg. 'He had a completely relaxed attitude to filming. He didn't say "I've got to go back and read my lines," he didn't say "I must have more sleep than this." He just said 'I'll do it on the day,' and he always, always did. I've been through that scenario before and actors turn up with terrible headaches and they can't function. I always knew he would do it. I always knew he knew his limits.' Ewan was totally professional, delivering the required performance on every take, not like some other young actors who expect the rest of the cast to come up with a decent performance each time while they search for their own personal performance by trial and error. There were none of the dark moods through which many actors go, often without the aid of alcohol.

Gregg got to know Ewan well during the location shooting in Oxford, though they have not kept in touch since then. It is difficult for those who have never been on location with a film unit to understand how intense and how temporary relationships can be. Old friends meet and renew their friendships only to lose touch again when filming is over. Affairs begin and then end with the shooting of the final scene. Cast and crew organise themselves into cliques, card schools and drinking crowds. 'He was a young bloke and that was what was on offer for the moment – you know, going out for a meal, having a drink,' says Gregg, 'and two weeks later, he might be doing the same somewhere else ... His social life that I know was just very spontaneous, very easy, and very whatever was going. And the company around him was similar.'

Also part of that crowd were a couple of attractive young actresses: Daisy Bates, the daughter of actor Ralph Bates, who became a regular as Kavanagh's daughter Kate; and Elli Garnett, who played David's girlfriend Sophie. One of the girls from the crew also drank with them, a member of the art department, the department responsible for designing and constructing sets and props, a petite, dark-haired French woman. She was five years older than Ewan and had considerable experience in film and television. While Ewan was still at school in Perthshire, she was in China working on Steven Spielberg's *Empire of the Sun*. More recently she had been production designer on *Bandit*

Queen, the highly controversial film about the contemporary Indian outlaw Phoolan Devi. Her name was Eve (pronounced Ev, with a short 'e') Mavrakis. At the time it seemed Ewan paid her no more attention than he did the others in the group. But in due course she would become Mrs McGregor.

McGregor's character in *Kavanagh QC* is also attracted to an older woman called Eve – Eve Kendall, a middle-class housewife who has hired him during his summer break to help dig a hole for a swimming pool in her garden. Her marriage has been going through a rough patch, she invites David in for beer and a sandwich and they have sex on the floor. The question is whether she consented. Alison Steadman is a fine actress, but it is hard to imagine her as a seductive temptress, and, given the constraints of prime time British television, it seemed beyond the capabilities of the programme-makers to portray her as such. The sex happens off-screen; nevertheless the Independent Television Commission upheld a complaint about the sound effects.

David Armstrong seems very much the sort of young man most girls would be delighted either to take home to meet their parents or take to bed. Ewan is seen in Eve's garden in cut-off denims with his long hair tied behind his head, in a shadowy nude scene at the police station and in court in a pin-stripe suit, with his hair flowing down to his shoulders and immaculately lacquered, so neat that Gregg sometimes felt obliged to ruffle it before a take. David is handsome and charming. He comes from a moneyed background, but is considerate and caring, very much the new man, and yet obviously capable of human failings. All the evidence suggests these failings amount to infidelity and poor judgment rather than rape. David even tells Kavanagh (Thaw), his lawyer, to go easy on his accuser as she is clearly emotionally unstable.

Throughout the court proceedings the camera continually turns to Ewan for reaction shots, just as it did in *Lipstick on Your Collar*. In court Eve says David had told her after the rape that 'no one would believe someone like him would go for someone like me.' David breaks down in the witness box, pleading with Eve to tell the truth. The jury opts for David's version of events. But the twist in the tale is a student who has been watching the trial and who approaches Kavanagh in a bar and tells him that David raped her too. She says David is just like his father, a wealthy industrialist, just helping himself to whatever he fancies. But we have seen the father and he is a boor. The problem is that Ewan plays the innocent party to perfection, there is no hint of boorishness, deviousness or deception, apart from the fact that we know he was unfaithful to Sophie; and Sophie is standing by him. The script does not afford Ewan the opportunity to hint at a darker side. The final twist is certainly surprising, but the reason it is such a big surprise is that it simply does not ring true.

Ultimately courtroom drama is a very static, very uncinematic form, because, by necessity, large chunks of it must simply be people talking in a single location. The demands of justice and the demands of drama are hardly the same. In which other genre does the audience get a summary of the story so far, before moving on to the denouement? And in no other form do scriptwriters consistently construct characters for the simple purpose of misleading the audience. *Kavanagh QC* was good of its type, which is not saying much. The series had been conceived as a vehicle for John Thaw when he decided that the highly popular *Inspector Morse* had run its course. 'Nothing But the Truth' attracted 13 million viewers when it was broadcast on 3 January 1995 – more than twice as many as *Lipstick on Your Collar*. It was subsequently released on video and Kavanagh proved a successful and long-running successor to Morse for Thaw.

Ewan's next job was another supporting role in a television drama, but he was choosing his projects wisely. Still only 23, he was consolidating the achievements of his early breaks in *Lipstick on Your Collar* and *Scarlet and Black*, by linking himself to projects that stood out from the rather uninspired TV norm. *Doggin' Around* was a feature-length drama written by Alan Plater, who, after Dennis Potter, was one of the most distinguished writers in British television. His credits included *Fortunes of War, The Beiderbeck Tapes* and *A Very British Coup*. It was a remarkable double for Ewan to appear in dramas by both

Potter and Plater in so short a space of time. *Doggin' Around* would also give Ewan the chance to appear with a genuine Hollywood film star. Cast as Joe Warren, an ageing American jazz pianist, on a tour of one-night stands in the north of England, was Elliott Gould, the doleful, dishevelled, former Mr Barbra Streisand. *Bob & Carol & Ted & Alice* and *MASH* had made him a major star at the end of the Sixties, and he was a brilliantly lugubrious and slovenly Philip Marlowe in Robert Altman's *The Long Goodbye* before his career began to fall away as the Seventies progressed.

Producer Otto Plaschkes had seen Ewan in *Scarlet and Black*, though he had mixed feelings about it. 'I thought he was actually miscast,' he says. 'He can't play period, Ewan. He's not a period actor at all.' But whereas he considered him wrong for Julien Sorel he thought he might be just right for Tom Clayton, the cocky, young double-bass player who is hired to provide accompaniment for Joe after he insults his original bassist by chalking the position of B flat on the neck of his instrument. Ewan did not read for the part. Plaschkes and director Desmond Davis cast him on the basis of a chat. 'His freewheeling attitude to life was what the part needed,' says Plaschkes.

Doggin' Around was very much a two-hander, focusing on Gould's brilliant but unpredictable musician and the minder who is assigned to look after him, played, coincidentally, by Geraldine James, who had just finished working with Ewan on *Kavanagh*. She meets Joe at the airport and leads him to her car, an old Citroen. 'That isn't a real car,' he snaps in mock indignation. 'You got it free with your breakfast cereal.' It is not the first time that Warren has toured these parts and as they make their way from town to town they are confronted with the legacy of his visit ten years earlier – unanswered criminal charges, a hefty gambling debt and even a paternity suit.

For *Doggin' Around*, Ewan retained the hairstyle he wore when working in Alison Steadman's garden – swept back and tied behind his head, though he had clearly given up on the razors since his acquittal and looked much more like a rapist now than he did in *Kavanagh*. He promptly informs Joe Warren that he is the best bass player there is. Joe wonders if he should not perhaps be in bed by now or doing his homework. Tom says he never misses a chance to play with one of the old-timers. 'In my neighbourhood we prefer to say living legend,' Joe retorts. Ewan does not try to match the charisma of Gould's performance. Joe Warren is the old showman, Tom the new kid on the block. Ewan keeps his own sense of humour in check and plays the lines straight, which is the only way to make his character work – talented, committed, arrogant. The drama requires a slightly uptight characterisation from Ewan to balance Gould's expansive performance. Gradually of course the two characters develop a grudging respect for each other.

The film shot for four weeks in the summer of 1993 on a budget of £1 million. Although it was set largely in northern England, most of the filming was done in London. Gould had undergone years of therapy and was prone to psychobabble, but he appreciated that Plater had provided him with a quality vehicle for his talents and he got on well with cast and crew. It was another relaxed shoot and Ewan felt comfortable bringing female company along to see some of the filming, though there was no sign of any great love affair developing with the future Mrs McGregor: Eve was still tied up on *Kavanagh*. 'He had a number of girlfriends, as I remember,' says Plaschkes, 'kept changing nightly. He's a very handsome kid obviously and girls flocked to him and he flocked to them.' His flocking days were, however, numbered.

The film's jazz venues were in London, including Ronnie Scott's club. Ronnie Scott is seen at the beginning organising Warren's visit. Anthony Etherton, in the role of the drummer Gary Powell, was the only member of Joe's band who played his own instrument. However, Ewan had to pretend to play his double bass and put on a show that would convince most viewers that he might well be a jazz virtuoso in the making. He was given expert advice and it helped that he had innate musical talent and could play guitar. He quickly picked up the necessary fingering patterns.

Doggin' Around is not one of Plater's major works. It exists almost as an extended stand-up routine for Elliott Gould, with

Geraldine James as his 'straight man'. He tends to talk the whole time in a florid, ironic, quasi-literary style that is obviously deliberate on the part of Alan Plater. If Geraldine James is the straight man, or straight woman, Ewan is the counterpoint. It is a small, but effective performance. *Doggin' Around* was broadcast in the *Screen One* slot on a Sunday night in October, so it went out before *Kavanagh QC* was broadcast or *Shallow Grave* opened. It attracted a disappointing 3.4 million viewers, it was not released on video and became little more than a footnote in the careers of most of those involved.

Ewan's next outing *Blue Juice* gave him the opportunity to try something new – surfing. It has long been an integral part of youth culture in the United States, from the Sandra Dee movie *Gidget* in the Fifties, through the music of the Beach Boys, the Silver Surfer comic superhero and John Milius's cult *Big Wednesday* movie, to *Baywatch* in the Nineties. Generations of Australian kids have grown up on sun-drenched beaches with surfboards under their arms. Mel Gibson made his film debut in a low-budget surf movie called *Summer City*, which was intended specifically for the 'surf circuit' – cinemas and halls in seaside resorts, where audiences would be composed mainly of surfers. But Ewan was going to neither California nor Australia. He was going to be closer to Wales than New South Wales. *Blue Juice* claimed to be Britain's 'first ever surfer movie'. Of course there may have been very good reasons why there had never been a British surf movie before. *Blue Juice* shot largely on location around St Ives, in Cornwall, but eventually had to relocate to Lanzarote in the Canary Islands to catch the really big waves.

Blue Juice also gave Ewan the chance to work with Sean Pertwee and Steven Mackintosh, a couple of the young actors who subsequently became known in certain circles as the 'Brit Pack', an allusion to Hollywood's 'Brat Pack', a term applied in the Eighties to a loose grouping of American actors including Tom Cruise, Matt Dillon, Charlie Sheen, Emilio Estevez and Molly Ringwald. And the film afforded him another chance to work with new British film-makers. Carl Prechezer and Peter Salmi started working on short films together while students at the Royal College of Art in London and made a black-comedy short called *The Cutter* for Channel 4. It got a cinema release supporting Louis Malle's *Damage* in 1993. Prechezer's flatmate introduced them to the surf scene in Cornwall. They were attracted by the incongruity of quaint little fishing villages populated by muscular, wet-suited surfers, went on a surfing course, became dedicated surfers and persuaded David Aukin at Channel 4 to allow them to make a £2 million drama about four friends, facing up to the realities of adulthood, responsibility and commitment, against the backdrop of the Cornish surf scene. It would be a British *Big Wednesday* they hoped.

Filming on water is notoriously difficult and expensive and you could hardly expect the weather in Cornwall that you would typically find in California, Australia and the Canaries. The brief British summer was over before *Blue Juice* began its ten-week shoot at the end of September 1993. The production team encountered grey skies and lost equipment in rough seas. On the other side of the world Kevin Costner was having problems with his $200 million oceanic drama *Waterworld*. Salmi, who wrote the script with Prechezer and took on the role of producer, joked that it was reports of Costner's problems that kept them going. 'Suddenly the days when our schedule was threatened by erratic weather didn't seem quite so bad.' Prechezer, who directed the film, says: 'Basically we learnt how not to make a first film. It should have been set in a flat, with few characters, shooting lots of interiors.'

The actors went through a short surfing course and Ewan and Sean Pertwee went down to Cornwall about a week before filming began to hang out with the locals and get a feel for the lifestyle. Pertwee, the son of former Dr Who Jon Pertwee and star of the football hooligan drama *ID*, is the central character JC in *Blue Juice*. Approaching 30, he is torn between the demands of his girlfriend Chloe (Catherine Zeta Jones, the *Darling Buds of May* beauty who arrived in Cornwall with a tabloid entourage) and his old mates who have come down from London (McGregor, Mackintosh and the portly Peter Gunn). In one early scene JC is faced with choosing between sex and surf and opts for the latter. Although Ewan and Pertwee are seen surfing in key scenes in the film, the actors were doubled by expert surfers for the long shots. Steve England, one of Britain's top surfers, was required to cut off his long hair and surf with towels wrapped around his stomach, beneath two wet suits, in order to double for Peter Gunn.

Ewan still had the long hair and beard from *Doggin' Around*, complemented by dark glasses, a ski hat and a wet suit in the black, red and yellow that suggests an outing by the Partick Thistle Surf Supporters Club. Ewan was thankful for the dark glasses the morning after the night before. 'Fuckin' hell, I've never partied so much in my life.' On one occasion he and a friend sat up drinking after the day's filming. They drank well into the night. When Ewan's driver arrived Ewan thought he was coming to join them for a drink, but he was there to take Ewan to the set for the next day's filming. Ewan had drunk right through the night without realising it and had missed his chance for any sleep. Somehow he still manages to deliver a highly effective performance in a role that was a brave departure for him, a role in which he pushes his familiar cocky character over the dividing line that separates mischievous rogue from complete prat.

Ewan plays a London drug dealer called Dean Raymond, to whom life is just a joke. He descends on JC and Chloe uninvited, lets off a distress flare outside their window instead of knocking on the door, sells the locals duff drugs and gives the staid Terry (Gunn) a little something that has him chasing cows, declaring his love for them and spraying himself silver to become a rather overweight Silver Surfer. He does not so much laugh at life, as cackle annoyingly. In the end he is beaten up by the locals and falls out with all his friends. He is, in his own words, 'a professional fuck-up' and he decides that he must redeem himself by surfing the legendary wave known as 'The Boneyard', though he lacks the skill and experience to do so and requires JC to come to his rescue. In the end JC settles down with Chloe, and Dean stays on in the community, taking a job in a workshop that makes surfboards.

Playing jerk to Pertwee's regular guy and Mackintosh's cool

dude, Ewan's performance is as selfless as his character is selfish, though it is not a performance that such a handsome and talented young actor, someone who had already played leading roles, would want to repeat too often, for fear of being typecast as the unhip loser. Pertwee, Macintosh and Gunn are also excellent. Catherine Zeta Jones never goes surfing, but still manages to get out of her depth. But the actors are fighting a losing battle against the script. The film-makers seem to have been carried away simply by the audaciousness of their idea of a British surf movie. Beyond that basic idea, the film does not seem to know what it is trying to achieve, mixing vague notions of mysticism with a creaking sense of humour that appears to have been lifted from the Carry On films – Pertwee with a sock on his willy, Catherine Zeta Jones throwing missiles at his privates, and dialogue along the lines of 'Shit!', 'What?', 'I've just stepped in cow shit.' Tarantino, this ain't. Sean Pertwee, Catherine Zeta Jones and some Cornish cream make for one of the least appetising sex scenes ever committed to film, a sort of *Last Tango in Newquay*.

The whole thing is disjointed and, despite a few nice shots of big waves, lacks visual flair. A few critics seemed to be fooled by the hype and *Blue Juice* was the sixth most successful native British film of 1995, but the figures only show up the incredible disparity between the No 1 slot and what you might expect to gross five places lower down. *Shallow Grave* took £5.1 million at British cinemas, 20 times *Blue Juice*'s £256,000 haul. A few years later Ewan managed to run right across the critical spectrum when he said: 'It's a good laugh. I mean, it's a bit muddled in the middle. It's just a shame. It's not really very good.' The truth is that *Blue Juice* is one seriously bad movie.

Ewan was not just speaking hypothetically when he told *Premiere* magazine, shortly before *Shallow Grave* came out, that he wanted to work with a director who used film as art. He was just about to begin filming *The Pillow Book* for writer-director Peter Greenaway. No one was making artier films than Greenaway and managing to get them shown in cinemas. Greenaway was a painter, who had been making short films since the mid-Sixties and who scored a considerable arthouse hit with *The*

Draughtsman's Contract in 1982. Described as a 17th-century thriller about class, sex and landscape, it was atmospheric and at times delightfully bamboozling. Janet Suzman played a moneyed lady who hires a draughtsman to provide 12 drawings of her husband's home, and possibly an heir as well. Greenaway has seemed obsessed with numbers: one of his most playful and amusing films is *Drowning by Numbers* (1988), but he is simply gross when his playfulness and humour misfire. *The Cook, the Thief, His Wife and Her Lover* (1989) marked the beginning of a decline, which seemed to reach its nadir with *The Baby of Macon* (1993), in which Ralph Fiennes was gored to death by a bull and Julia Ormond was raped no fewer than 208 times.

Greenaway maintains, in the press notes for *The Pillow Book*, that there may be only two things in life that can guarantee excitement and pleasure – sex and literature, a statement which shows how far removed he had become from everyday reality as experienced by those living in Britain's inner cities and suburban housing estates, who were deriving more pleasure from smack than Smollett. In *The Pillow Book* Greenaway attempts to mix sex and writing. The film was inspired by a 'pillow book', a sort of personal diary and notebook, kept by a 10th-century Japanese courtier, and by the whole tradition and art of Japanese calligraphy. It tells the story of Nagiko, a young Japanese woman, whose childhood birthdays were marked by her aunt reading extracts from the ancient pillow book and her father writing a greeting on her face in beautiful script.

As an adult in Hong Kong Nagiko attempts to find men who can emulate her father's skills with a pen by writing all over her body and who can also satisfy her sexually. Nagiko was played by Vivian Wu, a Chinese actress who had appeared in *The Last Emperor, Heaven and Earth* and *Teenage Mutant Ninja Turtles III*. Ewan, in another supporting role, plays Jerome, an English translator, who does not appear until 40 minutes into the film. He proves hopeless as a calligrapher, but encourages Nagiko to switch roles and write on his body instead. Nagiko's first attempt to have her writing published is met with rejection, but Jerome is having a relationship with a publisher, whom he entices to publish her work by presenting it written on his own body. The publisher is the man who published Nagiko's father's work in Japan, while at the same time insisting upon sexual favours from him.

'I thought it was the most beautiful story,' says Ewan. And the film-making process was unlike anything Ewan had encountered before. 'Greenaway really is an artist. It sounds wanky, but it's true, he paints with the camera. They light it, then he'll go and adjust things around the set as if he was about to sit down and paint them. You're as important as the leaves on the tree in the background. A lot of it was hand-held [hand-held camera], which surprised me. He'd tell me "You come in here and you end up here," and the rest of it is just up to you ... It was a fantastic movie script, reading it was a kick in itself – it was so detailed, he had drawings of the frames in it, because he's doing frames within frames within frames, again detail right down to the bone. And pages of description, as if he's forgotten to write dialogue. Then you find out he really didn't bother to write any. But you're doing the scenes, so you have to find the dialogue yourself ... I was scared to begin with, but I think you do your most interesting work when you're not sure how it will work out.

'Jerome is a complex and vain man. He shamelessly uses and manipulates the publisher, and really surprises himself when he falls madly in love with Nagiko. Generally not one to lose control, he starts off with a hopelessly romantic idea of his suicide (after a clash with Nagiko over the amount of time he is spending with the publisher).' The 'books' were devised on paper and mannequins before being transcribed onto the skin of Ewan and other actors. Their bodies were sectioned off in white pencil before the laborious process began of creating an extremely ephemeral work of art. Gold leaf was included in 'The Book of the Lover' on Ewan's body. 'I regularly spent between two and four hours having calligraphy applied all over my body,' he says. Ewan had to get up in the middle of the night and calligrapher Yukki Yaura would start painting at four in the morning to be ready for the first scene of the day. 'Very sensual,' Ewan continues. 'And something I will not forget in a long while ... I'd often get the Japanese extras to read me, so I knew what it said. It was a surreal experience.'

Sight and Sound magazine devoted four pages to the film and the *Daily Telegraph* carried a feature on Japanese calligrapher Yukki Yaura, but more column inches and public discussion have subsequently been devoted to Ewan's body itself than what was written on it, culminating in the legendary *Elle* headline 'Actually I do have a very large penis'. Interviewing Ewan for the *Face*, Sylvie Patterson admitted that it was unnerving talking to someone whose penis she had seen blown up to ten feet. Ewan shares some graphic sex scenes with Vivian Wu and it is perhaps surprising that it is not even larger, though he explained to Patterson that it was freezing in the studio. In a reversal of the usual ratios of female to male nudity, audiences certainly see plenty of Ewan's penis and those of other male actors in *The Pillow Book*. The actors and the penises come in all shapes, sizes and colours. There is a sumo wrestler and there is an American who is so fat that it is difficult to see whether he has a penis at all. 'There's two schools on this one,' says Ewan. 'There's the school that discusses the film's artistic content at great length. And there's the other people that come up and just, straight out, say "I saw your cock on screen."' He was pleased when one article described his penis as 'very handsome'. Ewan's parents often take their respectable Perthshire friends to see his films; he advised caution on this occasion, but subsequently received a fax saying they thought the film was beautiful. There was a PS from Ewan's father: 'I'm glad to see you've inherited one of my major assets.' Suffice to say Ewan does a very good charade of *The Elephant Man*.

Ewan, the other actors, and indeed the characters they play, appear to be no more than figures in Greenaway's landscape. Despite the display of flesh, they are never fleshed out. Greenaway does not favour Ewan with close-ups, at least not of his face. Jerome appears to want to fake his death, but manages to kill himself. Nagiko writes a final love poem on his corpse, but the publisher has the body exhumed and the skin flayed as a keepsake. Nagiko completes the promised series of 13 'books' on other men and sends them to the publisher. The narrative thrust, if such a phrase can be applied to Greenaway's films, slackens after Jerome's death. There is a coldness about Green-away's work that can be very offputting and his liking for numbers can count against him: counting down the number of 'books' is rather like waiting for the minute hand on a clock to shudder forward occasionally. The final book is 'The Book of the Dead'. The bearer secures the return of Jerome's skin and cuts the publisher's throat.

Greenaway had a considerable international reputation and *The Pillow Book* was supported by Channel 4, the Eurimages Fund of the Council of Europe and several other European backers. The budget of $2 million was modest for a film that was to shoot on location in Hong Kong and Japan, where the team felt the Kobe earthquake, and in the studio in Lux-embourg. It involved lengthy post-production work to accom-modate the intricate, tricksy images-within-images that Greenaway favours and *The Pillow Book* was not released in Britain until November 1996, coinciding quite nicely with the release of *Brassed Off*, and following the huge success of *Trainspotting*.

Ewan's growing reputation and full-frontal nudity obviously helped the film find a significant arthouse audience. 'If it takes my nadgers to get them in there,' said Ewan, 'then all's the better.' Ultimately, nadgers or no nadgers, *The Pillow Book* falls far short of Greenaway at his best.

11
Choose Stardom

THINGS HAPPENED QUICKLY . . . .That opening chase to the music of Iggy Pop's 'Lust for Life', reminiscent of the Beatles being chased by fans at the beginning of *A Hard Day's Night*, except Ewan, two stone lighter than usual, with his hair cut to the scalp, is being chased by store detectives. Ewan's opening monologue, 'Choose life. Choose a job ... Choose a fucking big television,' lampooning official anti-drugs campaigns. 'I chose not to choose life. I chose something else. And the reasons? There are no reasons. Who needs reasons when you've got heroin.' This is obviously not going to be an unrelenting, social realist portrait of the despair of drug addiction. Ewan disappearing down the worst toilet in Scotland in pursuit of his opium suppositories – no, definitely not social realism, more like social surrealism. Ewan and Jonny Lee Miller doing Sean Connery impressions and shooting the ugly brute of a dog in the park with an airgun. Spud on speed at the job interview. 'How many O Grades did I get? Could be like six, could be none. It's not important. What is important is – that I am. Yes?' Ewan picking up the girl in the disco, screwing her and seeing her next morning in school uniform and realising she is young enough to get him locked up. Spud waking up at his girlfriend's house to discover he has had an accident during the night, and attempting to deal with the bundle of sheets himself. It all happens so fast. Director Danny Boyle called those early scenes 'a rollercoaster'. Spud's girlfriend's mother rising from the breakfast table and attempting to take the odious package from him and spraying crap and puke all over the kitchen and everyone in it, except that is for Spud. The abortive excursion to the hills, where Ewan is asked if he is not proud to be Scottish, and he declares emphatically that he is not. The English are wankers, he says. 'We on the other hand are colonised by wankers.' Rarely, if ever, has a film opened with a series of scenes which are all so funny and yet so funny on so many different levels, from the intellectual demolition of the Scottish psyche to the sheer horror of covering your girlfriend's parents in shit.

And then the baby dies.

Renton (Ewan), Spud (Ewen Bremner), Sick Boy (Jonny Lee Miller) and Tommy (Kevin McKidd) have gone to the desolate flat of drug dealer Swanney (Peter Mullan). Allison (Susan Vidler) and her baby Dawn apparently live with him, though there is some uncertainty about the father of the child. Danny Boyle used twins in the role of the baby, which meant neither was forced to endure the repetition of take after take for too long. The actors used to play with the babies between takes. Some of the heaviest scenes in the film were shot in Swanney's flat and the actors would break the tension cooing to the infants. The babies always had a smile for Ewan or Peter Mullan or Jonny Miller at the end of the most harrowing and draining scenes and the actors grew very fond of them. Allison screams and the others rouse themselves from their drug-induced stupor. She cannot make herself understood, but the other characters – all except the ineffectual Spud – make their way to the cot where the baby was sleeping. They look into the cot where the baby lies with its pink elephant cuddly toy. Its eyes are closed and its mouth open, it is still, white and quite lifeless. Renton turns away, Swanney rubs his face and Sick Boy breaks down in tears and is left alone by the cot. Renton goes to 'cook up' and observes, in voice-over, that 'at least' they learned who the father was that day. It is an extremely moving scene that changes the whole tone of the film.

Of course the actors knew that this was the point in the story where the baby dies – cot death – and that it would be a dummy in the cot. But there was more to it than that, things that no one talked about at the time. It was only much, much later that Peter Mullan told me what really happened that day.

'The two twins were really important on the *Trainspotting* set,' he says, 'because you were playing with these two little darlings, and it lightened things up away from all the more depressing side of the film, with all the drugs and, you know, the shit lying around, and all that. So we had great fun. All of us would take turns playing with these twins, these wee bambinos. We'd literally just left them in the green room (hospitality/waiting room) to go on set to do that scene ... The camera was through to the cot, we had run through and it was really, really shocking – the dummy had been modelled exactly on the twins. And we are now looking at a dead baby and all of us without exception ... we cried outside in the other room. I think we wept for, Jesus, I don't know, ten minutes, something like that, just all of us in this ridiculous kind of huddle, because it was really genuinely, genuinely upsetting. And Ewan was no different. I mean we were all crying, crying our eyes out, you know it was genuinely horrible to have to do that.'

Things happened quickly. *Trainspotting* came out in February 1996. It was enormous, a phenomenon, hailed by *Empire* and *Time Out* magazines as the best British film of the decade, a major event in the cultural and social life of the nation, setting the agenda, prompting widespread discussion and debate on drugs issues. Unlike *Shallow Grave, Trainspotting* was a hit in North America too. It became one of the most successful British films of all time. And it turned Ewan from a promising young actor into a genuine star. His picture appeared on the cover of magazines. But before all that, in between the filming and the release, something else happened. Peter Mullan was wrong when he said Ewan was no different from the other actors gathered in anguish around the replica baby. They did not know it at the time, but before the film came out, Ewan would himself become the father of a little girl. The birth was one of the most emotional moments of his life, though he would later share Sick Boy's despair when his baby became desperately ill.

Ewan did not know whether she would live or he would find himself with another dead baby on his hands.

Things happened quickly, but let's go back to 1993. *Shallow Grave* had just finished shooting and producer Andrew Macdonald was casting around for another idea for a feature film. A friend gave him a copy of a book called *Trainspotting*, by a new Scottish writer called Irvine Welsh, and suggested it could make a good film. Its central characters were the junkies, low life and losers that visitors to Edinburgh would probably never see. Macdonald was an ex-public schoolboy, but he had glimpsed this netherworld when working as location manager on Scottish Television's drama series *The Advocates*. He was threatened with needles and had shit thrown at him when filming in the Muirhouse area of the city.

Welsh was familiar with this junk milieu, not as a visitor, but as a former resident. His book wallows in filth and degradation. Renton fishes around in a toilet full of shit for his lost opium suppositories; another character – in the book it is David Mitchell, not Spud – shits in his girlfriend's bed and ends up covering her, her parents and their Sunday breakfast in 'a pungent shower of skittery shite, thin alcohol sick, and vile pish'. It is disgusting, and yet more than that, it is very, very funny. Macdonald was never a great reader at the best of times. Reading had become something of a chore as he now saw every new book in terms of its film potential, but he was impressed with Welsh's unsentimental approach, his refusal to present his characters as victims, and the self-deprecating humour, energy and freshness of the novel. 'It's based in reality and it tells the truth, but it uses a different way of doing that,' he told me. 'That's something we're particularly interested in.' But whether it could be turned into a film remained to be seen.

Macdonald gave the book to director Danny Boyle and scriptwriter John Hodge early in 1994. Boyle loved it. It was left to Hodge to explain why it would not work as a film. As a doctor he understood the scientific detail of heroin, and while employed at Edinburgh Royal Infirmary he had come across patients who had contracted HIV from sharing needles. He had also lived in Leith, Edinburgh's port area, where much of the novel takes place; albeit that he lived in the port's up-market outskirts. But it was with neither the subject nor the setting that he had problems. The book was in a language that would be unfamiliar to many people in Edinburgh, let alone farther afield. It was written largely in the first person, and not even the same first person – different chapters are narrated by different characters. Much of it was interior monologue. There were far too many characters. No one, including Welsh, even seemed able to satisfactorily explain the title, with all sorts of possibilities on offer from the fact that injecting is called 'mainlining' to the way in which junkies became obsessed with the drug. And last, but by no means least, there was no central narrative. The book was a collection of short stories, with a recurring cast of characters.

By this time Hodge was already working on another original script, 'a romantic comedy with edge' called *A Life Less Ordinary*, later referred to by one careless journalist as *The Lifeless Ordinary*. It was that project that was being mooted as the team's next film when they took *Shallow Grave* to Cannes in May 1994. At that point Macdonald was talking about *A Life Less Ordinary* shooting in Scotland with a budget of under £2 million, though the plans were subsequently revised and it was intended to shoot in Britain and on the east coast of America, with a budget of £5 million and Hollywood stars in both lead roles. Uma Thurman, Patricia Arquette, Robin Wright, John Cusack, Johnny Depp – 'people our sort of age, early thirties,' said Macdonald.

But Macdonald, ever the astute businessman, wanted to keep his options open and persuaded Hodge to at least try to adapt *Trainspotting*. Macdonald, Hodge and Boyle visited Leith and met heroin users. For the most part, they were the victims familiar from social realist dramas and public health warnings, rather than the characters in Welsh's books. But there were occasional moments of surreal humour too. 'I remember meeting this guy who was called Floyd Paterson,' says Macdonald. 'And he told us this story about him being high on drugs and going into a shop in Leith and he wanted half a melon, not a whole melon. So he pulled out one of those big butcher's knives that some of them carry around and started cutting it in half. He thought he was doing something reasonable, and everybody else thought it was completely mental. The humour communicates a different kind of truth.'

Macdonald, Hodge and Boyle also made contact with the Calton Athletic drug rehabilitation group in Glasgow, survivors, people who had come out the other side of heroin addiction, who had replaced heroin with football. (They were an inspiration to the film-makers and would become consultants on the film, beneficiaries from it and extras in it – providing the opposition in the opening five-a-side match.) The third thing that Macdonald, Hodge and Boyle did was to lock themselves away for a series of brainstorming meetings. It was obvious that there was enough material in the book for three or four films, but was there enough for one really good one? They discussed their favourite characters and episodes, what should stay and what should go.

They decided to focus on a single character – Mark Renton, Rent Boy, Rents – and make the film his personal journey, so that he would link together various disparate incidents, leading to the final, lengthy episode in which he and his friends go to London for a drug deal. Many of the book's characters and storylines were dropped, including the death of Renton's brother, his funeral and Renton screwing his pregnant girlfriend. Other stories, such as 'Traditional Sunday Breakfast', were transferred from one character to another. The stylisation that characterises the film began with the script. Cinema is, by its nature, a more explicit medium than literature. Some episodes in the book had to be stylised, softened or omitted, because they would be unwatchable on film. Renton's diarrhoea and his visit to the worst toilet in Scotland are described in shitty detail in the book, concluding: 'Ah then wipe my arse wi' the clean part ay ma' pants and chuck the shite-saturated keks intae the bowl . . .' The disappearance of Renton down the toilet into beautifully clear blue waters is an early declaration that the film will not be hidebound by conventional notions of reality. Begbie's violence is also stylised, though to a lesser degree, with the freezing of the moment where he simply tosses a pint pot in the air in a crowded pub. Begbie remains a vicious psychopath, but Hodge also plays up the sad humour in the character, which would have been impossible with the inclusion of the episode in which he assaults his pregnant girlfriend, recounted by Begbie in the book: 'Ah punches it in the fuckin' mooth, 'n boots it in the fuckin' fanny.' Reflecting on the possibility that she may lose the child. Begbie consoles himself with the knowledge that: 'Ah've hud bairns before, with other lassies.' It is Begbie's pathetic delusions that are funny on the page, in the blackest of black ways, but such a scene on film could unbalance and undermine the whole. The novel's language was toned down slightly on the basis that while a reader dictates his own pace, a film is dictated by what happens on screen and the viewer cannot stop it to look up a word or re-read a section. Hodge dispensed with Welsh's precise geographical details and sectarian concerns, reduced Renton's passion for Hibs to a few bedroom decorations and tried to develop Welsh's underwritten female characters.

It was November 1994 before he had drafted out his first 40 pages and handed them over to Macdonald and Boyle. 'I remember reading it coming back home on the tube,' says Boyle, 'and I just roared with laughter. The feel of the book is surrealistic and he'd captured the tone brilliantly.' Hodge continued to work on the script over Christmas, exactly one year after Macdonald had first read the book, and he had completed it by early in the new year, passing it on to Macdonald and Boyle and to the man they wanted as Renton.

Ewen Bremner was winning acclaim as Renton in a stage version of *Trainspotting* and Robert Carlyle had grown up in a working-class Scottish community among people like those in the book. But the first choice for the role of Renton in the film was always Ewan McGregor, the ex-public schoolboy from Perthshire. He had played a drug dealer in *Blue Juice*, but that character had seen himself as a hip part of the London service industries. Renton was working-class, violent and an addict, very different from anything Ewan had attempted before. He was also the lead character in a film that would be dependent on the quality and conviction of his voice-over narrative to hold it together. He said yes at once. 'It's the most amazing part. I knew it would be something special. What it does for you in terms of career, I don't think about. I was just worried about getting him right.'

Macdonald, Boyle and Hodge were being courted by Hollywood, with promises of big bucks to make whatever they wanted. But Macdonald felt a certain loyalty to Channel 4. He also had the nous to realise that he was dealing with a very controversial subject and was wary of interference from a big studio. If they could make the film on a modest budget of about £1.5 million for Channel 4, they could insist on 'final cut' – the right to produce a finished version of a film, which the studio or financier must accept without amendment. Despite his initial scepticism, Hodge had produced a viable screenplay, Ewan had agreed to play Renton, Channel 4 were ready to put up the money, the film was ready to go. There was only one problem. And it was a fairly basic one at that. Another company had already bought the screen rights to the novel – Noel Gay, the company behind the *Red Dwarf* TV series. Macdonald knew this at the outset, but was convinced he could find a way round it, that he could bully them or buy them off. But Noel Gay simply refused to give up the rights. What they were prepared to do was to discuss the possibility of a partnership and in the end Macdonald and Channel 4 had to concede a deal that gave the Noel Gay Motion Picture Company joint credit for the film and a share of profits.

Once again things were happening very quickly. Hodge completed his script in January, it went to Channel 4 in February, a deal was in place in March, pre-production – the period in which actors rehearse, locations are finalised and sets are built – was scheduled for April, and filming was due to begin in May.

While Macdonald, Hodge and Boyle were shaping the script and negotiating a deal, Ewan was shooting *The Pillow Book* with Peter Greenaway in the Far East and Luxembourg. He would be going from a supporting role in an arthouse movie to the lead character in a film by the team who made *Shallow Grave*. He did not wait until he finished *The Pillow Book* before beginning his preparations for *Trainspotting*.

Luxembourg is not exactly famous for its drugs scene. But then Luxembourg is not exactly famous for anything much. Ewan asked around and found out there was such a thing as Luxembourgois junkies. He was told they hung around the railway station, so he went there on Sundays, and spent the whole day quietly watching the way they behaved, how they spoke to each other, the way they carried themselves, the way they moved. 'I got some of my look from them and some physical ideas,' he says. Irvine Welsh and John Hodge may have provided the character of Renton, but some anonymous, uncredited Luxembourgois junkie provided the physical model. 'I used this particular stooped posture for Renton which is an exact rip-off of a guy I saw in Luxembourg.'

Ewan read more books in preparation for *Trainspotting* than he did for any other film. He had read the original novel, but had not seen the play, and, after he was cast in the film, he made a deliberate decision to avoid it because he did not want to be influenced by Ewen Bremner's interpretation of Renton. The tone of the play was completely different from that of the film, much darker and more of an ensemble piece. Ewan had to shave his head and he had to meet one other vital condition, that he would lose weight, and a lot of it, down from his usual chunky 12 stones to a more slim-line 10. He went on a diet, supervised by girlfriend Eve Mavrakis, ate grilled food and gave up beer, but not drink. He switched to wine and gin and tonic. The pounds began to melt away.

Ewan's drugs of choice had always been alcohol and nicotine. 'Booze, lots of booze, but that was it,' he says. 'I wasn't involved in the rave scene when it kicked off in the Eighties. I can't remember where I was, but I wasn't there. I've never been in a drugs scene at all.' He briefly contemplated using heroin before making *Trainspotting*, but he had never been a Method actor and had little time for the extremes of their technique. Although his character in *The Pillow Book* is not a junkie, he dies of an accidental drugs overdose. Ewan told himself that he had not had to take an overdose or die to play that scene. There is a famous story from the set of *Marathon Man*, in which Dustin Hoffman keeps himself awake for nights on end in order to appear suitably tired in one particular scene, at which point co-star Laurence Olivier off-handedly suggests he might save himself a lot of bother by simply trying acting. Ewan opted for the Olivier approach. A month before filming began, he told the press: 'If we manage to make the film that John has pulled out of the bag, then it should be brilliant. And it will be interesting to see what people make of it, because it's such a horrific world and yet it's also very funny.' It would indeed prove interesting.

Macdonald and Boyle started hiring other actors and crew members, trying to preserve a sense of team spirit and continuity by bringing back many of those with whom they had worked on *Shallow Grave*, particularly behind the camera, though Keith Allen, the fourth flatmate in *Shallow Grave* became the London drug dealer in *Trainspotting*; Peter Mullan, one of the thugs in *Shallow Grave* was given the key role of Swanney, the Edinburgh drug dealer; and writer John Hodge, who was a policeman in the first film has apparently been reduced to a store security guard and is seen chasing Ewan at the start of *Trainspotting*.

Ewen Bremner, who came from Portobello, just along the coast from Leith, might have expected to be approached to repeat the role of Renton that he had already played on stage. Boyle did not think Bremner's goofy restlessness was right for Renton in the film, but wanted him to play Spud. Bremner did not take offence at this apparent downgrading in his status, he saw the film as an entirely different project and agreed to do it.

Robert Carlyle, who had been earmarked for Ewan's role in *Shallow Grave* before falling out with Danny Boyle, agreed to play Francis Begbie. He does not take drugs, wears a suit, a shirt and tie and white socks, and sports a moustache so neat that it suggests a certain terminal conformity, and yet he is arguably the maddest of the lot, a time bomb forever poised on the point of explosion, ready to beat the living daylights out of anyone who looks at him the wrong way. Originally Boyle had had Chris Eccleston in mind, but thought that casting a big man in the role was a little too easy and that the character had the potential to seem even more menacing if played by a smaller actor.

Sick Boy, the stylish, blond-haired ladies' man and expert on James Bond films, would be played by Jonny Lee Miller, the young English star of *Hackers*. He persuaded Boyle he was right for the part with the quality of his Sean Connery impersonation. Miller should know more than most about the James Bond movies: his grandfather was Bernard Lee, who played M to Sean Connery's and Roger Moore's Bonds throughout the Sixties and Seventies. Boyle spotted Kevin McKidd when he saw rushes for Gillies MacKinnon's *Small Faces* and cast him as Tommy, the clean-living one, who tries heroin only after being dumped by his girlfriend and ends up dying of AIDS.

One of the biggest problems was the casting of Diane, the self-confident, under-age schoolgirl. Boyle could hardly cast a 14-year-old in a role that required a nude sex scene. At the same time he did not want a familiar actress who audiences would know was much older. He distributed leaflets asking 'Are you the new Kate Moss or Patricia Arquette?' and held an open casting session in Glasgow that attracted several hundred hopefuls. Kelly Macdonald (no relation to Andrew) was a 19-year-old barmaid, who wanted to go to drama school. She did not think she had any chance of getting the part, but reckoned it would be a worthwhile experience going through the audition. She had her photos taken in a booth en route and nearly turned away when she saw the other glamorous applicants. But she possessed the sort of raw talent for which Boyle was looking.

He brought the principal actors to Glasgow for two weeks of rehearsals before shooting began and they met members of Calton Athletic, who told them their life stories and demonstrated the mechanics of heroin use – how to 'cook up' and how to inject. The actors were issued with syringes and paraphernalia and told to practise. 'This guy marched up and down telling us what we were doing wrong,' says McKidd. 'It was just like Bruce Forsyth's *Generation Game*.'

But *Trainspotting* was essentially a story about friends and the fact that most of them are drug addicts is almost incidental, in the way that the friends in Martin Scorsese's *GoodFellas* just happen to be gangsters. Boyle wanted his cast to get to know each other well during the pre-production period. He hired a flat, as he had done in the run-up to *Shallow Grave*, at the top of a Glasgow tower block, and they spent a lot of time together watching films which Boyle felt were in some way relevant, including *GoodFellas, A Clockwork Orange, The Hustler, Near Dark* and *The Exorcist* – some being more obviously relevant than others.

Shooting began on 22 May 1995, with four weeks on location in Glasgow and Edinburgh, three weeks in a temporary studio in the old Wills cigarette factory in Alexandra Parade in Glasgow, and finally a couple of days in London. Ewan had developed a solid working relationship with Danny Boyle. They worked quickly and easily together. Ewan rarely needed repeated takes, even though Boyle encouraged all the actors to improvise around Hodge's script. The camera loved him. Even as a grubby, skinhead junkie the camera loved him. 'Ewan has phenomenal technical skill, which allows him to use the camera to its full extent,' says Boyle. 'He's actually not the most gorgeous-looking person. He's not one of the drop-dead gorgeous Brad Pitt types. But there's something about him that's attractive because he's more human. He has that slight edge of boy-next door.'

The nature of his role meant Ewan was needed on set from breakfast time until night-time, virtually every day. He may not have been doing anything too physically demanding, like dancing or surfing, but he had to be there. 'Renton is often observing,' says Ewan. 'In a lot of scenes I don't have an awful lot to do physically, but at the same time he almost always has a critical edge about things in his mind, which is expressed in the voice-over which runs quite extensively through the film.' Ewan cites the dead baby scene as the toughest and describes it as 'a very demanding, horrible, emotional scene', but he also considered it a challenge. 'Sometimes it's more demanding sitting listening to other people have a chat about a biscuit or something because you don't know what you're supposed to be doing.' He defined the mystique of acting for one journalist visiting the set as 'fear of being crap', but Boyle reckons Ewan knew exactly what he was doing. 'There's a lot of difference between not doing anything and doing nothing,' says Boyle. 'Renton is very modern. He doesn't show much emotion. He becomes what you want him to be. Ewan has that thing that Caine or Connery had ... He lets the film happen around him.'

Apart from the trauma of the scene in which the baby dies, Ewan also had to steel himself for various scenes with needles. 'I was pretending to stick needles in my arm on and off for weeks. I got quite used to having one in there. For the close-ups, my arm was moulded prosthetically, with a plastic pipe going into a little pool of blood underneath, so you can see the pulse.' He was also required to appear naked, to which by this time he was well accustomed, he had to take a condom off his penis on screen, which was breaking new ground for a mainstream commercial film, and he had to disappear down the worst toilet in Scotland. 'That day was like "Please can I get off this set, it's disgusting."' Audiences tended not to look too closely, but if you re-view the film you will see that the shit in this scene and in the scene at Spud's girlfriend's house looks nothing like shit. The contents of the worst toilet in Scotland are in fact grey, as if someone has been mixing cement in it.

Trainspotting is set in Edinburgh but, as with *Shallow Grave*, most of the shooting took place in Glasgow. Several key scenes, however, were shot in the Scottish capital, including the opening in which Renton and Spud are running away from store detectives along Princes Street, one of the most famous shopping streets in Britain and one of the busiest. The film crew had their work cut out trying to keep the public out of sight while the scene was shot. Some shoppers simply refused to wait in the shops, demanding to get out and walking straight into the movie, creating enormous problems for the film-makers. It might not have been so bad if they had kept going, as they would normally do, but, no, they would have to take a good look into the camera as they went by. The shoplifting scene is picked up later in the film when Ewan is seen running up Hanover Street, with the Royal Scottish Academy building behind him, and is later apprehended going in the opposite direction down Calton Road, half a mile away. The magic of

locations! If he had been in Calton Road a year earlier he might
have met Julia Roberts, who was filming the ill-fated *Mary Reilly*
there.

Coming from a theatre background, Danny Boyle recognised
not just the privacy and control that studio sets afforded, but
also their potential to subtly stylise the real world. The dirty,
dilapidated Edinburgh flats, with bare floorboards and holes
in walls, that production designer Kave Quinn created for
Trainspotting were the flip-side of her elegant Georgian residence in *Shallow Grave*.

Boyle manages to present real characters, a real world, in a
stylised way, the degree of stylisation varying with the attendant circumstances, from Begbie's vaguely ludicrous moustache
and wardrobe to the excitingly original portrayal of Renton's
drugs overdose, as he slips blissfully into the ground to the
sound of Lou Reed's 'Perfect Day' on the soundtrack, and his
subsequent cold turkey in which he sees Spud in a prison
uniform and ball and chain, Allison's baby crawling across his
ceiling and, the worst nightmare of all, Begbie in bed with him,
offering his own particular brand of encouragement.

Boyle, Macdonald and Hodge had agreed at the outset that
they would keep the film down to an hour and a half and some
scenes that are in the published version of the script were
dropped from the film, including a whole sub-plot about
Swanney having a leg amputated and pretending to be a Falk-
lands veteran; others were curtailed, including Spud's speedy
interview. Speed is the essence of the film. Virtually everything
about it is fast, from the sheer pacing that captures the energy
of Welsh's original text and does indeed offer the visceral thrill
of a rollercoaster, to the cross-cutting and the soundtrack music
that courses through the film's veins.

At the end of filming the principal actors went straight into
a London studio for further shooting, for the film's posters.
'The actors were completely worn out by this film,' says pho-
tographer Lorenzo Agius, 'and they didn't want to do the photo
shoot, but that made it better for us, the fact that they looked
shit, that they hadn't slept. If they had had a few weeks
to recover, they probably would look too groomed and too

healthy.' Begbie gives a V-sign; Diane, in her little sparkly disco dress, curls up her nose and snarls; Sick Boy forms his fingers into a gun; Spud stares out through oversized glasses that make him look like a skinhead version of Joe 90 and appears to be challenging the viewer to fight, with all the menace of a skinhead version of Joe 90; and Ewan is dripping wet and has his arms around himself, presumably having just returned from his swim in the worst toilet in Scotland. His image is the odd one out – he is the only one who looks vulnerable. Individual black and white shots were encompassed into a poster announcing that 'this film is expected to arrive ... 23.02.96', with the title of the film in white on bright, shiny orange. It was so successful that it was imitated by other advertisers. *Withnail and I* was rereleased with a poster that was a straight copy, with a quote from *Premiere* saying that *Trainspotting* was destined to be the biggest British cult movie since *Withnail and I*. There were adverts for *Starlight Express*, computer training and training shoes – 'Trainerspotting'.

Masahiro Hirakubo found *Trainspotting* difficult to edit because of the lack of narrative flow. He worked 12-hour days shaping it and it was late summer before Ewan recorded his voice-over. The completed film was sent to the British Board of Film Classification – aka the censor – in the same week Leah Betts died after taking ecstasy at her 18th birthday party, intensifying tabloid interest in *Trainspotting*. The censors watched it several times and passed it without any cuts. But the distributors were not content to leave it to the tabloids to raise public awareness of the film and the publicists were wary of being sucked into an ill-informed debate on the morality of drugs.

It was not by chance that *Trainspotting* became the most eagerly awaited British film of recent times. Nor was it down purely to the success of *Shallow Grave* or *Trainspotting* the novel, even though it had become a best seller throughout the UK long before the film came out. Channel 4 had more than covered their £1.5 million production costs with deals set up prior even to the film's completion, including the sale of the British rights to Polygram and the American rights to Miramax.

But it would be coming out in Britain at a time when a lot of Oscar contenders were opening. Polygram believed it needed careful marketing to maximise its potential and spent about £850,000 on their campaign, a phenomenal amount considering the actual cost of the film. A teaser trailer went out months before the film, showing Ewan tied to train lines, footage that is not in and never was intended to be in the actual film.

Simultaneous world premières were held on 15 February at the Odeon in Renfield Street, Glasgow, and Edinburgh's UCI and Cameo cinemas, with the proceeds going to Calton Athletic. The Glasgow screening was scheduled for later in the evening, enabling Ewan to make personal appearances on both sides of the country. Tickets for the Cameo screening sold out within half an hour. The Cameo house record had been set by *Shallow Grave*, but *Trainspotting* was on its way to breaking it even before it opened, such was the level of advance sales.

As it turned out, *Trainspotting* did open in London the same week as two big Oscar movies, *Sense and Sensibility* and Martin Scorsese's *Casino*, but by then it already had its accolades from the vanguard of the British film press. In *Empire*, Ian Nathan decided to forego the conventional review in favour of the sort of uncritical praise that people might normally expect only when they die or are in the company of someone in a state of infatuation. He pointed out that the film's makers could have gone to Hollywood after *Shallow Grave*. But did they? 'No *sirree*. In a magnificent piece of artistic bravura they have stuck to their creative guns and opted for what, at first sight, seems like an insane choice: adapting Irvine Welsh's radical, near unfilmable, drug-infused novel ... If *Shallow Grave* was the best British film of the year, *Trainspotting* is the best British film of the decade,' he gushed. And if *Shallow Grave* was not the best British film of the year? But of course it was.

Philip Kemp took a more rigorously analytical approach and came to much the same conclusion in *Sight and Sound*, praising Ewan's 'fine weaselly performance, at once spiky and vulnerable' and the film's 'visual inventiveness and sheer visceral exuberance'. He even suggests that scenes featuring Swanney, who is also known as Mother Superior, because of the length of his habit, are bathed in reds and blues 'in ironic simulation of light through stained glass', a point that eluded most reviewers. Ben Thompson, in the *Independent on Sunday*, called it 'the most engaging, original and resonant cinematic portrayal of delinquent British youth since *Quadrophenia*.'

Unfortunately, too many critics in Britain seemed to be adopting a stance, rather than reviewing a film. *Trainspotting* was undoubtedly hip, it had a lot of drugs in it, and it suggested that they might even be pleasurable in the short term, which was enough for some critics to laud it and others to pan it, depending on the age of the critic and the nature of his or her publication. It reminded Alexander Walker, veteran critic of the London *Evening Standard*, of *A Clockwork Orange*. But whereas *A Clockwork Orange* made one think, *Trainspotting* made one puke, he said. Geoff Brown of *The Times* said: 'For young audiences willing to go with the flow, *Trainspotting* offers an adrenaline rush, a sense of life ripped from the gutters and the appeal of amorality.' On the other hand Christopher Tookey in the *Daily Mail* thought: '*Trainspotting* pours scorn on conventional values and pokes fun at capitalism.' Most critics acknowledged the quality of Ewan's acting. Ian Nathan wrote: 'McGregor, so good in *Shallow Grave*, matures immeasurably here, his defiant burr singing out the voice-over, his sullen, mesmerising presence the film's heart.'

Few films have relied quite so much on a voice-over. *Alfie* comes to mind, but Michael Caine simply enriched the film with his ironic asides to camera, whereas *Trainspotting* is effectively one long, dramatic monologue. Hodge defined Renton's character in the voice-over and it was absolutely essential that the actor get the delivery right. It would be so easy to overdo the passion, the cynicism, or the accent, but Ewan recognises the power of the words themselves and appreciates that he will maximise their impact by delivering them almost matter-of-factly, with just a hint of bitterness and sarcasm. He does not dwell theatrically on his lines, but delivers them quickly, as you would if you were telling a story or making a point. And he is making a point, about drugs. 'People think it's all about misery and desperation and death and all that shite, which is not to be ignored, but what they forget is the pleasure of it,' he says. 'Otherwise we wouldn't do it. After all, we're not fucking stupid.'

It seems fairly obvious, but it was to prove an enormously controversial stance. The line from the film most frequently quoted in the media was: 'Take the best orgasm you ever had, multiply it by a thousand and you're still nowhere near it.' Renton did not have a job, but he did have 'a sincere and truthful junk habit'. The film's acknowledgement that heroin must have a positive side or else people would not take it, did not amount to an endorsement. But it was too complicated an argument for the English tabloid press, never noted for their intellectual sophistication. They prefer not to muddy the waters of debate with information. 'The odious culture that killed Leah,' blasted the headline over a feature on *Trainspotting* in the *Daily Mail*. But no intelligent commentator could seriously accuse the film of ignoring the downside of heroin, represented in the deaths of Allison's baby Dawn and of Tommy. He dies alone and destitute, and his body is found only after neighbours complain about the smell.

'*Trainspotting* isn't the best film of the month, never mind the year, but, having sat through 90 harrowing minutes, I can say it is certainly the most odious,' ranted the *Mail's* Edward Verity. 'Not because of the language, which is unspeakable, the sex and violence, which are graphic, the crime, the alcoholism, or even the jokes about incontinence, although these are all unpleasant enough. The real reason *Trainspotting* is such a thoroughly nasty, insidious film is its deliberate and self-consciously irresponsible approach to drugs.'

The deliberate and self-consciously irresponsible approach that he is talking about is the fact that the film refuses to accept the simplistic official line that any experimentation with drugs must inevitably lead to addiction, misery and death. Sometimes it does, as in the case of Tommy and Leah Betts. Kids who grew up in the schemes, particularly in the Eighties, would probably know someone like Tommy, who took heroin and died, but equally they would know others, like Sick Boy, who took heroin, came off it and survived. Renton finds it incredibly difficult to kick his habit, but Sick Boy has no difficulty in giving up, which he does just to annoy Renton. Official campaigns had no credibility on the street because they refused to acknowledge that there was any pleasure in heroin or any hope for its users; because of their patronising tone; and because their basic message stemmed either from ignorance or dishonesty. *Trainspotting* did more to get across the dangers of heroin than any Government campaign ever did, because it presented a balanced picture and kids took it seriously. 'What makes *Trainspotting* a great movie,' says Ewan, 'is that it shows both sides of the fence – him having a good time on it and him nearly dying from it. By the end of the movie, too many nasty things have gone on for the audience to come away with a positive view of heroin.' Ewan subsequently reiterated his personal opposition to drugs when he provided the voice-over for an anti-drugs campaign by the Health Education Board for Scotland.

Renton goes to London and gets a job with an estate agent, Sick Boy becomes a pimp, Begbie an armed robber and Spud continues to pursue his career as a loser. Renton returns to Scotland for Tommy's funeral, after which the four of them go to London to sell a major consignment of heroin which they have acquired from two Russian sailors, via a dealer called Mikey Forrester, a cameo role for the author Irvine Welsh. He acts like he is acting for the upper balcony, but just about gets away with this outrageously bad performance, because the other actors are so good that the audience assumes that this must be some sort of colourful character who really does behave like he is acting for the upper balcony. His performance is closer in style to the dead baby crawling upside down on the ceiling than to any of the other actors.

They sell the drugs at a big profit. But, just as he did in *Shallow Grave*, Ewan's character ends up with all the money. He double-crosses the others, though he leaves some money for Spud, and he announces in the final voice-over that he is going to change, he is going to go straight and choose life, get a job, a family and a 'fucking big television'. John Hodge sums the character up well when he says: 'The film depicts his philosophy and his nihilistic, selfish way of life, which aren't particularly attractive traits, but at the same time he's charismatic, intelligent and attractive. One of the great things about the book is that amidst all these horrific circumstances this character is still alive and kicking, he's still got a smart comment to make and he's still got a heart, maybe a slightly damaged, bitter one, but he's still a human being, and so are the people around him.' Of course you read those final voice-over comments about going straight and getting a job either literally or ironically as you see fit.

Many viewers did not recognise the actor from *Lipstick on Your Collar* and *Shallow Grave*, with his head shaved, his face lean and his eyes gaunt and sunk in their sockets. The public schoolboy from Perthshire was totally convincing as the skinhead from Leith. Carlyle, Bremner and Miller are brilliant, but they remain satellites in McGregor's orbit. *Shallow Grave* made stars of Boyle, Macdonald and Hodge, with McGregor in a supporting role. This time round Boyle, Macdonald and Hodge may have constructed the rollercoaster, but McGregor was the one who was riding it. It was his face on the magazine covers. *Empire* and *Sight and Sound* even used the same shot. He appeared on Chris Evans's programme *TFI Friday*, defended the film and complained in general terms about the Conservative Government. His use of the word 'fucking' led to Channel 4 being censured by both the Broadcasting Standards Council and Independent Television Commission, but did his street cred no harm.

Trainspotting opened in London and Scotland on 23 February, coming into the British chart at No 5, behind *Jumanji, Casino, Heat* and *Sense and Sensibility*. Its opening coincided with the retail video release of *Shallow Grave*, which included a two-for-the-price-of-one voucher to get into *Trainspotting*. Two weeks later *Trainspotting*'s release was expanded across the UK and it went to No 1. The *Observer* noted that British cinema audiences were being divided into trainspotters and Janespotters, the two groups being delineated largely, but not entirely, by age. It quoted one skinhead as saying that *Trainspotting* was a great film about the youth of today. 'I'm not interested in seeing that Jane Austen crap,' he added. 'It's not *now*, is it?'

One oldie who did go to see *Trainspotting* was National Heritage Secretary Virginia Bottomley. She was urged to see it by her daughter, a junior doctor. 'It's a harrowing film that leaves you in no doubt about the ravages of drug addiction,' she said after seeing it in Cannes in May. The official festival had turned *Trainspotting* down, but Polygram went ahead and staged a private screening. By this time *Trainspotting* had grossed more than £10 million in Britain and producer Andrew Macdonald had persuaded the actors to re-record some of the dialogue for the imminent American release. Analysts believed *The Commitments* and *Shallow Grave* had failed to fulfil their potential in North America because of the accents. *Trainspotting* the novel was published there with a glossary, but that was not an option for the film-makers, so they decided to re-record dialogue in the early part of the film with clearer pronunciation to let American ears get used to it.

The film was never going to challenge *Independence Day* or indeed any of the big studio blockbusters. It was, after all, a low-budget, foreign (some would maintain foreign-language) movie. But it became *the* hip film, *the* film to see in more sophisticated circles. The *New York Times* devoted a page to it, *Variety* called it '*Clockwork Orange* for the Nineties', *Time* speculated that Renton, Spud, Sick Boy and Tommy could become as popular as the Beatles and the *Village Voice* carried a lengthy interview with Ewan, beginning with a story as disgusting as anything in Welsh's novel, in which Ewan recalled how he ate a plate of liver, felt a rumbling in his bowels and gave birth to a live calf 'through my arsehole'. The magazine described Renton as 'the slouching, scabrous offspring of Johnny Rotten and Margaret Thatcher', clearly unaware that the slouch's origins lay in Luxembourg. And Ewan got political again, enlarging on Renton's outburst against the English and the Scots. 'This anger against the English, but more than that, his anger against the Scots for putting up with it in the first place, is something I can really relate to. He's right. The Tories introduced the poll tax in Scotland a year before they did everywhere else to try it out on us. And what did we do? We marched and we moaned about it. But when they introduced it in England, there were riots in the streets and they had to repeal it.'

Ewan maintains, in his characteristic off-hand way, that he was only vaguely aware of the enormous excitement that the film was generating. 'When it opened in Britain I was in the States, and when it opened in the States I was in Ireland. So, apart from doing all the press, I missed the buzz, but I'm delighted it's been so successful. I was passionate about it, and it's a nice reflection of my taste that people think it's good as well.' And what does he think in retrospect of the character that made him a star? 'I quite like him,' he says. 'But I don't like the fact that he's given up on everything. The press release said something like "Mark Renton: a hero for our times". I never thought that. He doesn't give a shit about anyone.' Nevertheless Ewan had very good reason to quite like him.

The trade magazine *Screen International* reported early in 1997 that *Trainspotting* had been the No 1 'independent' film of the previous year in North America, with a gross of more than $16 million. It was a superb performance for such a low-budget film, but, to put it in context, it is worth pointing out that *Trainspotting* did not quite make it into the Top 100 for the year, ranking below such classics-I-don't-think as *The Phantom* and *Flipper*. It took more than £40 million worldwide and, by most definitions, became the second most successful British film ever, after *Four Weddings and a Funeral*. John Hodge's script was nominated for an Oscar. Not bad for an 18-certificate film on such a difficult subject as drug abuse. But it was, as the skinhead interviewed by the *Observer* said, *now*. It captured the mood of nihilism among British youth as surely as *If ...* had captured the mood of rebellion in the Sixties. *Trainspotting* was arguably not just the best British film of the Nineties, but the best British film since the Sixties, when social realism seemed fresh and relevant and Michael Caine, Peter O'Toole and Sean Connery established themselves as genuine international stars. That mood of nihilism was epitomised in the pictures of Ewan McGregor expressing everything from rage to a has-anyone-here-got-a-towel-please vulnerability. Danny Boyle was right: there was in Ewan an element of the boy next door, the mischievous boy next door, who has gone too far and fallen in the pond, or in this case the toilet. You do not know whether to cuddle him or run away from him. Ewan summed up the uncertainty of the age. Ewan was *now*, the man of the moment, the heir to the kingdom of Caine, O'Toole and Connery.

12
A Week in Dordogne

SUMMER SUNSHINE BATHED the courtyard in a warm glow. It was a fine day for a wedding. Young women in long black skirts and white aprons darted around laying out places for the guests who would soon sit down for the wedding meal. With its attractive climate and picturesque landscape of medieval castles, fertile valleys and mile upon mile of vineyards, France's Dordogne region has proved popular with English visitors, many of whom have bought homes there. Four rustic farm cottages had been converted into a single holiday home, with a farmyard, or courtyard, a huge garden and a pool. The property was owned by theatrical agent Jonathan Altaras. He had suggested to the groom, a promising young actor on his books, that he might want to use the house for his honeymoon. When the young actor and his fiancée went to the Dordogne to look at it they fell in love all over again, with the area and with the farmhouse. And they wondered whether they might not get married there, and have their reception at the house.

Altaras was happy to oblige and directed the preparations for the reception while the young couple visited the little town of Festalemps, where they would be married by the local mayor. The bride wore a simple, long, sleeveless dress of white chiffon, blindingly bright in the sunshine. Her curly hair fell loose upon her shoulders. The groom wore a beige linen suit and open-necked shirt. His hair was cut so short that it looked like someone had sprinkled his scalp with iron fillings. He apparently needed to have it like that for the film he had just finished making, something about trains. He was very handsome and very young, just 24 years old, five years younger than his bride. It was a short, simple ceremony, attended by family and friends. And when it was over the groom returned to the farmhouse with the new Mrs Ewan McGregor.

Ewan had been a ladies' man since his days in primary school in Crieff and he had led a full bachelor's life in London. 'I had this amazing bachelor pad in Primrose Hill,' he says. 'The things that went on there ...' And he lets the sentence drift away on the imagination of his listeners. He met set designer Eve Mavrakis while filming the pilot episode of *Kavanagh QC* and they went drinking together on location in Oxford, but it was some time before their relationship developed back in London. 'I did a lot of the initial chasing,' says Ewan, 'and we both then chased each other around London for a while.' Eve is much quieter than Ewan, possessed of attractive, dark, Gallic features, rather than stunning Hollywood looks, and possessed too of an inner steeliness and quiet determination. Eve's parents divorced when she was small, her mother remarried and Eve spent part of her childhood in China, where she demonstrated an early aptitude for languages. She returned to Asia as an adult, before moving on to London, where she worked as a designer on commercials, television programmes and films.

Ewan was beginning to feel a certain dissatisfaction with his wild bachelor lifestyle. 'I met Eve and it really did feel very, very different,' he says. This was more than a brief passionate fling. Ewan and Eve not only enjoyed each other's company; they felt comfortable with each other; they felt they could have a future together. 'We wanted to get married,' says Ewan. 'So we got married.'

Most of his immediate family were at the wedding, though his uncle, Denis Lawson, was in New York, with a play called *Lust*. Jonathan Altaras's holiday home was packed out with wedding guests, and various nearby properties were also hired to accommodate them. Ewan and Eve stayed at the farmhouse for a week and friends and relatives were encouraged to stop off for a few days. Ewan found himself at the centre of a little hedonist commune, surrounded by those who meant most to him. 'We all cooked for each other at nights, (and) drank fine wines in the garden,' says Ewan. 'It felt like absolutely what we wanted to do. That's very unusual, when you have a dream, to actually see it totally realised, which our marriage was. It was perfect.'

Ewan had always been very close to his family, particularly his mother. The family served as a support system, a source of advice and encouragement, a bedrock on which to build his life and career. After he moved to London, he was a regular visitor to the home of his uncle, Ewan's inspiration for a life in acting. And whenever Ewan had news his mother would be the first to know. Wives sometimes find it difficult to fit into such close families, with their long histories in which a wife has no part, other perhaps than that of audience. Ewan's family was close, but it was not tight, it was not exclusive. It was a gregarious, welcoming social club. Denis is by nature a quiet, even shy individual. Ewan may have followed his uncle into acting, but in looks and temperament he is very different. Ewan's mother Carol and his grandmother Phyllis were by nature sociable and talkative, to say the least, and in many ways Ewan took after the Lawson womenfolk. He felt no need to keep friends and family separate, even after he became a star. Many stars feel slightly uneasy about the family that nurtured them, but not Ewan. At a première Ewan's mum, dad and granny would find themselves sitting alongside celebrity friends like Jude Law, Sadie Frost and Jonny Lee Miller.

Eve slipped easily into Ewan's family, Ewan's support system. She would routinely accompany Ewan to film locations and to functions. Sometimes she would retire to bed early leaving her husband to sup away in the bar with his friends, or just whoever happened to be around, until the small hours. They trusted each other. Tabloid speculation about the intensity with which Ewan and his *Rogue Trader* co-star Anna Friel were seen kissing in a photograph left Ewan unfazed. Shortly after the picture appeared, he felt sufficiently comfortable in his marriage to joke – in the company of his wife, his mum and his granny – that he had fallen in love with one of his co-stars, not Anna

Friel, but Julianna Margulies from *ER*. But Eve was the girl he chose to marry. 'So we got married,' he says. 'Then I got really, really excited about having children.' Looking at the petite little Frenchwoman, in her white chiffon dress, on her wedding day in the summer of '95, no one would have guessed, but their first child was already on the way.

Ewan was now so busy that it was all he could do to squeeze in his wedding and a short holiday between the completion of filming on *Trainspotting* in July and the start of his next film in August. Once again he was playing a shiftless, deceitful character and once again his friends were a bunch of wasters, except this time instead of having names like Sick Boy, Spud and Swanney, they were called Mr Elton, Miss Smith and Mr Knightley. The most accomplished con trick of these costumed wasters was to convince the world that they were not low life, but rather the cream of society, and to persuade the English public to allow them to retain their wealth and their heads.

Emma was another comedy-drama, as light as *Trainspotting* had been dark. Instead of being set among the under-classes in Scotland in the late 20th century, it was set among the upper-classes in England in the early 19th century. Many regarded the source novel as Jane Austen's finest comedy of class and manners. The film was written and directed by Douglas McGrath. A veteran of the *Saturday Night Live* TV programme and Woody Allen's co-writer on *Bullets Over Broadway*, he knew his comedy, though there was scepticism from the outset about the prospect of an American production of such an intrinsically English work.

These concerns were exacerbated by the news that the title role would be taken by Gwyneth Paltrow, a young New York actress who was making a name for herself in Hollywood with a series of strong supporting performances, including the role of her then real-life partner Brad Pitt's wife in *Seven* – in which her character is beheaded. To make matters worse, Emma's friend Harriet Smith would be played by the Australian Toni Collette, best known as the ugly duckling in *Muriel's Wedding*. No one seemed to mind or even notice that the supporting cast was dominated by Scots, with Alan Cumming as the vicar

Mr Elton, Ewan as Frank Churchill, and James Cosmo making his second film in a row as Ewan's dad; and in retrospect it seems that the worries were slightly misplaced.

McGrath had studied Austen at university and was a great fan of the novel, in which the characters have little else on which to spend their time other than gossip, and in which the socialite of the title attempts to match-make for various friends with unfortunate results. 'Thousands of readers around the world have come to see that the people she characterised and sent up so sardonically 180 years ago are still here,' said McGrath. Among those readers was Amy Heckerling, who took Austen's story and updated and relocated it in Beverly Hills as *Clueless*. It went into production first, appeared in cinemas long before McGrath's version and proved a major hit on both sides of the Atlantic.

Hollywood had altered the period slightly less dramatically in the 1940 version of *Pride and Prejudice*, with Laurence Olivier and Greer Garson, to avoid the Regency dresses, with their waistlines just below the bust, quite the most hideous English fashion garments along with those from the glam rock era. For the following half a century cinema had neglected Austen, but McGrath suddenly found himself part of an Austen boom, prompted perhaps partly by the success of recent film versions of other English classics, led by Merchant Ivory's adaptations of E.M. Forster. Not only was McGrath up against an updated version of *Emma*; he was also faced with a rival ITV version, with Kate Beckinsale in the title role; and with Emma Thompson, the darling of English period cinema, in *Sense and Sensibility*. It could have been worse – McGrath was initially misinformed about Emma Thompson's project and told that Emma was making *Emma*. In the event *Sense and Sensibility* would probably help create an audience for McGrath's film. And although he did not have Emma Thompson, he did have her mother Phyllida Law and her sister Sophie Thompson as token English women in the supporting roles of Mrs and Miss Bates.

Ewan was cast as Frank Churchill, who is much talked about in the early part of the film, but is not seen until halfway through when he comes to the rescue of Emma, whose carriage is stuck in a ford. From between the overhanging branches of a tree, he appears mounted on horseback and hiding his *Trainspotting* crew-cut with a top hat and a wig that he has quite clearly purloined from Worzel Gummidge the scarecrow. Frank becomes the toast of local society and sings a duet with Emma at a party. Ewan and Paltrow did their own singing and even worked out the harmony themselves. Ewan fancied himself as a singer, but enthusiasm could be no substitute for precision in such a dainty little number. What did his co-stars think of his singing? 'Compared to a strangled cat,' says James Cosmo, 'it was a bit better. It made me laugh a lot anyway, because all I had to do was sit and listen to him. I was just grateful it wasn't me.'

It was simply coincidence that Cosmo was once again playing Ewan's father. Because they knew each other from *Trainspotting*, they tended to socialise together, drinking and playing darts in the local pubs in the Dorset area, where much of the film was shot. 'He's a very low-key guy,' says Cosmo. 'He's not bon viveur by any stretch of the imagination. He's a very earthy sort of normal young man, and very easy to get on with. So it worked out very well.' Cosmo felt more comfortable in the pub with Ewan than he did in the movie. Although the subject matter and characters were lighter than *Trainspotting*, the project had stresses of its own.

'Ewan wasn't as comfortable in the part as some other parts he's done, but I didn't see any signs of stress or whatever: he just wasn't as cheerful as he would have been in something else ... I felt very much the same. It's something that I don't think I'd ever want to do again – that sort of period and that sort of script. For some actors it's their bread and butter and for others it's a much harder job. I know that I found that, and I think that Ewan probably felt the same.'

Cosmo is a big man best known for action roles from *Battle of Britain* to *Braveheart*. He looks and sounds slightly awkward as the Regency gentleman, like a boxer in a straitjacket, but that awkwardness seems consistent with his character. Ewan's awkwardness is less easy to justify, given that he is meant to be a dashing young blade, the heartthrob of Highbury society. Emma imagines herself in love with him, though Frank has secretly become engaged to someone else. He does not want his aunt to know and so flirts with Emma, much to the annoyance of her friend and admirer Mr Knightley (Jeremy Northam). Graceful, elegant and long-necked as a swan, Paltrow manages to inhabit the formal, mannered language of the piece as if born to it, whereas Ewan's delivery, in a slightly effete English accent, seems as stilted as the language itself, lacking any sense of spontaneity, flair or indeed personality. For once Ewan turns in a mediocre performance, though he is given very little material with which to work: the character remains sketchy and his most important moments happen off-screen.

Ewan was shrewd enough to acknowledge his shortcomings in the role. 'I was under the fucking sofa when I was watching *Emma*,' he says. 'I think the film's alright, but I was so crap. I was terrible in it. I didn't believe a word I said. I just thought "Shut the fuck up, Frank." ... We were forced into doing this very clipped, proper English accent, so as a result I wasn't really talking *to* anyone. I was just trying to sound right.' It is hardly surprising that Ewan never quite came to terms with his character, for he had found the novel impossible to read – 'It really bored me to death' – and clearly had no empathy with the material. He should never have accepted the role, but it was a chance to appear in an American production, with a rising American star; and the experience did not put him off period roles.

His performance, in what was very much a supporting role, is not the film's principal problem. Nor is the lighting, which at times makes it seem that characters' faces are illuminated by torches. The principal problem is that the audience is expected to accept Emma's good intentions and her social values, when all the evidence points to her being an appalling and often ill-willed busybody and an irredeemable snob. It is true that she helps the poor, but she sees it very much as charitable work. She persuades the extremely silly and impressionable Harriet Smith that she should reject Robert Martin because he is a farmer rather than a gentleman. 'A family like the Martins are

From Irvine Welsh to Jane Austen. In the film which followed *Trainspotting*, Ewan played the dashing young heart-throb, Frank Churchill, in an adaptation of *Emma*, opposite rising Hollywood star Gwyneth Paltrow.

Peter Greenaway, director of such 'art house' classics as *Prospero's Books*, *A Zed and Two Noughts*, and *The Cook, The Thief, His Wife and Her Lover*, cast Ewan in his 1996 film *The Pillow Book*. Deliciously photographed, McGregor plays Jerome who falls in love with a Japanese calligrapher and lets her paint his whole body.

In the *Serpent's Kiss* a star cast was assembled for Philippe Rousselot's fable of sexual intrigue in the 17th century, filmed in Ireland in 1996. McGregor played garden designer Meneer Chrome, with a rather bizarre Dutch accent.

The Clan McGregor descend on
Glasgow for the Scottish BAFTA
awards. Ewan collected Best Actor
Award for 1997.

In *Brassed Off* Ewan co-starred with Stephen Tompkinson from *Drop the Dead Donkey* and *Ballykissangel*, and Pete Postlethwaite fresh from his Hollywood triumph in *The Usual Suspects*. This delightfully crafted film displayed a gentle side to McGregor's acting talent. Ewan plays Andy who, with a group of mates, loses his job and regains self-respect by playing in a local brass band.

McGregor and wife Eve Mavrakis attend the 1997 Empire Awards

Rogue Trader is the true story of Nick Leeson who lost over £850 million of Barings bank's money and broke the company. Anna Friel, late of *Brookside,* played his wife Lisa.

The seventies ride again in *Velvet Goldmine.* Glam rock with glitter, flares and outrageous male make-up. About as much fun as you can have with your flares on.

precisely the sort of people with whom I have nothing to do,' she says. 'A degree or two lower and I might be useful to their families, but a farmer needs none of my help and therefore is as much above my notice he is below it.' Mr Knightley scolds her for interfering, not because he feels Harriet is really in love with Robert Martin, but because he feels that Emma is overestimating Harriet's position in society. Ultimately Emma marries the sensible Mr Knightley, and Harriet finds that her natural station in life is indeed with Robert Martin.

McGrath proves exceptionally loyal to his source, probably too loyal. He does nothing to dilute the obsession with social position and presents slabs of dialogue in the form of dinner party conversation. The fact that his film works as well as it does is largely down to the humour in his script, the charm and ease of Paltrow's performance and the memorable characterisations of some, but by no means all, of the supporting cast.

Reviews ranged from good to excellent: *GQ* called it 'brilliant' and *Newsweek* suggested it was a 'triumph' for Paltrow. They were not necessarily so enthusiastic about Ewan's performance. Angie Errigo singled him out for criticism in her review in *Empire*, suggesting he looked out of place, a view echoed in *Sight and Sound* by Peter Matthews, who thought him 'too shaggily anachronistic a presence to be entirely convincing'. It grossed a respectable $22 million in North America, more than *Trainspotting* and more than double its production cost, though less than half the grosses of *Clueless*, and *Sense and Sensibility*, which boasted stronger performances overall and a sharper script. Despite the reservations, *Emma* was a major hit in Britain and outgrossed the likes of *The Birdcage* and *Casino*.

Its appearance in American cinemas, hard on the heels of *Trainspotting* certainly did Ewan no harm. Jeremy Northam gives a more assured performance and yet is overshadowed by Ewan's charm and sheer screen presence: some actors have it and some simply do not. 'It was certainly more Ewan than Austen,' concludes James Cosmo.

Having played a daring, post-modern anti-hero for the 1990s in *Trainspotting*, it seemed almost perverse of Ewan to follow it up with first a Jane Austen adaptation and then a film on that most parochial, anachronistic and seemingly uncommercial of English pursuits – the brass band. It was hardly the traditional stuff of Hollywood hits. Even musicals have tended to steer clear of brass bands, preferring to adopt the format of auditions for a Broadway chorus line or to embrace the fashions of the current hit parade. The Brighouse and Rastrick Brass Band may have taken 'Floral Dance' into the British Top Ten in 1977, but in the year of punk rock the 'Floral Dance' never seemed quite as cool on the streets as the Sex Pistols, the Jam and Iggy Pop. Ewan was only six when safety pins and saliva were in vogue, to him Elvis meant Presley, not Costello, and in the rarefied environs of Crieff and Morrison's Academy he found it perfectly possible to combine a love of pop music with a passion for French horn.

Ewan did not share the smug Tory complacency of many of his Perthshire neighbours and bridled at the blatant social injustices of the Thatcher years. He was attracted to *Brassed Off* not only by its story of a colliery brass band competing in national championships, but also by its politics. 'From the moment I read it, I knew I had to be part of the project,' he says. 'I loved the politics of it and I thought it was brilliant ... Sometimes you get a script and you think – "Well, there's something here and I like it, but it'll take a lot of work from the actors to get it kick-started." Then there are the special scripts – they're totally unlike the ones where things *might* come alive. They are the ones where you read it and think "Bloody hell, that's got a bit of zip to it." And that was most definitely the case with Mark's work on *Brassed Off*.'

Others might have felt that, on paper, the project did not seem that promising – a low-budget Channel 4 drama about brass bands and pit closures written and directed by a man whose only other feature was the risible Dudley Moore farce *Blame it on the Bellboy*. The critics were of the opinion that as writer and director the blame lay with Mark Herman rather than the poor bellboy. After that debacle, Herman had wanted to do something more serious, a film about Thatcher's systematic shut-down of the British coal industry and the tens of thousands thrown out of work, but he realised that that in itself was not going to have film companies fighting for the rights. 'I needed something to hang it on,' says Herman, 'and then I heard about this brass band up in the north-east, and it was exactly what I needed.' The small Yorkshire mining community of Grimethorpe was torn between despair and pride when their colliery closed and their brass band reached the national finals at the Albert Hall in the same week. It is difficult perhaps for outsiders to understand how much that could mean to such a small, tight-knit community, but one band member compared it to reaching the FA Cup final. The conductor inspired the band by telling them that they were playing for all their mates who had lost their jobs. They won the title.

Channel 4's cash was doubled by Miramax, the American company that had bought the rights to *Trainspotting*, giving Herman a decent £2.5 million budget that enabled him to secure a distinguished cast of British actors and to shoot on location in Grimethorpe, though the name is changed to Grimley in the film. Ewan plays Andy Barrow, a young miner and horn-player who has grown up in the town, though the central character is the band's conductor Danny Ormondroyd, played by Pete Postlethwaite. A British theatre actor, Postlethwaite had, with the support and encouragement of his close friend Daniel Day-Lewis, been gradually building up his reputation as a leading character actor in films and had won an Oscar nomination the previous year for co-starring with Day-Lewis in *In the Name of the Father*. Stephen Tompkinson, from the TV series *Drop the Dead Donkey* and *Ballykissangel*, was to play Phil, his son and the band's trombonist. And Ewan would get a belated chance to act with Tara Fitzgerald, the rising star of *Hear My Song* and *The Camomile Lawn*, with whom he would have made his screen debut if he had opted for *Six Characters in Search of an Author* instead of *Lipstick on Your Collar*. She would play Gloria, the granddaughter of legendary band member Arthur Mullins. She returns to the town, joins the band and picks up with Andy where she had left off in their teens when the relationship was restricted to 'top half only'.

Depressed by the lack of jobs and disenchanted by an earlier television programme about the community, the locals did not exactly welcome the film-makers with open arms. 'It was never the easiest of locations,' Herman admits. At times it could be downright dangerous. 'They're bored stiff up there. On 5 November, bonfire night, I saw a couple of kids in the street and asked what they were doing that night. They said they were going to burn down the co-op, which I thought was funny. But when we turned up the next day it was gone. We naïvely expected the police to defend us, but there's only one policeman there. He's about 40 but looks 80. And he told me: "They know where I live." ' But the location filming brought home to the cast the despair of long-term unemployment and added a hard edge to what might otherwise have been a frothy comedy in which the powers-that-be may rob the Ealingesque working folk of their livelihood, but cannot take away their joie de vivre.

Ewan described Grimethorpe at the time as 'a sad old place. They've shut down the pit and filled it with concrete and left all the miners there ... If you're going to take away people's livelihoods, you have to replace it with something, but our government doesn't care about anyone except themselves ... I saw three-bedroom houses for sale for £5,000, people desperately trying to get out of there ... I was there for seven weeks and at the end I was just so saddened by it all that I was dying to get away.'

The songs on the soundtrack were played by the Grimethorpe Colliery Band, though, as was the case with *Doggin' Around*, the actors had to look sufficiently convincing on screen and were coached by the real band. Ewan found it easy enough, while Tara Fitzgerald had played the flute at school and learned how to play the flugelhorn for the film. Her character has to prove herself with a solo from Rodrigo's *Concierto de Aranjuez*, or 'Concerto d'Orange Juice' as it is known to the miners. The real band were not quite the hopeful amateurs portrayed in the film. They were handsomely sponsored by British Coal and included many outsiders who were not miners; their practice rooms were considered much too grand for Herman's needs. Frank Renton, the conductor who led the band to their finest moment at the Albert Hall, attacked the film's inaccuracies and bad language, leading to a slightly surreal debate in the press about the extent of swearing among band members.

Herman might simply have used this most unhip of musical forms as a backdrop for his story and his politics, and it is to his credit that he did not take the easy option. The music is as central to *Brassed Off* as it is to any musical and includes renditions of 'Floral Dance' and 'Danny Boy', the latter played by the band outside Danny's hospital window, after he has collapsed in the street. In another particularly memorable sequence, Herman presents a whole series of powerful, wordless images while the band are playing, cutting between the band's performance at their regional heat in Halifax, the result of the ballot to close the pit, Phil's wife comforting their children as their furniture is taken away, and the miners – and the wives who have maintained a protest at the pit gates – walking slowly away with defeat etched on their faces ... Then Herman spoils it with a shot of the band, back in Grimley, spread out across the street at significant intervals that suggest they are doing some sort of impression of the Magnificent Seven awaiting the arrival of Eli Wallach's Mexican bandits.

While it would have been simple to produce either a depressing political drama about pit closures and the evils of Thatcherism or a frothy feel-good comedy, it was much more difficult to produce a drama that suggested hope within the despair, without covering up the extent of that despair and, for the most part, Herman achieved this balance. In an attempt to earn a little extra money Phil dresses as a clown, with red nose and enormous, awkward shoes, and provides entertainment at children's parties. One of the most powerful scenes in the film is Phil, still dressed as a clown, dangling at the end of a rope when he attempts to hang himself.

But, despite its strengths, *Brassed Off* is a patchy film. The strongest characters are Danny and Phil, father and son, who represent the continuity of the mining tradition within the community. Fitzgerald's character is returning to the community after many years away. A surveyor, she is carrying out a survey for management on the viability of the pit. It would seem prudent for her to be entirely honest and open about her work at the outset, rather than being evasive. Surely 'This and that, keeping busy' was never going to suffice. If she did feel ashamed of the assignment, would she really be so desperate to blow her flugel with the lads? It is inconceivable in any case that, in such a small, tight community, everyone would not know exactly what she was doing there, particularly as she is working at the colliery itself. The sound of the Grimley band alternates with the creaking of the dialogue and the plot – would the entire band really fall asleep on the bus on the way to the final? And yet Herman just about manages to keep the whole thing afloat.

Andy's background is never fleshed out to the same extent as the backgrounds of the other main characters, and the easy sexual relationship between him and Gloria is unconvincing. It is a small triumph for Ewan that he manages to provide such an effective performance, complete with working-class Yorkshire accent, with so little material. And he carries it off despite another bad hair day. Tompkinson had obviously grabbed the rights to the skinhead in this one and poor Ewan is landed with a bouncy bouffant affair that would seem more appropriate to an interior designer than a miner. Like the film, Andy alternates between humour and a dour, frowning pessimism, which is quite uncharacteristic of Ewan's roles. He quietly builds his character without any show or fuss or great cinematic moments. 'He's very restrained,' says Herman. 'He hardly moves, but you watch him all the time. He has amazing eyes. You can tell so much through the eyes. Isn't that what makes a movie star?'

Channel 4's distribution company were so confident about *Brassed Off* that, unusually for them, they took out prime-time TV adverts in order to reach older viewers who might not be regular cinemagoers. They also devised a trailer which was split into segments to be slotted in between rival trailers. The film received largely positive reviews, though Ian Freer in *Empire* suggested it would play more comfortably on television. It opened in November 1996 and held its place in cinemas as positive word of mouth spread. Dennis Skinner, the left-wing

Labour MP, did his bit for the film at Parliamentary question time, asking Virginia Bottomley: 'Does the Secretary of State agree that one of the best British films of the past few months is *Brassed Off*?' In traditional parliamentary fashion, she declined to give a straight answer, waffling on instead about lottery grants for brass bands. Nevertheless, within two months of release, *Brassed Off* had grossed more than £3 million, providing Ewan with his third commercial hit of the year. With *The Pillow Book* opening a week after *Brassed Off* and playing concurrently in arthouses, Ewan was very much in the public eye as 1996 drew to a close.

It is the nature of cinema that anything between a few months and a few years may elapse between a film's production and its release. During the interim, editing and other post-production processes are completed, distribution deals are struck (if they were not in place beforehand), a suitable slot is found in release schedules and the actors will, hopefully, have gone on to other projects. By the time *Brassed Off* was released Ewan had already completed another two feature films and was working on a third.

He had also become a father, the pre-production, production, post-production and release schedules for which are much more rigid than those pertaining in the film business. That is not to say, however, that there is not a large degree of uncertainty and worry in the baby business too, and Ewan became increasingly nervous as he waited for the birth. He pulled out of some of his *Trainspotting* promotional commitments to spend time with his wife. One journalist who did get an interview reported him as saying that the anticipation was killing him and that he was 'falling to bits'. She noted that his hands were shaking as he lit a Marlboro. Ewan rushed Eve to hospital at four in the morning and waited for the baby to come. For two days they waited for the baby to come. 'I just got more and more frightened, the longer it went on, that something was going to go wrong,' he says. 'I wasn't prepared to be that frightened.' Eve was in labour for 24 hours before it was decided that she would have to have a Caesarean section. 'I had to go in there,' says Ewan, 'and all I was thinking was "Oh no, I'm not big enough for this, not quite sure if I can handle this one." '

A few hours later he returned to their London flat alone. Things would never be the same again. 'It was like walking into somebody else's life ... The sheets were pulled back where we'd rushed out of bed, all the things we'd dropped were lying everywhere and, I don't know ... you feel like a completely different person. You've gone through the biggest emotional experience of your life and this is what you left behind – this is "Before" and you're already in the "After". You can never go back there now.' He was a father, and the first thing he did after he got back to the flat was to phone his own parents to tell them that the McGregor clan had one new small female member, Clara Mathilde.

Some would argue that a wife, let alone a wife and baby, was an encumbrance for an ambitious young actor, but not Ewan. 'We're happy,' he said in an interview after the birth. 'We can travel around together. She'll have young parents. You're building up a future together. People are so sceptical and I think that makes it all the stronger.' Not everyone was sceptical. *She* magazine ran a feature on 'the 40 sexiest dads in Britain', with Ewan at No 1, just one of the various assorted accolades he was picking up from the media. The magazine quoted him as saying he was much happier than he used to be. 'Having children is the most amazing thing in the world.' In the space of a few weeks at the beginning of 1996, *Trainspotting* opened, Ewan was acclaimed Britain's brightest young star and he became a father. And he was still only 24 years old.

13
A False Start in Hollywood

ALMOST EVERY ACTOR has his wilderness years. Who remembers *The Next Man, The First Great Train Robbery, Meteor* and *Cuba,* the films made in the second half of the Seventies by Scotland's greatest-ever film star Sean Connery? Ewan had his wilderness period too, after making *Trainspotting, Emma* and *Brassed Off. Nightwatch* had the sort of starry cast and highly rated script that should have ensured a glorious Hollywood debut, but it was still awaiting release two years after it was made. It was not the first time Ewan had made something specifically for the American market. He had already starred in 'Cold War', an episode of the long-running cult television series *Tales from the Crypt,* but it was not a success and HBO cancelled the series. Ewan returned to costume drama in *The Serpent's Kiss,* which followed *Nightwatch* into post-production limbo.

And then there was *Sleeping with the Fishes.* Don't worry if you have never heard of it. No one has. It was about Cypriot fish-and-chip-shop owners in Eastbourne. Even Ewan seemed unable to remember the title. During his interview with Sylvie Patterson for the *Face* the film was repeatedly referred to as 'Swimming with the Fishes', and so has entered some filmographies, sight unseen, under that erroneous title. Ewan was always a man in a hurry and in his accelerated version of time the wilderness period spanned not years, but months, and it was effectively over by the time *Brassed Off* actually opened. No one even noticed that it had happened.

Nightwatch did not start out as a Hollywood movie. It began life in Denmark as *Nattevagten*, a tight, highly atmospheric thriller from writer-director Ole Bornedal about a student called Martin (Nikolaj Coster Waldau), who takes a job as a night-watchman in a mortuary. He finds himself in a world of dark passages, flickering lights and dead bodies – which were apparently a big attraction for one of his predecessors, dismissed many years earlier for taking advantage of the dear departed ones. It is a busy time for the morgue, with a serial killer on the loose – he likes to scalp his victims. The alarm goes off in the morgue and when Martin goes to investigate he gets the shock of his life to see the sheet fall away from one of the corpses. It turns out to be his friend Jens, with whom he is playing a perverse game of challenges. Martin gets to know Peter Wormer, the police inspector investigating the serial killings; and as part of his game with Jens he sees Joyce, a young prostitute who reveals that one of her clients likes her to pretend she is dead while having sex. Weird things start happening at the morgue – OK, weirder things start happening at the morgue – bodies appear to move by themselves and someone has intercourse with one of the corpses. Martin's semen is found at the scene of the crime. Although that could be innocently explained away by his compulsion to have sex with his girlfriend in the morgue, he discovers he has become the chief suspect for the serial killings. But, if he is not the killer, who is? With such a small cast of characters, it is not terribly difficult to guess and Bornedal confirms audience suspicions long before the end.

This is dark, dark stuff. It is not the killings and butchery that make it so different from Hollywood thrillers, but the line-up of characters, nearly all of whom seem to have 'unusual' sexual desires, to say the least. But at what point does the unusual become the downright grotesque? And how much do we really ever know about our friends, our partners, ourselves? *Nattevagten* makes *Shallow Grave* seem like a Carry On movie. That is not to say it is a better film – it is not – but it is a much more serious film, unrelieved by the black comedy of *Shallow Grave*, an unrelenting journey into the dark side of the psyche.

Miramax thought they could turn it into a $10 million Hollywood thriller, with Bornedal as director, an American setting and an English-speaking cast. The task of translating and adapting the script was entrusted to Steven Soderbergh, who, in the late Eighties, had been hailed as a major new talent on the strength of his remarkable debut feature *Sex, Lies and Videotape*, though his personal wilderness period seemed to take in every film since then. Certainly *Kafka, King of the Hill* and *The Underneath* had fallen a long way short of repeating *Sex, Lies and Videotape's* success.

Bornedal hired Ewan for the role of the nightwatchman, now played as an American, after seeing him in *Shallow Grave*. Patricia Arquette, who had recently starred in the hip Tony Scott–Quentin Tarantino film *True Romance* and was, at the time, even hotter than Ewan, was cast as his girlfriend. The detective was to be played by Nick Nolte, whose recent films included Scorsese's *Cape Fear, Lorenzo's Oil* and *The Prince of Tides*, for which he had been Oscar-nominated for best actor.

Ewan was happy living in London and on a rational level very much against the idea of moving permanently to Los Angeles, though he did feel a tremendous excitement to be flying into the film capital of the world, which in childhood had seemed as distant from Crieff as Oz or Never Never Land. He rented a 1966 Buick Skylark convertible, describing it as 'sex on wheels' and 'the real America', and drove around LA, feeling that he was already in a movie, because the city was so familiar from American films he had seen. The driving and the weather were the two aspects of LA he enjoyed most. He remained uncomfortable with valet parking, however, and reckoned it would never catch on in Britain – 'Thanks very much, see ya.'

He was in LA when the Oscars were handed out and Mel Gibson's Scottish historical epic *Braveheart* won best picture. 'It was like Christmas,' he says. 'We had a brilliant time, went to all these parties, behaved really badly. I was doing heroin and cocaine and booze.' And he trusts that his audience will interpret the last comment as a joke. Los Angeles was a very different environment from London, though Ewan was surprised at how little difference there was in the actual process of making films. 'The technicians have got much bigger tool belts than we do back in Britain, they have got much more equipment hanging on their bodies, but apart from that it's kind of the same process.'

Filming of *Nightwatch* began only weeks after Clara's birth and mother and baby were with him in LA. 'Things have changed for the better,' Ewan told journalist David Eimer who interviewed him during the making of the film. 'Some things maybe, but not his interview technique,' Eimer noted in *Scotland on Sunday*. It is difficult to find anyone with a negative word to say about Ewan, among old friends, in the film industry and even in the media. Eimer's article is one of the few even vaguely negative pieces to have appeared in his early years of film stardom, though some American interviewers considered him a rather dull interviewee. On the other hand Ewan considered their endless questions about his attitude to drugs dull and uninspiring. 'McGregor is earnest and friendly,' Eimer admitted, 'but his guard hardly ever drops and he seems unwilling to analyse himself or his work.' Eimer quotes him as saying 'I just see what happens at the time on the set ... and then let it out.' Other journalists have sometimes complained, at least to me, about the actor's tendency to try to be funny or clever when they would have preferred a straight answer. Ewan is certainly not one for wordy analysis at the best of times, particularly on the subject of acting. Eimer found that the only subjects that drew any sort of animated response from Ewan were the politics of *Brassed Off* and motorbikes. 'I've got an old '74 Moto Guzzi,' he said. 'It's nice, a bit heavy for town, but it's a good bike. I saw a really nice Harley the other day, a sweet one. I'm thinking of taking it home, but I don't know if it'll be suitable for London. It would be good to go round Europe on.' Ewan is not a great interview. But, in fairness, his profession is acting not interviewing.

Eimer may have been particularly 'brassed off' by the fact that he had an interview on the set of what was supposed to be Ewan's big Hollywood breakthrough, yet as months went by there was no sign of the film. Its release was put back several times. Andrew Macdonald and Danny Boyle did see some footage from it because they wanted to see how Ewan fared as an American. Accents had always been one of his strengths, but when they saw the *Nightwatch* footage, Macdonald and Boyle decided to change his character in *A Life Less Ordinary* from American to Scottish.

When asked what he thought of *Nightwatch* by Chris Heath for the October 1997 edition of *Neon*, Ewan said: 'Don't know. Haven't seen it finished properly,' and then added: That's my polite answer.' It seemed certain to open in the United States in November 1997. A few months later Ewan was telling people that it had done so badly that he doubted whether it would ever come out in Britain, whereas in fact the American release had been postponed again. There had been speculation that *Nightwatch* would herald a permanent move to Hollywood, despite Ewan's denials. Instead of hastening his departure, the *Nightwatch* experience, and the attendant disillusionment and lack of exposure, made it all the easier for him to stay in Britain. The film finally opened in the United States in April 1998 and turned out much better than one might have feared, given Ewan's comments and Miramax's apparent reluctance to release it at all. John Hazelton of *Screen International* felt it did not quite add up as a suspense thriller, but worked as a stylish and grisly slasher movie. Jim Bartoo of *Hollywood Online*, said: 'While there are flaws, there are plenty of knee-jerk scares as well.' But you could hardly say there was a buzz about the film, it never really stood much chance at the box office and did not even make the Top 20 in its first week of release.

Nightwatch has all the strengths and weaknesses of the original – for the simple reason that it is essentially the same film. The word 'remake' is habitually applied to new versions and updatings of old films when the word 'reinterpretation' might be more accurate. However *Nightwatch* truly is a 'remake' of *Nattevagten*. It follows the original storyline, virtually scene for scene; it looks – and even sounds – like the original. Not only does *Nightwatch* have the same director, but the same producer, the same cinematographer and the same composer. The only elements that are substantially different are the language and the cast. Ewan brings a hard edge to the young man whose boyish good looks hide darker urges, the innocent who is not entirely innocent. He produces an acceptable American accent – it is certainly easier to accept than the Dutch one he would use for *The Serpent's Kiss*. Ultimately however there is a feeling that Ewan's situation is akin to that of an actor who takes over the lead role in an established play in the middle of its run.

The movie, in fact, marked Ewan's second American production in a row. He began 1996 by making an episode in HBO's long-running television series *Tales from the Crypt*, although it was shot in Britain. The stories were based on the notorious horror comics, which had been banned in Britain and which had prompted the introduction of the 'Comics Code' in the US in the Fifties. The comics had previously inspired a British film of the same name in 1972 and a sequel *Vault of Horror* the following year. The HBO version was a series of half-hour stories presented by a crypt keeper and embracing horror, science-fiction, magic and twist endings. Guest stars had included Arnold Schwarzengegger, Whoopi Goldberg, Joe Pesci and Christopher Reeve. Partly to inject a little freshness into the series and largely in an attempt to keep costs down, HBO decided to film an entire series in Britain, and Ewan was cast alongside Jane Horrocks, Bubbles from *Absolutely Fabulous*, in an episode entitled 'Cold War'.

The budget was so low that production took only about a week. 'It was quite rushed, but a lot of actors just did it for the fun of it,' says Horrocks. Among the many other distinguished Brits in this season were James Wilby, Julia Sawalha and Denis Lawson. 'They were mad stories,' says Horrocks. 'I wanted to work with Ewan and that's why I decided to do it.' She remembers that Ewan had been to see her in *The Rise and Fall of Little Voice* (they would subsequently appear in the film version together) and that he bought her champagne for her birthday. 'We'd hardly known each other and he brought me some champagne. He was very sweet about my birthday and I thought that was quite charming for somebody of such young years.'

After a couple of botched robbery attempts, Cammy

(Horrocks) walks out on the vain Ford (Ewan). She picks up a stranger called Jimmy in a bar and brings him home. Ford threatens and insults the stranger, for being a mere human. It turns out that Cammy and Ford are zombies but, unbeknown to them, Jimmy is a vampire. In the ensuing scuffle all three fall out of the window. Jimmy turns into a bat and flies away (off-camera, to keep costs down). Cammy and Ford survive. Ford's good looks have been ruined by his fall, the flesh horribly stripped from one half of his face. Cammy too has suffered horrendous injuries. But at least they have each other.

Guest director was Andy Morahan, who made *Highlander III*, which seems like serious drama compared with this. 'Cold War' was adapted from one of the original William Gaines comic stories. It is essentially a short story, a macabre joke, and Horrocks and Ewan approach it in the spirit in which it is intended, with performances that are considerably more expansive than the production values. Horrocks in particular is a delight, screeching like a provincial English banshee beneath a big blonde wig. Ewan seems to have taken it quite literally when told that his character has been sentenced to walk the Earth forever – his accent here certainly does a fair amount of globetrotting, with frequent journeys from Scotland to the States and back. Not that it matters much; this isn't exactly social realist drama.

Having worked with Peter Greenaway on *The Pillow Book*, Ewan returned to Greenaway country with *The Serpent's Kiss*. Like Greenaway's best film, *The Draughtsman's Contract, The Serpent's Kiss* is a cerebral 17th-century thriller, set largely in the grounds of a grand English country house. It shares the elegant costumes, sexual intrigues and elaborate deceits of the earlier film. In the first, Anthony Higgins is a draughtsman hired to make drawings of a stately home; in the second, Ewan is hired to design a garden around a stately home. The only element missing was Greenaway himself. Instead *The Serpent's Kiss* had Frenchman Philippe Rousselot making his directorial debut after establishing himself as one of cinema's foremost cinematographers with his work on films such as *Dangerous Liaisons* and *A River Runs Through It*. It would have proved a difficult shoot for any director. The Irish weather never seemed to suit – ironic, given that one of the key elements in the film is man's attempt to control nature.

Ewan's character draws up grand designs for a garden that includes paths and patterns in different colours of little stones, statues, ironwork, a few patches of grass and the occasional bush. When asked if there will be any flowers, he replies that garden design has 'progressed' beyond flowers. Ultimately the film-makers could no more control nature than the characters in the film could. Changing light was a continuing challenge for the camera team. But that was the least of the weather worries. Ewan is not alone in thinking that the storm created by wind machines to wreck the garden is not quite as dramatic as it should have been. Meanwhile nature proved that it could do it much more effectively. Rousselot shot first with the garden in a state of wilderness, then spent a little over a week on interiors and shots elsewhere, while production designer Charles Garrad and a team of 25 helpers laid out the Dutch parterre garden on boards held above the ground by scaffolding and covering an acre of land. The details came from Dutch paintings and authentic gardens. Just before shooting on this section of the film began, the garden was hit by torrential rain, the boards warped and characters found themselves not so much walking through the garden as bouncing. Alert viewers might still spot at least one shot in the finished film in which the ground is seen to bounce up and down. The film was not done on the cheap – it was an international co-production with a budget in excess of £10 million.

It was not just on screen that the cast were bouncing. Stuck for weeks on end in the wilds, on the west coast of Ireland, leisure and cultural activities revolved largely around alcohol. The film was a godsend to local publicans and Ewan rates the parties as the best he has ever encountered on location. According to him, the film company phoned round the cast to check on particular requirements for accommodation and Richard E. Grant's wife said that he disliked big modern hotels, jokingly adding that he liked to stay in historic buildings, surrounded by beautiful antiques, so he ended up in a castle, which became known as 'Reg's Castle' or 'Reg's Place'. One night he hosted a glam rock party, in which several hundred cast, crew, extras and locals turned up in suitably drab Seventies costumes and partied the night away. 'All the boys were girls,' says Ewan, 'and all the girls were sexy girls.' And 'Reg' himself turned up in a silver wig, platform boots, a pink lycra outfit and a diamonte codpiece. Ewan, Eve and daughter Clara shared some quieter moments too. He enjoyed sitting on the golf course outside his hotel just looking at the stars – the ones in the sky – with his family beside him.

The start of an eight-week shoot in County Clare in July 1996 marked the end of a lengthy search for the right location which had taken producer Robert Jones on fruitless trips through England, France, Italy and even South Africa, and had enforced postponement from the previous summer for want of a venue. Ewan had a long-standing commitment to the project, which was conceived by writer Tim Rose Price in 1990 after a storm destroyed the garden around his house in Gloucestershire. He decided to do some research on the sort of gardens that would have been fashionable when the house was built at the end of the 17th century and discovered a brief craze for Dutch parterres, very formal, symmetrical gardens, from which plants were all but banished. He wrote his screenplay around this central idea of a 'false' garden, creating a story in which at least some of the characters are also false – period conmen.

Ewan is, or at least pretends to be, Meneer Chrome, a leading Dutch garden designer. He is recommended by the flamboyant Fitzmaurice (Grant) to industrialist Thomas Smithers (Pete Postlethwaite) to design a garden for his wife Juliana (Greta Scacchi). But Fitzmaurice knows that Ewan's character is not the real Meneer Chrome. Fitzmaurice has romantic designs on Juliana, who is his cousin, and has forced the young designer into a plot to create a garden so grand that it will ruin her husband. However both Juliana and her daughter Thea (Carmen Chaplin), a strange girl who seems to be at peace only in the wildness of her father's grounds, are attracted to 'Chrome'. Price had a great-grandfather who tried to protect his garden in Cornwall by constructing a hill to divert the wind. It became known as Price's Folly. Price built this element into his plot. Blowing on a dandelion, Thea seems to create a storm that destroys Chrome's garden. Fitzmaurice persuades Smithers to re-lay the garden and build not just a hill to protect it, but a grass-covered pyramid, with steps and a monument on top, though Chrome is becoming increasingly disturbed by the progress of events. 'I wanted to do this very badly,' says Ewan. 'It was one of those scripts that comes along that you know is very rare. I was offered a lot of other films, but I was always going to do this.'

The film-makers needed a substantial 17th-century house, which did not already have a garden around it. Continuing his search for a location, Robert Jones saw Mount Ievers Court at Sixmilebridge, in County Clare, in a 1958 copy of *Country Life*. 'The house and surrounding grounds looked as if they were built to order,' he says. It had been in the same family for three centuries and, although the house was substantial, the owners were not rich, they ran the property as a dairy farm and, most importantly, there was no existing garden. The son of the house was a fan of *The Usual Suspects*, on which Jones had been executive producer, and the family gave the film-makers free rein inside and out. The interior had changed little over the centuries, walls were repainted, carpets lifted and virtually the whole film was shot on location at Mount Ievers.

For all the detail that has gone into the historical accuracy of the garden and house, there is a curious carelessness in other areas of the film. The film-makers may have shown an admirable lack of colour prejudice in casting Charlie's grand-daughter Carmen Chaplin, who is half-Trinidadian, as Thea Smithers, but in doing so they seem to have created a further, presumably unintentional puzzle as to how Pete Postlethwaite and Greta Scacchi ended up with a daughter who does indeed look like she has just arrived from the West Indies. The film seems to get carried away by the cleverness of its metaphors and ideas, the plot itself is ponderous and convoluted. When, near the end, Smithers says he is confused, he could well be speaking on behalf of the audience. And yet one suspects that by this time the audience may be past caring. The tidiness of the resolution seems as unreal as the garden. Chrome and

Thea elope together, Smithers and his wife are reconciled and Fitzmaurice takes the poison that he had intended for Chrome. A gold star for neatness if nothing else.

Ewan did get to wear some lovely clothes. He turns up on Smithers's doorstep in a flowing wig, a flowing yellow coat and what looks like an enormous white stetson. Costume designer Consolata Boyle enthuses about how comfortable Ewan seemed in his outfits: 'His nonchalance when he wears a costume is exactly what I wanted. He is completely underwhelmed by it.' Ewan may have felt comfortable in his outfit, but that does not stop him taking all his clothes off for a discrete nude scene while walking in the wild grasses, watched by Thea. Ewan enjoyed the 'taste' of his Dutch accent too. 'It's nice in your mouth,' he says. A voice coach recorded all his lines in a Dutch accent on tape for him. Ewan, who finds it very difficult to stop working, did have three weeks holiday before filming began, but he played the tape constantly during that time. Despite his apparent comfort with the accent, there was some sniggering at the belated British première of the film in Glasgow in February 1998 when Ewan's character announced himself as being Dutch. It may be doing him an injustice to suggest it prompted memories of Peter Sellers, but obviously some viewers had difficulties in accepting Ewan as a Dutchman.

Reviewing the film in Cannes in May 1997 Allan Hunter of *Screen International* gave it only two stars, rating it as fair, and noted that Ewan was 'once again uncomfortably cast in historical fare'. James Cosmo had said they both felt uncomfortable on *Emma*. Ewan's own agent had been questioning his suitability for period roles since *Scarlet and Black*. So why does he persist in doing them? I put the question directly to Ewan himself, and his answer was interesting to say the least. He insisted that he made no distinction between period and contemporary roles. 'They are all people,' he told me. He seems quite proud of the fact that he 'does not act period', though in reality this is exactly what the critics have been saying all along. There is another, very simple reason why he likes doing period dramas – he likes dressing up. He insists, quite seriously, that every actor does, whether they admit to it or not.

He had been attracted to *The Serpent's Kiss* not just by the prospect of dressing up in fine clothes, but by what he considered a beautiful script. He feels it lost something in its transition to the screen. 'I don't know ...' he says, carefully weighing up his words. But Ewan has always been one to call a spade a spade. 'The director just missed the point really ... It was a much more complex story than we were doing; just little details, which was a shame. That was to do with him being very ... difficult and arrogant. I shouldn't be saying all that. But he was.'

Ewan could be outspoken, but he also showed tremendous loyalty to those he felt had earned it. He had a month off between finishing *The Serpent's Kiss* in Ireland and starting *A Life Less Ordinary* in the United States and he chose to devote a week of it to making a short film in Eastbourne, for an old pal. Justin Chadwick was a jobbing TV actor, whose credits included *The Bill* and *Casualty*. He was hoping to establish himself on the other side of the camera and had directed Ewan in the Lloyds Bank Film Challenge short *Family Style* 18 months earlier. Chadwick wrote and directed *Sleeping with the Fishes*, a nicely shaded character drama about Cypriot immigrants running a fish-and-chip shop in England. 'I believe in him,' Ewan said in an interview at the time. 'I've got this weird loyalty thing going on, mates and friendship and all that nonsense.'

The title *Sleeping with the Fishes* comes from a phrase in *The Godfather*, meaning that someone has been killed and the body dumped in a river or the sea. But Chadwick's short might equally well have been entitled *Sex with the Fishes*. Ewan plays Billy, son of one of the immigrants. By this time one actor had made the role of Ewan's screen dad pretty much his own. 'I'd already played his dad twice,' says James Cosmo, 'and he phoned me up and said "Will you come and do it again?" because it was a friend of his that was directing it.' So Cosmo reported to Eastbourne to fulfil his paternal duties for the third time in a little over a year. He regards *Sleeping with the Fishes* as the most enjoyable of their three films together. 'We just had such a lot of fun,' he says. 'There wasn't the stress of making a big feature movie.' An interview from the location reveals that Ewan was enjoying himself too, knocking back beer and whisky between takes.

His character, Billy, is caught having sex with the daughter of the chip-shop owner, in the back room, in an explosion of fish fillets. 'Four years of training,' Ewan laughed as he watched the rushes of the fishy sex scene in Eastbourne's Grand Hotel. For this crime Billy must sleep with the fishes, says the boss, who clearly fancies himself as the Cypriot community's Codfather. The film was only a quarter of an hour long but it managed to touch upon clashes between different cultures, between different generations and between individual characters. It was lodged with the British Council for festival exhibition. But, despite its star name, there was little interest in showing it, yet another reminder that these days a star name is not in itself enough to open a film.

14
Pervert in Utah

THE BACKLASH BEGINS here. The date is 24 October 1997, the day *A Life Less Ordinary* opened. John Hodge had begun writing it four years earlier as the intended follow-up to *Shallow Grave*. However producer Andrew Macdonald pushed for *Trainspotting* instead. Hodge found *A Life Less Ordinary* an even more challenging assignment than *Trainspotting*: it was an original story, a post-modern romantic comedy, and there were countless changes in plot and detail along the way. Official press notes suggest there were 18 drafts for *A Life Less Ordinary* compared with two for *Trainspotting*. You can interpret that in two ways – either Hodge was aiming for perfection or he was in trouble from the start. *A Life Less Ordinary* had been set in Britain, France and the east coast of America before finally settling for Utah. The critics were of the opinion that it was not just the setting that was all over the place.

If *A Life Less Ordinary* had been the team's first film it would surely not have been subjected to quite as much negative criticism, but critics were using the yardstick of films that they themselves had hailed as the best British film of the year and the best British film of the decade. *A Life Less Ordinary* is a brilliant piece of cinema, not perfect, but brilliant in terms of its vision, its ambition, and, most certainly, its dialogue. It is without doubt Ewan's most underrated film and it has a special place in his affections as one of the most enjoyable films on which he has worked and as the one which provided him with the character he felt was closest to his own personality.

Hodge had Ewan in mind when he wrote the story of the sensitive office cleaner who kidnaps a wealthy heiress, more by chance than design, and finds himself caught up in a battle of wills between her and her father. The project had been conceived to shoot in Scotland on a budget of £2 million, but on the back of *Shallow Grave* the budget rose to £5 million and the whole production moved across the Atlantic. The characters have to escape to the middle of nowhere and Hodge thought America's wide open spaces provided a more effective setting than anywhere in Britain. At this point the film-makers were also talking about American stars in both lead roles. After *Trainspotting* Boyle, Macdonald and Hodge were inundated with offers from Hollywood. Hodge was approached about a remake of the black detective movie *Shaft*, and Boyle and Macdonald got into fairly detailed negotiations about the possibility of taking on the fourth *Alien* movie with Sigourney Weaver and Winona Ryder, but decided to go with *A Life Less Ordinary* instead.

The trio were now in a position where they could set up a financial deal that gave them a budget of £8 million, still very modest by Hollywood standards, and complete creative control – something they would not have had on the *Alien* movie. Brad Pitt asked for, and got, a meeting with the film-makers, but Macdonald was maintaining that the part had always been destined for Ewan – which is not entirely consistent with his previous mentions of Johnny Depp and John Cusack as possibilities. But by now Ewan was well on his way to becoming a star himself, thanks largely to his association with Boyle, Macdonald and Hodge. He jumped at the chance to work with them on a comedy and was confirmed for *A Life Less Ordinary* in spring 1996. Numerous young American actresses were considered as the female lead before Boyle met Cameron Diaz, the former model who had made a big impact in a supporting role opposite Jim Carrey in *The Mask* in 1994. He wanted someone who was not only right for the role, but right for Ewan. 'She was unlike any of the other actresses I had met,' says Boyle, 'very natural, very fun-loving, and with a great sense of humour.'

It was at a dinner at the Cannes Film Festival that Danny Boyle met Holly Hunter, the diminutive star of *The Piano* and David Cronenberg's controversial film *Crash*, and he asked her there and then if she would play one of the angels whose job it is to make the two main characters fall in love. Her partner would be Delroy Lindo, fresh from another kidnap film, Mel Gibson's *Ransom*. Sean Connery, who Ewan and Jonny Lee Miller had mimicked in *Trainspotting*, was approached for a one-line role as God, but said no and so the film ended up godless. Utah was chosen for its landscape of desert, mountains and city, within a few hours drive of each other, and for its pool of film technicians, though many key posts were filled by people with whom Boyle had worked before.

One new face was 'art department associate' Eve Mavrakis, aka Mrs Ewan McGregor. And baby made three. 'I have always made sure they come with me,' says Ewan. 'There are too many wrecked marriages in this business for mine to be one. I am in a position to insist that they come. And if anyone doesn't like that, then I won't make the film. It's important – I don't want to miss my daughter growing up because of a film. As it is I'm usually away to work before she's up and back after she's gone to bed. But at least she knows I'm around.'

As usual Boyle and his principal actors spent part of the rehearsal period watching movies, before the film began its nine-week shoot at the end of September. He was particularly keen for them to see two which he felt had shaped his vision of *A Life Less Ordinary*. One was *It Happened One Night*, Frank Capra's archetypal screwball comedy of 1934 in which Claudette Colbert plays a spoiled heiress running away from her father and Clark Gable the reporter who agrees to help her make her way from Florida to New York in exchange for her story. 'One of the things that I learned from Capra's film, and continued to learn during the editing process,' says Boyle, 'is that in a romantic comedy you can't stray too far from your lead actors.' The second film was *A Matter of Life and Death* (1946), aka *Stairway to Heaven*, one of the films of Michael

Powell and Emeric Pressburger, Macdonald's grandfather, a bizarre romance, with David Niven as a downed airman, arguing for his life in front of a celestial court on the strength of his love for Kim Hunter. 'It's one of the boldest, most imaginative films I know of. The way it makes the extraordinary and supernatural concrete is something I wanted to achieve in our film.'

Boyle also took the actors to a shooting range, which was a real eye-opener for Ewan. 'It was fucking terrifying,' he says. 'It was huge, like a supermarket, just full of things to kill people. I mean, why is it such a major issue in America, the right to have a gun, the right to kill?' The life of Diaz's character, Celine Naville, is so dull and pointless that she tries to amuse herself by shooting apples off the heads of minions and suitors. Ewan's character, Robert, also has to handle a gun. He gets hold of the pistol of one of the security guards who set upon him after he goes to protest about his sacking to his employer, Celine's father (Ian Holm). In a show of righteous indignation Robert tries to throw the robot that has replaced him through a window, but it bounces back and continues its cleaning work. Robert gets the pistol, but loses it, and it takes Celine to surreptitiously kick it back to him. He points it at her father and demands his job back … by the time he has counted to five. He hesitates after 'four' and is so surprised when Celine says 'five' that he shoots Mr Naville in the leg. Despite his country upbringing, Ewan had never fired a gun before, though Diaz was a crack shot, a state of affairs which was consistent with their characters.

That early sequence reiterates Hodge's talent for black comedy and establishes the sweet ineptitude of one character, the exciting recklessness of another and the bitterness of the relationship between Celine and her father. It also determines the balance of power between Robert and Celine. That balance, and the nature of the characters, is quickly, skilfully and amusingly underlined when Robert assures Celine he is not going to hurt her, but he wants to make it clear that he is the kidnapper and she is the … She butts in with the word 'victim' and reveals that she has been kidnapped before. Robert is horrified. She assures him it was a long time ago. Regaining his composure he asks her how he is doing.

Celine determines that they should join forces in an attempt to extort a ransom from her father. They warm to each other and sing and dance together in an elaborate production number in a local bar in what was to become one of the most heavily criticised scenes in the film. Liese Spencer in *Sight and Sound* considered it 'a belated rip-off of a Dennis Potter musical moment'. The lavish style and choreography are reminiscent of Potter, though the sudden shift in tone from reality to fantasy could also be attributed to Powell and Pressburger. But what is more important than the exact nature or inspiration of the set-piece is the fantastical quality of it. It is followed by Robert waking up next morning, so viewers may read it as reality, memory or fantasy, in whichever proportions they choose. It serves as a gentle prelude to the magic realism at the end of the film.

There was a sense of, if not magic realism, then certainly surrealism when Boyle took Ewan and Diaz to a country-and-western bar in Salt Lake City and asked them to sing Bobby Darin's 'Beyond the Sea' in front of the assembled rednecks. 'When I got there they said "Oh, it's a rehearsal for your dance,"' Diaz recalls. Despite the numerous revisions, there had been no song-and-dance number in the script Diaz had read. 'Not wanting to look like an idiot, I didn't ask where was the dance scene. I held out for a while, then I asked Ewan finally "Is there a dance scene?" And he said "I don't know." So then I felt I was pretty much in the same bag.' Boyle promised that if Ewan and Diaz sang 'Beyond the Sea' he would do a number too, and managed to top their performance with a rendition of 'My Way' in the style of Sid Vicious, conjuring up memories of John Belushi and Dan Aykroyd's discomfort when they are forced to play in a C&W bar in *The Blues Brothers*. Some customers patted Boyle on the back, some congratulated him, one suggested he go fuck himself. Diaz encouraged her party to discreetly withdraw and head for their car – it was not difficult to find as it was the only vehicle in the parking lot that was not a pick-up truck.

Undeterred by this introduction to local culture, cast and crew regularly let off steam in another Salt Lake City bar on Friday nights. Ewan enjoyed shooting pool with the locals, or at least he seemed to at the time. He later upset some of them with his comments about their locality. 'It's a weird, yet beautiful place,' he said.' 'It has some of the best skyscrapers I've ever seen, but the whole town is built in this bowl where you do not have to think about the rest of the world – you are absolutely safe from any normal people. It is built next to this huge, stagnant and stinking lake, which says rather a lot about the people who live there ... the Mormons ... I'd walk to the supermarket with my wife and baby and be stared at because we weren't dressed like them. They looked at me as if I was Satan himself. I have this woolly hat with "Pervert" written on the front and I'd deliberately put it on my daughter's head and walk around, just to get a reaction.'

As anticipated, Diaz and Ewan hit it off on screen and off. 'He just comes in and he does his work and he makes it look so easy,' says Diaz. 'But you know it's not. You know it's not like he just whipped it up.' During one press interview, shortly before filming began, Ewan came across as being so naïve and unaffected by stardom that he could not even remember his co-star's name, despite the fact that the style magazines were touting her as the hottest young actress in Hollywood. He suggested Carmen Somebody or Karen Something, before the interviewer helped him out. The incident duly appeared in print. But Ewan later told another journalist that he was simply trying to be cool. 'It's embarrassing when men gush about someone like that. What they [interviewers] are fishing for is "She's fucking amazing," which now I can tell you she is. But I'd only seen her in *The Mask* and I hated *The Mask*. But of course I remembered her, ha, ha, ha.' Ewan has a tendency to play jokes on journalists, often leaving them unsure how to take him. He gleefully recounts one occasion on which an interviewer was pressing him about his relationship with Cameron Diaz. 'He was pushing, pushing, and I said "Oh, she's great" and everything. And then his tape ran out. So I looked at him and said "That's when I fucked her." ' The story illustrates not only how well Ewan got on with Diaz, but also his confidence in his marriage.

Boyle says, 'These two, fortunately, got on like a house on fire and it shows in the film. You can't buy that kind of relationship. Not all the money in the world can give you those moments when they look at each other and you think "Yeah, these people really do like each other." It's fantastic and they are bouncing off each other and Ewan is helping Cameron with some of the scenes because he's much more familiar with John's writing and the way that I work than she was.' After three films together Boyle and Ewan could just about read each other's minds. 'You always know what you are trying to achieve with Danny,' says Ewan. 'And with some other directors you don't, because they don't even know what they're trying to achieve.'

On this occasion, however, the critics were not at all convinced that Boyle knew what he was trying to achieve and seemed unsure about the relationship between Ewan and Diaz. 'They are entirely lacking in sexual chemistry,' wrote Liese Spencer in *Sight and Sound*. 'With their blamelessly bland faces neither is capable of suggesting the ingenuity or passion his or her role demands … Diaz is nasty without being vulnerable, while McGregor lacks the roguish charm necessary to make him attractive rather than just plain dim.' Caroline Westbrook in *Empire*, however, thought that Diaz was 'luminous', that Robert was Ewan's most sympathetic character to date and that they held the film together. Reviews of the film ranged from, at best, balanced to at worst Liese Spencer: 'Poorly paced, incoherent and uneven, this ambitious film is fascinating only for the comprehensiveness of its failure.' In one of the more thoughtful reviews, Damon Wise of *Neon* argued that the script was 'fantastically funny', but the film was let down by Boyle's directing.

Ewan has never been more natural, and even a haircut which suggests a Bay City Roller caught in a shower of rain does not undermine his charm. Diaz delivers a steely performance that no one could expect of an ex-model relatively new to acting. She is like a Hitchcock ice-maiden. And, although comedy is perhaps the most subjective of all film genres, Hodge's script positively sparkles with wit and banter, not just in its smart one-liners, but in the whole seductively daft way the humour develops in scenes such as the one where Robert works up his aggression for the ransom-demand phone call, dials a wrong number, and is easily diverted into chit-chat with the lady on the other end before Celine cuts him off.

The film is a flawed masterpiece. It is *It Happened One Night* for the Nineties. It is not however *A Matter of Life and Death* for the Nineties. Boyle is right – as soon as you switch attention away from the central couple you are in trouble and the sub-plot about two hard-boiled, gun-toting angels called Jackson and O'Reilly never quite engages as it should, despite strong performances from Lindo and the totally manic Hunter, 'Cupid as Terminator' in the words of Damon Wise. It is a reflection of the success of the central relationship that we cannot work up the same interest in Jackson and O'Reilly. But there is also an in-built flaw in the whole idea of the angels getting themselves hired by Celine's father as hitmen in an attempt to drive Robert and Celine closer together through shared adversity and danger. Robert and Celine may not know that they are their guardian angels, but we, the audience, do, and consequently there is no tension in the situation.

If Boyle is guilty of anything – and he is – it is of being over-ambitious. He sacrifices coherence to artistic ambition and ultimately asks too much of the audience, particularly in a finale in which Celine's bullet passes harmlessly through Ewan's heart and kills Naville's henchman, a finale which teeters just a little awkwardly between magic realism and cop-out nonsense. The audience is then subjected to an embarrassingly misjudged sequence in which Robert and Celine discuss the nature of love and fate, to camera, while a succession of brief scenes from the film are replayed behind them. The final sequence, in which animated models of Robert and Celine go on honeymoon in Scotland, has a certain charm, but it looks like an afterthought tacked on to tie up various loose ends left by the main part of the film, including the fate of the ransom money. It looks like an afterthought because it was an afterthought, a response to negative comments from preview audiences. *A Life Less Ordinary* is an extremely bold and very funny film. Unfortunately most of its weaknesses are concentrated in the final few minutes, the minutes that would be freshest in audiences' minds as they left the cinema.

A Life Less Ordinary is very different from its two predecessors from the same team and yet, for the third time running, Ewan ends up with a bag full of money. Sadly the public were not quite so forthcoming with their cash. The movie opened simultaneously on both sides of the Atlantic, with a big promotional push behind it. It was preceded by heavy advertising, a soundtrack album and no fewer than three versions of the story in print form – the script, a novelisation and a comic-strip serialisation in *2000 AD* magazine. There was also a film about the making of the film, which eschewed the art, insight and wit of Kevin Macdonald's *Digging Your Own Grave* in favour of star sound bites, film excerpts and pure puff. *A Life Less Ordinary* entered the British Top 10 at only No 4 behind *The Full Monty*, *Hercules* and *The Peacemaker* and got no higher than No 9 in North America, prompting *Screen International* to headline its report 'A Gross So Ordinary'. It took about £4 million in Britain and considerably less in the United States.

Strange though it may seem, given his phenomenal work rate, *A Life Less Ordinary* was the only Ewan McGregor film to open in 1997 and it provided magazines with a peg for lengthy interviews with and profiles on the man who was taking over Alec Guinness's mantle in *Star Wars*. Suddenly he was on the cover of the style magazines. There was a very definite backlash against Boyle, Macdonald and Hodge for failing to match the standards they had set with *Shallow Grave* and *Trainspotting*. But the backlash was directed very specifically against the men behind the camera and Ewan emerged untarnished. *A Life Less Ordinary* and, more so, the attendant publicity made Ewan a bigger star than ever.

By the time *A Life Less Ordinary* came out he had completed another production in the United States, which had already reached a much bigger audience with only a fraction of the media publicity. A special episode of *ER*, the United States's top-rated television show, was built around Ewan and series regular Julianna Margulies. Ewan was a passionate fan of the series which had been created by Michael Crichton, an undistinguished film director who became a best-selling novelist and author of *Jurassic Park*.

ER is essentially a soap opera, following the lives and loves of a small group of regular characters, just like any other soap. Their stories are told however, not against the neutral backdrop of the local boozer, but within the context of a Chicago hospital. The frantic pace and life-and-death dramas of the emergency room gave the series an importance and urgency that other soaps lacked, while explicit shots of medical procedures and extensive use of jargon, and indeed blood, seemed to ground it in reality, as if it were a documentary. It helped too that it had excellent actors, writers and directors, with Quentin Tarantino supervising one early episode. It made a major star of George Clooney, who subsequently played Batman on the big screen.

Ewan's appearance on *ER* was given an added poignancy by a life-and-death drama within his own household. His one-year-old daughter Clara had become a familiar figure on Ewan's film sets, but because he was going to be in America for only a short time for *ER*, he broke his usual rule of taking the family with him. He got back to find Clara seriously ill in hospital. She had fallen desperately sick and was running a fever. Tests confirmed she had meningitis. Ewan and Eve were terrified. An inflammation of the membranes that cover the brain, meningitis can prove fatal. Stardom meant nothing to Ewan compared to the joys of fatherhood. He was not a patient man and he waited despairingly for signs of improvement. This was one life-and-death drama that did have a happy ending. At the end of a year in which Ewan appeared on *ER* and made four feature films, including the first *Star Wars* prequel, he regarded Clara's survival as the biggest blessing of 1997. Her illness and recovery had been 'the scariest thing that's ever happened; the happiest thing when it was over'.

'The Long Way Around' was a major departure from the usual *ER* format, abandoning virtually all the regular cast and the usual hospital setting until the final scenes in favour of a tight

character drama in which Ewan's character robs a neighbourhood store, shoots the owner dead and holds his customers
hostage. One of the customers just happens to be Nurse Carol
Hathaway (Margulies), who sees through the façade of an
armed robber to the sensitive character within. We know
Ewan's character, Duncan Stewart, is a sensitive individual
because he shot the owner only after the old man appeared
suddenly with a gun and blasted Duncan's cousin James. We
know he is sensitive because he shows due concern for the old
man's welfare when Nurse Hathaway operates on him with
straws and a screwdriver, and because he is clearly upset by his
death. And most of all we know he is sensitive by the way in
which he takes James's mind off his injuries with his wistful
descriptions of the Scottish homeland he left to visit his cousin,
of the Firth of Clyde, the islands of Great Cumbrae and Little
Cumbrae and the purple mountains of Arran. 'Sounds beautiful,' says Nurse Hathaway. But it turns out that Duncan has
never actually been to the islands. 'Never even seen the firth,'
he says. He worked in the Glasgow shipyards, like his father
before him, but he was laid off and has come to America, land
of opportunity. Now he is thinking maybe he should have gone
to Little Cumbrae instead.

Close-ups of Nurse Hathaway tending the cuts that disfigure
his handsome features while he witters on about his homeland,
like a refugee from a Housman poem, shimmer with the possibility and the impossibility of romance. The idea of Carol
feeling any sympathy for this killer, no matter how lyrical he
might wax about his land of lost content, would seem absurd
were it not for her own personal situation. And this is the
episode's master stroke. When Duncan screams at James 'I
killed a man. Do you know what that feels like?', Carol is able
to respond 'I do.' If only Duncan had been following the series
he would know she had just been suspended for killing a man
by giving him the wrong blood. 'You didn't mean to kill him,'
says Duncan. 'You didn't mean to kill Mr Novotny,' says Carol.
He takes her with him when he attempts to escape from the
store via a circuitous route, 'the long way around', into a
backstreet. When challenged by a solitary policeman, he turns

and runs, despite Carol's pleading. The cop shoots him three times in the back.

Carol makes a high-profile return to the hospital pumping Duncan's chest and commanding operations in a valiant attempt to save him, finally calling time of death at 13.48. At the end Carol spends a few moments alone with Duncan, who lies bloody, naked, but for a sheet, and lifeless in the green-tiled emergency room of the title, a surprisingly unsettling image of wasted youth. This is corn. But it is corn of the first order, thanks not so much to the quality of the script as a whole, but specifically to the script device that makes Carol's empathy for an armed robber at least half-way believable. It takes Ewan's performance to take the episode the rest of the way. Whatever Liese Spencer of *Sight and Sound* may think, the one quality that Ewan most certainly possesses is roguish charm, but too much roguish charm here would upset the balance of the character. He has to keep the charm in check, offering only enough hints of an intelligent and sensitive inner self to support the abundant evidence provided by the script. It is the balance between Duncan's sensitivity and his anger and frustration that makes this such a brilliantly shaded performance.

In the United States NBC broadcast 'The Long Way Around' in February 1997 in a week when stations put out what they regard are their strongest episodes, because audience figures will determine advertising rates for the following quarter. 'The Long Way Around' emerged top of the TV pops with an estimated 23 million homes or 37 million viewers tuned in. Ewan was nominated for an Emmy for best guest performance in a drama series. He had picked up various minor awards for *Shallow Grave* and *Trainspotting* from critics, magazines and newspapers, but the Emmies, television's equivalent of the Oscars, were undoubtedly the most prestigious awards in which Ewan had been mentioned, though he lost out to Pruitt Taylor Vince from *Murder One*.

'The Long Way Around' attracted 4.4 million viewers on Channel 4 in April, making it the station's most popular programme of the week, though some critics did voice reservations about the departure from the usual format. For Scottish viewers the most incredible aspect of the plot was not the nascent romance between nurse and gunman, but the idea of a Glaswegian who had worked in the shipyards, but had supposedly never seen the Firth of Clyde. Glasgow is built on the River Clyde and it broadens out into the firth just beyond the city. If Duncan was working in the shipyards, he must have kept his head turned firmly towards Edinburgh the whole time to avoid seeing the firth. No wonder they got rid of him.

Ewan admits there was an element of, as he puts it, 'Look at me, mammy' about appearing on *ER*. 'It was as intense as shooting a movie in a short space of time. It was so brilliant. It was weird though – there were the people that I've been watching on TV for years, standing round asking for five milligrams of such-and-such and ECGs, and you're lying strapped to a trolley like a lump of meat.' It underlines just how young Ewan is when he refers to George Clooney, who was born in 1961, as 'very fatherly'. 'Your eyes are closed so you can't see any of it either. At the end of the day, it's like having bad seats at a football match. It's much better to watch it on TV.'

Ewan was due to return to Morrison's Academy for a drama workshop at the end of January. He had to postpone the visit because of *ER*, but duly fulfilled his pledge a week late. It was a strange experience to return to the school, where latterly he had been so unhappy, to teach a class of his own, and to be mobbed by teenage girls, all neatly turned out in school uniform, though some seemed determined to test the dress code by having Ewan autograph their shirts. At least one teacher, who remembered Ewan as a pupil, was bewildered by girls almost fainting with excitement at having been 'touched' by him. There was a big press contingent, including four television crews, and an article in the school magazine compared the visit to that of the Queen 12 years earlier, when Ewan was a pupil at the school. He gave tips on stage fighting to the actors in the school's forthcoming production of *Tom Sawyer* and delivered a lecture to the sixth year on the British film industry.

Having fulfilled one schoolboy fantasy in becoming a film

star, Ewan got a chance to fulfil another by playing a pop star in *Velvet Goldmine*. He had lip-synched to Elvis in *Lipstick on Your Collar*, but he would get the chance to really sing, in front of an audience of hundreds of people, in *Velvet Goldmine*, a hymn to the glam rock era of the early Seventies when English popular music was dominated by yellow, purple and pink flares, silver platform boots and a whole new concept of 'gender-bending'. Glam rock was pioneered by Marc Bolan and David Bowie. After initial public indifference, Bowie exploded into public consciousness in 1972, when Ewan was no more than a baby. He had four albums in the charts that year, including *Hunky Dory* and *The Rise and Fall of Ziggy Stardust and the Spiders from Mars*. Glam quickly mushroomed from cult to mainstream fashion and its influence was such that the group Slade got rid of their skinheads in favour of long, flowing hair and mirror-effect top hats and the Rolling Stones wore lipstick and feather boas. The movement spawned Freddie Mercury and Queen and it revived the career of America's Iggy Pop, who had retired to Florida to play golf, after a brief but spectacular singing career that included drug problems and arrest for indecent exposure. Under the influence of Bowie, Iggy Pop reformed his band, the Stooges, and moved to London. Within a few years glam was dead and Iggy Pop was being acclaimed 'the grandfather' of punk. Two decades later his music was still considered sufficiently hip to open *Trainspotting*.

Ewan has catholic tastes in music. Sadly they do not extend to glam rock. 'It's really annoying music,' he says. His own preference at this time was Oasis. When he got the chance to try out his concert technique at John Hodge's wedding early in 1997 he opted for Oasis's 'Champagne Supernova' rather than anything from the glam era. 'I liked the Stooges, but I've never been into Bowie,' he adds, with perhaps a hint of uncharacteristic diplomacy given that Ewan sings a couple of Stooges classics in *Velvet Goldmine*, 'Gimme Danger' and 'TV Eye', along with a new song written by original band member Ron Asheton, whereas Bowie refused to allow his songs to be used – though the film's title is taken from a Bowie song.

Glam rock was never the mainstream fashion in the United

States that it was in Britain. At school in California, Todd Haynes was vaguely aware of Bowie and Ziggy Stardust, but it was not until he went to college that he appreciated that they were part of a phenomenon that reached beyond music and fashion to question accepted notions of sexuality. Haynes, who is gay, explored notions of deviation in his debut feature film *Poison* (1991). It established him as one of America's more controversial film-makers. Haynes styled his hair in the fashion of Ziggy Stardust, dyed it bright red and took to wearing platform shoes and tight little tops when he was researching and writing *Velvet Goldmine*. Method actors may be common enough, but the idea of Method directors would seem to break new ground.

It was Ewan's performance in *Trainspotting* that convinced Haynes he had the energy and volatility for the role of Curt Wild, an American pop star in London. Haynes felt the new generation of young American stars were too internal and 'skulking' for the role. Although the characters in the film are fictional, it does not take a genius to work out that Curt Wild was inspired largely by Iggy Pop, though there is a little Lou Reed in there too, and it would not have done Ewan any harm that his first scene in *Trainspotting* is accompanied by Iggy Pop's 'Lust for Life' on the soundtrack. Haynes went to Ireland to see Ewan while he was shooting *The Serpent's Kiss* in the summer of 1996. It was a typical 'meeting Ewan' experience. 'We drank a lot of pints,' says Haynes, 'and I met his parents, because they happened to be visiting that day, and we just had a really nice chat. I thought he was so down-to-earth, so easy, very approachable and very smart. And he seemed to be someone who was excited by experimentation and people trying to do something a little bit out of the ordinary.' Haynes's track record suggested a director less ordinary. Previous films included a biopic of Karen Carpenter, in which she was played by a Barbie doll. On this occasion his professed intention was to make a film that would play like a drug trip, told largely in flashback, with throwbacks not just to the 1970s, but to the previous century, with references to archetypal glam-rocker Oscar Wilde.

Ewan kept Haynes hanging on while he deliberated over the

script. The length of time he took to read it and make his mind up became a rather strained joke between them. He was keen to do the film, but thought he might rather play the androgynous, mysterious, Bowiesque singer Brian Slade. Haynes managed to convince him there was more meat in the role of Curt Wild and saved himself the headache of coming up with someone else to play the American role that he had already decided was beyond the capabilities of young American actors. The role of Brian Slade went to Jonathan Rhys-Meyers, the young Irishman who appeared in *Michael Collins* in the small, but significant part of the man who killed Collins. Slade's wife is played by Toni Collette, with whom Ewan had appeared in *Emma*. The last of the four principal roles is a journalist, in the more conservative 1980s, who is investigating Slade's disappearance years before. Haynes recruited Christian Bale, who had been the juvenile lead in Steven Spielberg's *Empire of the Sun*.

There was the further complication that, far from slowing down after the success of *Trainspotting*, Ewan was taking on so many films that they were now beginning to overlap. His scenes on *Velvet Goldmine* were going to have to be crammed into long, arduous days in the first half of the eight-week shoot to free him up for a film dealing with another, very different chapter in the history of 20th-century arts. One day he was Iggy Pop, the next he would be James Joyce in *Nora*, the story of the Irish novelist, seen through the eyes of his partner Nora Barnacle. *Nora* was not going to be a respectful tribute, filled with beautifully narrated passages from the works of the great writer. The emphasis was going to be not on literature, but on sex and the relationship between Joyce and Barnacle. Ewan described it as 'a really dirty, sexy script' and was promising to bring out 'the true nastiness in the man'.

Previous projects had left Ewan feeling more than a little homesick. *Velvet Goldmine* was shooting in London, which meant Ewan could get home at nights, eventually. It was an exhausting shoot, with an unusually large number of very short scenes, which required patience and great technical discipline. The musical numbers were a rare opportunity for Ewan to really go for it. 'I heard him singing in *Emma*,' says Haynes. 'But this is a completely different kind of singing and requires more performance ability. I felt confident about his performance ability and I was proven right.'

'I watched a lot of Iggy (on video),' says Ewan. 'He's like a small kid, thrashing around in sporadic bursts, not even in time with the music sometimes. It's like he has to let it all out ... I ended up in front of 400 extras, with my trousers round my ankles, pulling my cock and showing them my arsehole, going "Fuck off", at four in the morning, in a field somewhere south of London.' It was Ewan's live singing that was used on the soundtrack. Ewan regarded it as one of the most enjoyable and physical roles he had ever done. Although glam rock was not his sort of music, he enjoyed the dressing up and make-up. He does not look like Iggy Pop, but, with long blond hair, bare chest and a spaced-out, slightly pained expression, he becomes eerily reminiscent of him.

He also has a long, physical scene with Christian Bale, though it was not intended to be quite as long as it ended up. 'I come off stage,' says Ewan, 'and he's in the wings there, and I take him up on to this roof-top and we have sex. And it's this roof-top in Kings Cross, and Christian and I are both straight guys trying not to make too big a deal about this. And we were actually giving it "full legs", which was brilliant. But it was going on for a very long time, I thought, with nobody yelling "Cut" ... I kept going, kept going, kept going, and by this time we're going so quick there was hair flying round and (moaning noises). And people on the street are going "What the fuck's going on there?" Finally I said "Well, I'm going to look", because Christian couldn't figure it out either. And I looked on the roof-top and people were picking up the tracks and cables and wires. And they just never said "Cut". They hadn't bothered to stop us ... Bastards.' Todd Haynes tells much the same story, except he makes the point that the camera crew were actually on a different roof-top, taking a long shot, and his version ends with him screaming 'Cut! Cut!' at Ewan and Bale, but they were so far away, or so into their work, that they did not hear him, and so just kept going. These days the media just cannot rely on celebrities to get the facts right.

After packing all Ewan's scenes into the first half of *Velvet Goldmine*, the Joyce film *Nora* collapsed. *Velvet Goldmine* had been teetering as well when part of the finance fell through shortly before filming was due to begin, but some alternative funds were secured, and it went ahead in March 1997 on a reduced budget of £4.5 million. Channel 4 had put up its share at the outset, convinced that *Velvet Goldmine* would not be restricted to a nostalgia market. With Seventies fashions making a revival, both Haynes and Channel 4 believed it would appeal to the same sort of young audience that had made *Trainspotting* such a phenomenon. A major advertising campaign was prepared to support its release in April 1998. But technical problems during editing forced a delay, and rearranging the release for May or June would mean competing with the World Cup. Channel 4 were not that confident, and the British release was postponed until the autumn.

Velvet Goldmine received its world première at the Cannes Film Festival in May 1998, where it proved one of the most exciting films in competition, both in terms of entertainment and sheer cinematic accomplishment. It opens with a caption saying that the film should be played at maximum volume, a reference to the instruction carried on records of the time. The camera descends through space to a shot of roof-tops, over which appears a flying saucer. A baby is found on a doorstep in Dublin in 1854, wearing a strange green brooch. The baby is Oscar Wilde who, as a schoolboy, declares his intention to become a pop idol. A hundred years later another schoolboy, Jack Fairy, is bullied, abused and abandoned in the playground, where he finds the brooch. Jack smears blood across his lip, as if it were lipstick, and a narrator informs us that Jack would discover others like himself and that 'one day the whole stinking world would be theirs' ... And all this happens before the credits.

The belated title sequence is an explosion of energy as colours clash together in the lettering of the credits, and the tank-tops, feather boas, platform boots and make-up of the fans who have embraced the new fashion of glam rock. The fans rush around like dislocated atoms and include in their number the young

Arthur Stuart (Christian Bale). They pass the dark, mysterious, romantic figure of Jack Fairy, who has apparently become a seminal figure in this new craze. Pseudo-documentary footage introduces us to the characters of Brian Slade (Rhys-Meyers), and Curtis Wild (Ewan), who questions the motivation of all these fans who are all suddenly claiming to be bisexual. Brian Slade stages his own mock-assassination and disappears from public view. Ten years later, Arthur Stuart, now a journalist, is commissioned to find out the truth behind the legend.

It is easy to understand why Ewan might have preferred to play the role of Brian Slade, for that is the more iconic role, the elusive focus of the entire story. Nevertheless Ewan could not have wished for a more memorable scene for his character than that which comes after Brian Slade's gentle acoustic music is jeered off stage at an outdoor concert. Slade is about to leave when his attention is captured by Curtis Wild's performance.

A bare-chested Ewan screams, waggles his tongue lasciviously, sticks his hand down his leather trousers and throws himself into a raw and gutsy rendition of *TV Eye* – to which he proves infinitely more suited than the dainty little ditty in *Emma*. He sprinkles glitter, drops his trousers, falls over and finishes off by setting fire to the stage and leaping through the flames on to the audience. Brian Slade tells his wife Mandy (Toni Collette) that he wishes he had thought of that. 'You will, love,' she says. 'You will.'

When Slade's career begins to take off he insists on meeting Wild. Rhys-Meyers may have the more iconic role, but Ewan has a more demanding one, requiring him to go through a series of transformations. When next we see him, his character is struggling with heroin addiction, collapsed on the floor of a club, spaced out of his head, with a cigarette hanging forgotten from his lips. Slade is determined to help Wild revive his career and invites him to a posh restaurant. Slade's eyes light up with little hearts; the eyes of his manager Jerry Devine (Eddie Izzard) light up with dollar signs. Mandy tells the journalist, Stuart that Devine saw Slade and Wild as a Tracy and Hepburn for the Seventies.

Very soon Slade and Wild are a couple and Mandy is no more

than a previous instalment in the Brian Slade story. Rhys-Meyers and Ewan have several intimate scenes together – a long close-up screen kiss, a shot of them asleep, naked in bed, and one in which Ewan is thrashing away on his guitar and Rhys-Meyers drops to his knees in front of him and plays the instrument with his tongue. But their happiness cannot last, because – and this is a central point in the film – it is all a fiction, all a pose, all make-believe. At one point Jerry Devine announces that 'the secret of becoming a star is knowing how to behave like one'. Brian Slade constructs an elaborate alter ego – Maxwell Demon. Just as Slade is based on Bowie, Maxwell Demon is obviously Ziggy Stardust. Bowie killed off Ziggy in song, whereas Brian Slade goes one stage further, leaving those who knew him abandoned and betrayed. Finally Arthur Stuart meets up with Curtis Wild – though we learn that it is not their first meeting. He finds out what really happened to Brian Slade and ends up with the strange green brooch.

Velvet Goldmine deliberately recalls *Citizen Kane* in its use of documentary footage and the way in which it tells its story through a journalist and his interviewees. Stuart's interview with Mandy Slade in a deserted bar is particularly reminiscent of Joseph Cotten's meeting with Kane's former wife. But *Velvet Goldmine* is more than a glam-rock homage to *Citizen Kane*. With enormous skill and confidence, Todd Haynes interweaves the stories of his various characters and the whole glam rock movement, cutting back and forth through time and space, jumping from scene to scene with breathless speed, audacity, and scant regard for cinematic and narrative convention. In one scene Slade and Wild are represented by dolls, a little in-joke reference to Haynes' Karen Carpenter film, and yet it does not undermine the film, possibly because of the implied suggestion that Slade and Wild are manipulating the dolls themselves.

Todd Haynes traces glam rock back through Brian Slade, Curtis Wild and Jack Fairy to Oscar Wilde and ultimately to outer space. But the fantastic approach suits the fantastic quality of his subject. Glam rock drew on multiple sources for inspiration, looking back to earlier moments in popular culture and forward into an unknown dimension of space oddities. Haynes's documentary footage makes it clear that many earthlings did regard glam rockers as if they came from another planet.

Velvet Goldmine divided critics at Cannes and received only one of the minor awards from the festival jury, for 'artistic contribution', but often great films are not recognised as such at the time. By luck or design Ewan had again managed to attach himself to one of the most outstanding and remarkable films of its time. And his association with spaceships was only just beginning.

15
Obi-Wan McGregor

IT WAS THE summer of 1983 before *Return of the Jedi* opened, completing George Lucas's initial *Star Wars* trilogy. Luke discovered Leia was his twin sister and Darth Vader's daughter. Darth Vader killed the evil emperor. Leia killed Jabba the Hutt and fell in love with Han Solo, which was just as well because he was the only remaining human character to whom she was not closely related. Leia, Han, Wedge and a sleuth of intergalactic teddy bears blew up another of those Death Stars. And Wedge's nephew enjoyed his final weeks of freedom before moving up to the big school, with his brother and his dad. Ewan and Colin tired of the light-sabres that once were their pride and joy and turned their minds to weightier matters, more so Colin, perhaps, than Ewan. Lucas too seemed to outgrow light-sabres and lose his enthusiasm for the other two *Star Wars* trilogies he had promised.

Lucas no longer needed the money. Instead of taking a straight fee for the original *Star Wars* film he had gone for the riskier option of a share of the profits, and the rather nebulous commodity of merchandising rights. No one knew at that stage of course that *Star Wars* would become the highest-grossing film of all time and that sales of merchandising would exceed $2 billion. *Star Wars* was duly joined in the upper reaches of the All-time Top 10 by its sequels, neither of which Lucas directed himself. His interests now lay in film production, through his company, Lucasfilm, and in the development of new hi-tech special effects at another of his companies, Industrial Light and Magic. Rumours of new *Star Wars* films would occasionally surface as Ewan worked his way through secondary school and college and followed his uncle, Denis Lawson, into the acting profession. But the years passed without any official word of events in the galaxy far, far away that was Lucas's brain.

And then something happened. 'When the lights came up, we were all crying,' said Lucas. 'We knew that nothing would ever be the same.' What was it that had such an effect on its audience? *Schindler's List*? *Philadelphia*? No, Lucas was talking about the first ever screening of the dinosaur stampede that ILM had created in a computer for *Jurassic Park*. And he was right. Nothing would ever be the same again.

Jurassic Park came out in 1993, it duly became the new highest-grossing film of all time and Lucas began to show signs of renewed interest in *Star Wars*, tinkering with the original films, restoring them and adding new computer effects, with the intention of re-releasing them, one after the other, in 1997 to mark the 20th anniversary of the series. Rumours intensified about new episodes and by July 1995 a casting director, Robin Gurland, was in place. Stars are often attached to projects from the outset. These days projects frequently depend on star names, and if the stars pull out the projects collapse. Gurland, however, was given an entirely free hand to suggest candidates – they may be stars, up-and-coming actors or complete unknowns.

She had the luxury of a two-year lead-in time before the start of principal photography, during which she considered literally thousands of actors. 'I had thumbnail sketches of the characters from George to start with,' she says. 'Two months later I was working from the script itself.' The prologue at the beginning of *Star Wars* had introduced it as 'Episode IV', partly in the spirit of the old Saturday morning cinema serials and partly because it was always intended that the original three films would comprise the middle part of a trilogy of trilogies. Lucas now intended to make three more films, depicting events long before most of the familiar *Star Wars* characters were born. The new trilogy would however focus on two of the older characters from the original series – Darth Vader and Obi-Wan Kenobi. It was Gurland's job to find actors to portray them. It was relatively easy in the case of Vader, who spends most of his time behind a mask in the original films. He is just a boy in 'Episode I' and, in the nature of the story, a completely different character, Anakin Skywalker, before he is corrupted by the dark side of the Force. It would be more difficult in the case of Obi-Wan Kenobi, who had been played so memorably and distinctively by Sir Alec Guinness.

Proceedings were shrouded in secrecy from the outset, though it was widely reported Guinness's shoes would be filled by Kenneth Branagh, whose stage and screen pedigree was impeccable. Gurland subsequently said that Branagh's possible involvement had been nothing more than a rumour started by the tabloids, possibly on the grounds, quite simply, that Branagh seemed like a natural heir to Alec Guinness. Ewan McGregor, working-class, junkie anti-hero of *Trainspotting*, was a much less obvious choice. Gurland began the casting process by assessing actors for the roles of Anakin and his future bride, but Ewan was one of the first she met to discuss Obi-Wan Kenobi. It was almost exactly a year after that initial meeting before he was recalled. Meanwhile Gurland had been assessing other possible Obi-Wans and Ewan was not to know that she had felt instinctively that he was right and that he had become the yardstick against which others were measured.

Gurland had been given free rein and a lot of time in coming up with actors, but ultimately it was going to be George Lucas who decided on the film's stars. Ewan met Lucas and his producer Rick McCallum. 'George Lucas was very relaxed, very calm,' says Ewan. But then there was no reason for Lucas to be anything but calm – it was not as if Ewan was auditioning Lucas for the job of director. Finally Ewan had to do a screen-test with another actor, who turned out to be Liam Neeson, the Irish star of *Schindler's List* and *Rob Roy*. 'I did three scenes with Liam Neeson,' says Ewan. 'That was really scary. I was more nervous for that than I have been for a long time. Sitting there, feeling really scared again, it was great.' He felt he had done everything possible. He simply had to wait, once again.

By this time Ewan's name had replaced that of Branagh as the focus of media speculation. He was just about to start filming *Velvet Goldmine* when he got a call from his agent to say he had the part. His first reaction was to tell his wife and, as ever, his mum and dad. But he was immediately caught up in the Lucasfilm web of secrecy and was not allowed to tell anyone on the *Velvet Goldmine* set, despite the media speculation, which was beginning to look increasingly reliable, given Lucasfilm's refusal to deny it. Ewan recalls that he spent the day going around with an enormous Cheshire cat grin on his face. 'God knows what everyone thought I was so happy about,' he says.

Not only had Ewan made a name for himself in low-budget British films, but he had also attacked the 'abomination' of big-budget Hollywood movies. He had railed against sledgehammer American morality, the power of the gun lobbies and the curse of clichés and special effects. He suggested that everyone involved in *Titanic* and 'that kind of film-making' should be ashamed of themselves and that those actors involved in *Independence Day* should have their Equity cards withdrawn. 'I would never taint my soul with that crap,' he said. *Star Wars* apparently was not that kind of film-making, contrary to the impression that some viewers may have had that it was a big-budget Hollywood movie, built on a simplistic, distinctly American notion of good and evil, an unashamed reverence for cliche and a surfeit of special effects and guns, albeit in the form of lasers. In fact Lucas bears more or less sole responsibility for the predominance of special effects in modern Hollywood cinema.

Denis Lawson had mixed feelings about his involvement in the first three films. He had been Ewan's mentor since child-hood and advised him against appearing in the new trilogy. Ewan says: 'He just said "Don't do it. I'd like you to have a career after you're 30." He doesn't look back on them with any sense of anything, I don't think. He's rather annoyed that people keep referring to him being in them, because it was just a bit of work – he only had wee parts in them all.' Quizzed on his attitude, Denis says, 'They are extraordinary films and they are a huge part of cinema culture. But as an acting job, for me, they were completely non-existent. They were one of the most insignificant jobs I have done in my whole career and the fact that I get more fan mail for that than anything is a little irritating.' He acknowledges Ewan's is a much more substantial role.

Ewan felt the power of the mysterious 'Force', a phenomenon that promised fame and wealth on a truly intergalactic scale. He had no intention of saying no. '*Star Wars* is like fairy tales or legends,' he says. 'You can't turn it down.' The die was cast. The boy from Crieff would once again take up his light-sabre as a Jedi knight. And this time it was for real.

Star Wars was indeed a Hollywood legend, a great fairy tale, if not a great film. Universal did not think much of it. They turned it down, despite the fact that they had had an enormous hit with Lucas's previous film *American Graffiti*, which cost $750,000 and made a *profit* of $50 million in North America alone. It would have been all too easy for Universal to get carried away with the flash-in-the-pan success of this movie brat, who had made his name with student shorts while studying film at the University of Southern California and had had one hit feature. *American Graffiti* was a wholesome light drama that tapped into the nostalgic memories of adolescence that Lucas shared with an entire generation of young Americans. *Star Wars* was going to cost more than ten times as much, at a time when science-fiction was box-office poison. Stanley Kubrick's *2001: A Space Odyssey* had taken years to recoup its costs. There was no reason to believe Lucas could reverse the trend. After all, he had already tried once. His only other feature, apart from *American Graffiti*, was a sci-fi film called *THX 1138*, set in a future world of 'droids and sparkling white uniforms, and it flopped at the box-office.

United Artists also passed on *Star Wars*, but Alan Ladd Junior, one of the most astute film executives of modern times, saw the potential in Lucas's proposal and gave him the backing of 20th Century Fox. The odd truth was that *Star Wars* was much closer in spirit to *American Graffiti* than *THX 1138* or *2001*.

It was not predicting the future, but tapping into the same wholesome nostalgia for simpler times as *American Graffiti*, and then coating it with layer upon layer of special effects. Certainly Lucas seemed to devote more attention to effects than to actors or script details. Carrie Fisher recalls his directions to her were nothing more sophisticated than the instruction to 'act more like a princess'. Alec Guinness complained that he did not know who his character was meant to be and threatened to walk off the picture when Lucas rewrote the script and killed him off before the climactic battle. Mark Hamill compared the experience of being in *Star Wars* to being a raisin in a fruit salad and not knowing who any of the other fruits were. Harrison Ford, who had been in *American Graffiti*, had reservations too. He told Lucas: 'You can type this shit, George, but you can't say it.'

Star Wars cost $11 million, a third of which was spent on special effects and models of spaceships and robots. From the outset the audience was captivated by the slow tracking shot along the length of the apparently awesome 'Star Destroyer' spaceship. They were then charmed by the comedy double act of R2-D2 and C-3PO. In reality it was the detail and imagination that made the effects so successful rather than the technology, which was often quite primitive in that first film. The Star Destroyer was a model of course, with supposedly a quarter of a million individual portholes. And C-3PO was simply a male version of the robot from Fritz Lang's silent movie *Metropolis*, way back in 1926. Both C-3PO and R2-D2 had actors inside them. Much of the time the motor that drove R2-D2 did not work, and when it did it was so noisy someone had to bang on the outside to let little Kenny Baker inside know when a take had been completed. Lucas appeared to have borrowed scenes and images from everything from the western *The Searchers* to *Triumph of the Will*, the most remarkable film from the German studio popularly known as the Nazi Party. But essentially *Star Wars* was a cross between a Saturday morning serial writ large and a fairy tale, complete with princess. It was a master stroke to throw the audience straight into the story as if they were coming in halfway through.

'The story really is an action adventure,' said Lucas, 'a fantasy hero's journey. It's aimed primarily at teenagers, the same audience as *American Graffiti*.' Ultimately *Star Wars* was as monumentally empty as a cheap children's serial, but as fast, flashy and exciting as the best theme-park ride, which in due course it would become. By 1980, three years after its release, *Star Wars* had grossed more than $500 million.

The principals were all on percentage deals. As the biggest name in the picture, Guinness got 2.25 per cent of the profits, which at that point amounted to $3.3 million. Harrison Ford was on two-thirds of 1 per cent, which brought him $1 million. As unknowns Carrie Fisher and Mark Hamill got only one quarter of 1 per cent each, but even that was worth $368,750 apiece. Lucas and his producers got $60 million and Fox's profits were close on $90 million. Alan Ladd was still picking winners 20 years later when he championed the story of an obscure medieval Scotsman and guided *Braveheart* into production. United Artists were determined not to miss another moneyspinner from an emerging young director and bankrolled Michael Cimino's follow-up to *The Deer Hunter*. *Heaven's Gate* cost around $40 million, it made about $1.5 million in North American rentals and it effectively bankrupted the studio. That, as they say, is show business.

Lucas had said that he was more of a film-maker than a film director. He provided the storylines for *The Empire Strikes Back* and *Return of the Jedi* and oversaw their production, but he hired others to script and direct them. He poured money into special effects, costumes, a menagerie of aliens and mock space technology. When *Return of the Jedi* came out, a Lucasfilm executive told *Time* magazine: 'I can't think of anything that we know how to do, that we didn't do for this movie.' It was a triumph, but its very success marked the end of the road, at least for the time being. Lucas had done everything he knew how to do and he did not want to repeat himself. He concentrated on production, working on projects as varied as the dinosaur cartoon *The Land Before Time* and the heavy arthouse Japanese drama *Mishima*, repeating his enormous commercial success with Indiana Jones and spectacularly failing to repeat it with Howard the Duck, who turned out to be a turkey in disguise. And, having done everything he knew how to do in *Return of the Jedi*, he and his special effects team at Industrial Light and Magic worked on ways of doing the things he previously did not know how to do.

'One of the reasons I've waited so long [to make another *Star Wars* film] is that I needed the technology to advance to a point where I could do the next group,' George Lucas said in an interview with the American *Sci-Fi Entertainment* magazine at the opening of the *Star Wars* exhibition at the National Air and Space Museum in Washington in 1997. 'Fantasy and science-fiction is really a literary medium. They're primarily designed for that, and they're perfect for that because you can create any kind of world that you get in your mind. You can describe things and do things that don't have to become reality. Once you have to make them real at some point, you get into a real problem.'

Computer animation had been around since the early Eighties when it was used to create a planet in *Star Trek II*. But it was *Jurassic Park* that proved that convincing living creatures could be created in the computer. ILM subsequently created a dragon with the mannerisms of Sean Connery for the film *Dragonheart*. In one scene where the dragon appears to pick up the actor Dennis Quaid in its mouth, not only was the dragon a computer graphic but Quaid was a computer graphic too.

The extensive electronic refurbishment of the original *Star Wars* trilogy, including the addition of a scene with a computer-generated Jabba, was intended largely as a dry run for the new *Star Wars* films and everyone was taken by surprise at just how well the films did at the box-office. *Lawrence of Arabia* had taken $7 million when it was restored and rereleased, whereas *Star Wars* took $100 million in its opening three weeks in North America, the sort of gross that only a handful of blockbusters can expect each year. Paramount postponed the release of *The Saint* to avoid competition with the sequels and Fox would probably not have released the three films so close together if they had appreciated the potential. *Star Wars* ended up grossing $255 million around the world, making it the seventh highest-grossing film of 1997, which augured well for the new episodes in the series.

Lucas told the official *Star Wars* magazine that he was *depending* on further breakthroughs in technology to make the new films work. 'ILM has spent the last nine months trying to reinvent some of these techniques,' he said. 'We have to write new software to do some of the things I want to do. We have a truly synthetic cyber-character ... We made some very lifelike creatures in *Jurassic Park*, but nobody's ever made a lifelike creature that *acts* – you have a performance from the character, and he's a regular character. We're doing that.' Environmental features were also created on computer. At a press conference during location shooting in Italy Lucas reassured any worried human actors that humans were 'still the best way to portray people'.

The effects may have been new, but there was no pretence that the story was. 'The story was written 20 years ago,' said Lucas, 'and it's pretty much the same story.' It would show Anakin Skywalker as a child and Obi-Wan Kenobi as a young man; it would introduce the young queen whom Anakin marries and would feature a lot of Jedi action and adventure. R2-D2 and C-3PO would also be back, as would the emperor Palpatine, who would be the principal villain of the piece. The new trilogy was to follow Anakin through childhood, love and marriage, to his corruption by the dark side of the Force. Ewan was on board for all three episodes, guaranteeing him employment into the next century. It meant he did not need to work on anything else in between and he would still be right there, back in the limelight, every few years. But then that is not Ewan's style at all. Lucas had originally hoped to do the films at two-year intervals, but post-production and the process of marrying animation and action were taking so long that that time-scale soon began to seem unrealistic.

Ewan was joined on the cast list by Liam Neeson as another Jedi knight. Jake Lloyd, who had appeared in *ER* and co-starred with Arnold Schwarzenegger in *Jingle All the Way*, was cast as Anakin and Natalie Portman as his bride-to-be. Although still in her mid-teens she had appeared with Robert De Niro and Al

Pacino in *Heat* and Woody Allen in *Everyone Says I Love You*, and had played Anne Frank on Broadway. Principal cast members had to sign secrecy agreements preventing them from discussing the film or the script in public. The story may have been 20 years old, but Lucasfilm were taking no chances – information was released on a 'need to know basis' only. Actors of the calibre of Terence Stamp, the Sixties pin-up from *The Collector* and *Far From the Madding Crowd*, were given only those sections of the script in which they appeared. Another big-name supporting actor was Samuel L. Jackson, who had co-starred with John Travolta in Quentin Tarantino's *Pulp Fiction*. Hollywood agents were desperate to secure cameo roles for clients, but Lucas felt that too many star faces would detract from the story.

Ewan did not meet Alec Guinness, but watched him in *Star Wars* again and again and in a lot of his other movies too. 'I found a new one I'd never seen called *The Card* – it's brilliant,' Ewan enthuses. Years before *Room at the Top*, Guinness played a penniless young man who used his wits to achieve wealth and power. 'I had to play Alec Guinness's character as a young man, so I mainly worked on his voice,' says Ewan, 'trying to take his voice, which is very, very distinct, and put it into a young person's body ... It's weird because it's a voice that I associate with an older man. The voice coach I was working with said the voice doesn't age all that much. So it will be more or less the same voice, and I didn't overdo it ... I didn't want to do an impersonation of him, but you had to be able to see that I would become him.' Although Ewan was taking on Alec Guinness's role, Lucas was looking to Ewan to provide the sort of excitement that Harrison Ford had brought to the originals and was impressed by how relaxed and confident he seemed.

Three months of principal photography began in June 1997, almost two years ahead of the projected release date of May 1999, under the working title of *Episode 1: The Beginning*. It was reported that costs for the trilogy would run into billions. Lucas was financing them himself and, rich though he was, he did not have that sort of money. He sold the merchandising rights for toys and games in a deal with Hasbro and Galoob that was reported to be worth $235 million and which would underwrite a budget of about $70 million per film. Shooting was split between Tunisia, Italy and Leavesden Studios, the former Rolls-Royce aircraft engines factory outside London, which had hosted the James Bond film *Goldeneye* and which was so big that Lucas's team used bikes to get around. It was yet another childhood fantasy come true for Ewan when he first stepped onto the set. 'It was overwhelming the first time he [Lucas] said: "OK, you come in the spaceship, you start it up and ..." And we were suddenly on the floor, laughing. You come in the spaceship and start it up? I wonder how you did that. Is there a key?'

Ewan worked with Kenny Baker, the diminutive actor returning to the role of R2-D2. 'I went home one day,' says Ewan, 'and my wife was sitting with a lot of her mates, and I go "I worked with R2-D2 today." And they all looked at me and went "Who?" I guess it's a boy's thing.' Every morning before going to Leavesden he watched scenes of Guinness in *Star Wars*. 'I just used his voice really and some looks that I thought might work here and there.' He took Denis Lawson onto the set one day and he met George Lucas again. 'And the first thing he [Lawson] said was "You're wearing the same shirt you were wearing when you directed the first one." And apparently he was.'

A lot of the Jedi scenes were shot in Tunisia, which doubles for the planet of Tatooine, as it did in *Star Wars*. 'We will finally get to see Jedi do what Jedi were designed to do,' says Lucas. 'In the first one you had this very old Jedi who was ready to go and one who had been reconstructed and who was half human and half machine. The only other Jedi who comes along is Luke, who is sort of semi-trained by Yoda, but never really gets the full training. So you've never seen a real Jedi doing what the real Jedi do. Until now.' As in the original, the Tunisian set was hit by a terrible storm. Plaster buildings were destroyed and 'droids were scattered around the desert – 'like corpses on a battlefield', said the official Lucasfilm release.

Lucas used the Caserta Royal Palace near Naples as the young queen's residence in the film. He gave a press conference there at which he made it clear that he intended to do as he did with the first trilogy and hire other directors to direct the second and third instalments. Lucas had only ever directed three films before. This was his first since *Star Wars*, when he had been a young director on whom a studio was taking a gamble. To the cast of the new film he was a cinema legend. He was also, according to Ewan, a 'lovely' man. 'I really enjoyed working with him,' he says.

The film was a whole new experience for Ewan. He told Marion Ross of *Film Review*, 'It's not quite as performance-based as the films I've been doing in the past. I've never done a movie that big before. I've never done anything with special effects or blue screen (the blank canvas on which a background is later imposed). So it's a different process. It was much more tiring. It was a hard film to make because so much of it's not there, and the pretending is so much of it.'

While the technical wizards were performing their technical wizardry and Ewan was enjoying a short visit home to Scotland, he was rather more candid about the experience. He admitted that, after his initial excitement, the film had turned out to be 'boring as hell' to make. There was a lot of hanging around and little challenge in terms of acting, beyond copying Guinness's voice. 'I was just frowning a lot,' he says. 'It was just a frowning exercise, the whole thing.' He adopts the demeanour of a Jedi knight. 'We know everything,' he says. With a frown. 'Jedis are cool. We aren't worried about anything.' Reverting to the more relaxed demeanour of Ewan McGregor, he adds, 'There's nothing to do, but that ...' And he puts on his Jedi frown again.

Although Ewan got on well with Lucas, he did share some of the reservations of the original cast about the quality of the dialogue, which he felt was rather less than spontaneous. 'Everything is very deliberate,' he says. 'It's all about "We're gonna go do this now," as opposed to what you're thinking. So the key is to just get it out.' Asked if he had discussed his reservations with Lucas, Ewan says, 'What am I going to say? "George, your dialogue's crap"?' That is exactly what Harrison

Ford told Lucas two decades earlier. But Lucas had rewritten the record books since then and Ewan knew that *Star Wars* was not about witty dialogue and soul-searching.

16

'When the curtains open and the lights go down'

MOST ACTORS MIGHT feel they could ease up a little after starring in such a surefire blockbuster as the new *Star Wars* movie. But not Ewan. Principal photography on *Star Wars* concluded at the end of September 1997 and the film of *The Rise and Fall of Little Voice* began shooting in October. All Ewan's scenes had to be crammed into the first half of its nine-week schedule to free him for *Rogue Trader*, the story of disgraced financial dealer Nick Leeson, which began in November and continued into the new year, with location filming in the Far East. Ewan was needed for additional work on *Star Wars* before going to Canada for the thriller *Eye of the Beholder*. He seemed to function like a car battery – the more he ran, the more charged up he became.

But chinks began to appear in the armour later in the year when he admitted he was suffering from exhaustion and that his workload was putting a strain on his marriage. 'I've had enough,' he told Jan Moir in an interview for *Harpers & Queen*. 'I have become tainted with the whole thing. I've pushed my career as far as I could, made as many films as possible in a short space of time, but it has become totally mad, just mad.' He regretted being abroad when Clara was ill with meningitis and then having to go back to work soon after she recovered. 'Eve dealt with it on her own and so did I, which was a mistake. We should have done it together. You can't just breeze through those kinds of things – there are a lot of feelings that have to be dealt with and thrashed out afterwards ... I just want more time with Eve, to make it better. It's quite a strain on many relationships when you are denied time and space together.'

There were to be no more films that year – no feature films at least – and Ewan spent much more time with Eve and Clara. But his idea of relaxing would leave most mortals in need of a rest cure. In the wake of the *Harpers & Queen* interview, it was reported he was enjoying 'a well-earned holiday' in France. In fact Ewan was sitting through film after film as a jury member at the Deauville film festival. No sooner was he back from France than he was launching the Children's Hospice Week at Butterfly World, near Edinburgh. At the beginning of the following week he was off to South Africa for Comic Relief. And then it was straight into preparations and rehearsals for the play *Little Malcolm and His Struggle Against the Eunuchs* at Hampstead Theatre.

Ewan seemed incapable of doing nothing ... or keeping a low profile. While in Deauville, he attacked working practices in the film industry and, more controversially, criticised Sean Connery. 'I do not like to be told by anybody what it is like to be Scottish. And nobody has the right to tell me, especially someone who has not lived there for twenty-five years.' A week later the *Daily Record* presented it as 'Ewan Feud with Sean' across pages one, two and three, with readers invited to phone in with their views. The Scottish tabloid claimed Ewan had become bored with Connery's politics when the two met in a bar in Paris before the Scotland–Brazil World Cup game. Ewan subsequently rubbished the story and said his politics were private and that he did not want to be held up as a figurehead against independence. He also apologised to Connery.

Ewan may have stopped making films, but his outspoken comments were generating more column inches than ever before. In the *Harpers & Queen* interview he attacked British stars who sell out to Hollywood, and one in particular – Minnie Driver. 'She's gone mad, mad,' he said. And he went on to provide detailed evidence: 'She goes to the opening of an envelope ... She wears those little dresses all the time ...' Her defence team might argue that the evidence was less conclusive than, say, appearing in a trio of *Star Wars* movies. Having attacked Driver in *Harpers & Queen*, Ewan subsequently apologised to her in *Vanity Fair*. In the interim he told the *Observer* how he used to masturbate over pictures of Madonna. 'Can you imagine if I met her now?' he added. Eh ... awkward moment perhaps, Ewan?

By early 1998 Ewan had six films in the can awaiting release. No one expected much of *The Serpent's Kiss* or *Nightwatch*. But hopes were higher for *Rogue Trader*, *Velvet Goldmine* was being lined up for the Cannes Film Festival, Miramax were already planning an Oscar campaign for *Little Voice* in 1999, and Lucasfilm were planning their entry into the record books with the new *Star Wars* film later that year.

Ewan was now in enormous demand, not just from British companies but from Hollywood as well. He was prepared to play ball, but it had to be on his terms, with the obvious exception of *Star Wars* – and even then he joked that they moved the whole production from Hollywood to Leavesden so he could get home at night.

The Rise and Fall of Little Voice was a quintessentially English play with working-class Northern characters. It was written specifically for the actress Jane Horrocks by Jim Cartwright, one of the most exciting English playwrights to emerge in the Eighties, but the film version might well have been relocated in America had it not been for Ewan's involvement.

It is the story of a painfully shy young woman, whose voice has been reduced to a squeak by an overbearing mother, but who possesses an incongruous ability to impersonate famous singers, including Judy Garland, Shirley Bassey, Gracie Fields and Edith Piaf. Her mother and her mother's boyfriend, a sleazy showbiz agent, force her onto the stage in an attempt to exploit her for their own profit. The play opened at the National Theatre in London in 1992 and transferred to the West End, a singular personal triumph for Jane Horrocks, who was required to provide the character of the mousy Little Voice and the range of larger-than-life impersonations. One critic was convinced she was miming to records and another speculated that the play would not have much of a future 'in the unlikely event of Jane Horrocks falling under a bus'.

Horrocks was under the impression that she would recreate her stage role on film for Miramax, when news broke in the summer of 1996 that the part was going to be played by the American Gwyneth Paltrow. Paltrow's then partner, Brad Pitt, was to be the male lead and Meryl Streep was reportedly being lined up as the mother. Horrocks went public in her attack on Miramax's volte-face, calling their proposals 'farcical', though the company subsequently came full circle when it was announced that the film would go ahead in England, as previously intended, with Horrocks and Ewan in the main roles. One newspaper report at the time said: 'No one at Miramax would discuss what casting negotiations had taken place, but sources say it was felt that the story of a back-street Cinderella in a bleak British seaside town would have seemed curious played by Hollywood superstars.' Horrocks is well known in Britain as Bubble in the television sitcom *Absolutely Fabulous*, but virtually unknown in the United States, and Miramax wanted a star name. Miramax boss Harvey Weinstein was, however, prepared to keep Horrocks and the British setting if he could also get as her co-star, Ewan McGregor. Miramax had already backed several of Ewan's films: they were the American distributors for *Trainspotting*, they were co-production partners with Channel 4 on *Brassed Off* and they financed *Emma*, in which Ewan co-starred with Gwyneth Paltrow and on which Weinstein was executive producer.

Fortunately Ewan had a window of opportunity in October and November 1997, albeit a very brief one. 'He was a linchpin for the whole film,' says Horrocks. 'Everybody had to work round Ewan's availability ... I'd just had a baby ... I really only wanted to do one job last year, so I was just going to fit in with what they wanted. So it wasn't a problem for me, but it might have been for the other people. I know, for instance, they were quite interested in Pete Postlethwaite doing it again. [He had played the agent on stage.] But his dates didn't fit in with Ewan's, so they couldn't have Peter.' The roles of the overbearing mother and her boyfriend went to Brenda Blethyn, who had won an Oscar nomination for Mike Leigh's *Secrets and Lies*, and to Michael Caine. Ewan would play the quiet, unassuming telephone engineer who becomes Little Voice's friend and saviour. The £4 million film marked a reunion for him with Mark Herman, director of *Brassed Off*.

Although the suggestion of Brad Pitt had been anathema to many, there were some doubts about the wisdom of replacing an American heartthrob with a Scottish one. 'He usually plays these hunks and sexy boys,' says Horrocks, 'and he's the total opposite in *Little Voice*. [The film's title was habitually abbreviated by everyone involved and it was no surprise when Miramax officially shortened it for the film's release.] I think we all wondered how he was going to do it really, how he was going to seem ordinary and plain. But I think the combination of a very good make-up artist and his good acting was totally convincing.'

From Ewan's first appearance, talking gently to his pigeons, it is clear that this is a new, quieter addition to the McGregor repertoire. This is a character at odds with his outgoing, outspoken predecessors. Ewan's smile, usually so confident, suddenly looks slightly hesitant. The eyes that normally fix an audience take on a distant quality. 'Is there anybody there?' Blethyn asks him when they first meet. Giving Ewan a naff hairstyle to complete the image was no problem, of course, and a greasy number with side-parting fits the bill. *Little Voice's* younger characters contrast with the vainglorious monstrosities created by Blethyn and Caine. This is a world turned upside down, where the young folk play Judy Garland records and keep pigeons, and the oldies play their pop music too loud, get drunk and generally misbehave.

Horrocks's progression from doe-eyed, open-mouthed mute, traumatised by the death of her father, to Bassey big voice, belting out 'Big Spender', always seemed a likely candidate for the awards season. One particular tirade which embraces Cilla Black and the Munchkins lingers in the memory long after the final credits. Nevertheless her singing does not have quite the same impact on screen as on stage, where there would be no chance of a retake and director Mark Herman almost allows Michael Caine to steal the show with a lengthy, self-pitying and tuneless rendition of 'It's Over' in the style of Sid Vicious's

'My Way'. It requires a closing credit saying 'Jane Horrocks performed all her own songs' to ram the message home. The blowzy Blethyn and Michael Caine's take on the oldest swinger in town are perilously close to caricature, making Ewan's discipline and restraint all the more praiseworthy. Herman makes a brave attempt to open out Jim Cartwright's play with panoramic views of Scarborough and evocative sets, ranging from Little Voice's room above the record shop to Mr Boo's seedy nightclub. But the fundamental structure of the drama and the big, formal set-pieces betray the film's origins and ultimately its limitations.

Ewan had to work long days and nights in Scarborough to keep to the schedule, and he had some demanding scenes, including one in which he rescues Little Voice from a fire, in a cherry-picker, with flames leaping around them. The demands of film production have driven lesser mortals to the point of nervous breakdown, yet Ewan never even seemed tired. 'He still went out partying in Scarborough,' says Horrocks. 'Ewan's stuff was mainly in Scarborough. I think he only had one week in London and he finished our job on Saturday night and started Nick Leeson [*Rogue Trader*] on Sunday morning ... I couldn't cope with that, just because I like to think for longer about a part, in between jobs, but I think that Ewan does hop from one thing to another very well ... He's thriving off that really.' That was the impression everyone had until Ewan suggested otherwise.

Having played a pop star in *Velvet Goldmine*, Ewan had a top-ten hit of his own without even having to find time in his hectic schedule for a recording session. The London group PF Project used excerpts from his *Trainspotting* voice-over on the single *Choose Life* and it was released under the credit 'PF Project featuring Ewan McGregor'. Ewan did, however, find time to go into the studio to work with another band. He recorded the narrative for a documentary on the Irish band Ash, who had performed the theme song from *A Life Less Ordinary* and also provided the music at the *Star Wars* wrap party. It was quite a party. And Ewan loved to party.

Paul Raphael might have been speaking about Ewan when

he said: 'He was a character, a charmer and a bit of a lad ... probably quite a good bloke to go out and get drunk with.' In fact he was talking about the character in his next film, *Rogue Trader*, which Raphael was producing. Ewan plays Nick Leeson, the son of a Watford plasterer, who became the young star of the Far East operation of Barings merchant bank and led a millionaire lifestyle before events turned sour in 1995, when Leeson's golden touch deserted him. Barings collapsed with losses of more than £850 million. Leeson was convicted of fraud and sentenced to six and a half years in prison. Production began in London and at Pinewood Studios, before going on location to Singapore and Malaysia. Filming continued on several nights until five in the morning, at which point Ewan would go drinking, knocking back the margaritas, in sessions which, according to his young co-star, Anna Friel, shocked the natives.

Journalist and sometime film producer David Frost bought the rights to Leeson's autobiography, *Rogue Trader*, after interviewing him in 1995 for his programme *Breakfast with Frost* while Leeson was in Germany awaiting extradition to Singapore. James Dearden, who wrote *Fatal Attraction*, was hired to write and direct the film, and he developed a script in which the two main strands were the working-class wheeler-dealer making millions for his upper-class bosses back in London and the love story between Leeson and Friel's character, Lisa, who he met and married while working in the Far East. Leeson, who had been a quiet, responsible school prefect, became flash and arrogant, thinking he could get away with anything. During one heavy drinking session he dropped his trousers in front of a group of women at a disco. One threatened to report him to the police. He said she would not dare and handed her his phone. The incident ended with a fine for indecent exposure and provided yet another opportunity for Ewan to drop his own trousers. It seems that Singaporean girls were less impressed than those in the West by the McGregor bottom. 'It's OK,' said sixteen-year-old extra Racquel Wong, 'but we'd rather see Tom Cruise's.'

'While [Leeson] was making money for Barings, no one

wanted to look too hard at what he was doing or how he was doing it,' says Raphael. 'It's Leeson's point of view, but we try to be objective and make it a story that has more than one side. He definitely fucked up and did things he shouldn't have done ... It is a rollercoaster of a film about a streetwise guy who just got way out of his depth.'

Dearden managed to get into prison to meet Leeson, who always denied he squirrelled away money for himself, but Ewan's application for a prison pass was rejected. Ewan admits he was embarrassed by the idea of the film star asking the jailbird for advice on how he should portray him, though he did watch video footage of Leeson, met several of his friends and wore his tie in the film, along with the uniform blue and yellow striped jacket. Ewan had been attached to *Rogue Trader* from an early stage, and his involvement helped raise a budget of about £10 million. 'Leeson's a fascinating guy,' Ewan told a local reporter in Singapore, 'but I don't want to say what my full impression of him is. I just want to play him without any judgement.' The daytime shoots were long and hot, and Ewan was knocking back the beers to keep cool.

Friel was cast only shortly before production began. Intimate location pictures of her with Ewan led to speculation in the tabloids about the extent of their relationship. Friel did nothing to dispel the rumours in interviews promoting the BBC adaptation of *Our Mutual Friend*, in which the twenty-one-year-old actress played the female lead. Instead of simply denying any impropriety, she made comments like, 'I'll let them think what they want.' She enthused about Ewan, saying, 'Ewan is the best, he's a wonderful guy ... We are male and female versions of each other ... We've given a great performance together.' *Our Mutual Friend* and *Rogue Trader* represented enormous breaks for an actress whose ambition was somewhat greater than her judgement, her modesty or her previous achievements. Her most notable appearances had been in *Coronation Street, Emmerdale* and *Brookside*, in which she was the lesbian father-killer Beth Jordache. Cynics might suggest it was in the soap star's interests to maximise publicity for herself. Back in Britain, Ewan was too busy enjoying himself with his wife, family and old friends to spend too much time worrying about such tittle-tattle.

He had never felt any great awkwardness with the opposite sex and frequently flirted with female co-stars, getting on especially well with Cameron Diaz, but Eve was never far away. If things had gone any further than flirting, it seems unlikely Ewan would have continued to be so open in relationships or careless in interviews. 'I'm married and have a kid, but I'm certainly not settled down,' he told Gavin Edwards of *Details* magazine. It sounds like an open invitation to any girl who might fancy her chances. Ewan was, however, referring not to sex, but to his appetite for partying. 'I like going out and she [Eve] likes staying home. So there's some balance there.' It sounds too good to be true and, as an afterthought, Ewan adds: 'Also a lot of arguments.'

Ewan is famous for his partying. It is the one factor, from his teenage years through to *Little Voice* and *Rogue Trader*, that interviewees invariably mention. When he made *ER*, he was surprised at how little the Americans drank; they, on the other hand, were gobsmacked at how much he consumed. People came up to him on set next day and quietly inquired if he was all right. Ewan drinks not because he is insecure or unhappy, but because he *likes* to drink. 'I'm very, very, very partial to the margarita.' He is not stupid; he is fully aware that drink can destroy a career, a marriage, a life more effectively than infidelity, and insists his consumption is not unusually high, not by British standards at least.

Ewan admires Richard Burton's work and is fascinated by his life and the role drink played in it. 'No way do I drink like that,' he says. 'I don't drink spirits.' He turns that claim over in his mind, perhaps reflecting on what exactly goes into a margarita – and we are not talking pizza here – then he adds the word 'necessarily' to his declaration. 'I couldn't handle three or four bottles a day,' he says. The very fact that this is Ewan's interpretation of problem drinking is in itself enlightening. 'But it fascinates me because it's extreme and I like extremes.' No one has suggested to me during my researches for this book or, indeed, at any other time that he has a serious drink problem – it was more a case of marvelling at his capacity for drink and his ability to appear on camera a few hours later and turn in a professional performance, complete with close-ups. But there has to be a limit, and Ewan must be very close to it. Perhaps he will cut down. If he goes the other way, he could find he has a dependency problem every bit as serious as that of Mark Renton.

Ewan is and always was a family man. It is a family of which Eve became very much a part when she married. And Ewan delighted in taking Clara to see his parents in Scotland, strengthening the ties across the generations. Sometimes he would sit down with Clara to watch a video of out-takes from *A Life Less Ordinary* and she would point and say, 'Papa! Papa!'

It has become almost *de rigueur* for actors to thank their mums when they pick up an award, but Ewan was prepared to go a lot further than that. Carol and Jim McGregor took early retirement from their jobs as teachers in the summer of 1997, and Carol became Ewan's personal assistant, a role which many other mothers might also argue they fulfil for their offspring. The difference here was that it was official, paid employment. The job offer did not even come directly from Ewan. 'Ewan's agent phoned me up and asked me if I would be prepared to do this PA work,' says Carol. 'I think possibly just to make it more official.' She took on responsibility for dealing with fan mail, for sending out photographs – 'He signs them all' – for keeping his diary and for assessing requests for personal appearances – 'He's so busy, most of them he has to refuse.'

Sacks of mail were redirected from London to Perthshire. In his later years at Jonathan Altaras Associates, Ewan's personal agent had been Lindy King. When the agency split up, Ewan went with King to Peters, Fraser & Dunlop, despite the obvious temptation to switch to one of the big international agencies with more Hollywood muscle, though he did sign up in the United States with CAA, the same agency as Sean Connery. Ewan even continued doing voice-overs for advertisers such as Virgin Airways, not for the money, but because he felt a certain loyalty to his voice-over agents, Yakety Yak. He did discover, as many American stars had done before him, that there was serious cash to be had from Japanese adverts and he lent his face to the promotion of the rather less than legendary Bobson jeans. There was the added advantage in Japanese adverts that no one on your home turf ever saw them.

Ewan was taking a very pragmatic approach to the glittering prizes that Hollywood had to offer. He made it clear that he would judge every project on its merits, irrespective of its origins. Certainly he had no intention of moving to Los Angeles, which, he felt, lacked any culture or personality outwith cinema. He called London 'the best city in the world' and spent well over £1 million on a big house in St John's Wood, one of its leafier areas. It was to become his base. His next film in America was not in Hollywood, not even in the United States, but in Canada. *Eye of the Beholder* is a small independent film based on a weird, out-of-print 1980 thriller by Marc Behm. Behm was primarily a film writer whose work ranged from the Beatles' movie *Help!*, through the Cary Grant comedy-thriller *Charade* to the Sylvia Kristel soft-porn version of *Lady Chatterley's Lover. The Eye of the Beholder* was written originally as a screenplay for a Spanish studio and it was only when the film fell through that Behm turned it into a novel, relocating it from Europe to the United States. And it is a very strange novel at that. The central characters are a private detective, the 'Eye' of the title, and the woman he is trailing. They spend years criss-crossing America, leaving a trail of corpses behind them. The woman is quite literally a *femme fatale*, a serial killer, and the Eye could just become her next victim. But would that necessarily stop him? Behm said: 'It's the story of God in disguise as a private eye, searching for his daughter.' Author and publisher Maxim Jakubowski described it as 'a heartbreaking love story, a most puzzling thriller, the story of a descent into hell'.

The novel met with large-scale indifference in Britain and America, but won an award as the thriller of the year in France, where it was filmed as *Mortelle Randonnée* (known in English as *Deadly Circuit* or *Deadly Run*). That version was directed by the celebrated French director Claude Miller, who made *An Impudent Girl* and *The Little Thief*, with an outstanding cast headed by Michel Serrault as the Eye and Isabelle Adjani as the object of his obsession. *Mortelle Randonnée* remained virtually unseen in Britain and the United States, though the novel did begin to acquire a cult following.

Stephan Elliott had already managed to turn odd material into an unlikely hit as writer-director of *The Adventures of Priscilla, Queen of the Desert*, the story of a group of transvestites in the Australian outback. He wrote a fresh adaptation of Behm's novel, acquired the backing of MDP Worldwide, a £10 million budget and the services of two of cinema's brightest young stars. Playing opposite Ewan would be Ashley Judd, who, like Ewan, had a mind of her own and relished difficult material. She had been a survivor in Oliver Stone's bloody *Natural Born Killers* and seemed to have stepped from some strange Gothic fairytale as a woman who lives in the woods in Philip Ridley's weird and almost wonderful *The Passion of Darkly Noon*.

Ewan was beginning to feel the pace of the previous few years and found it difficult to establish a relationship with both his leading lady and his director. The star who had charmed a string of actresses simply did not get on with Judd at all. He felt she had 'a very Hollywood way of looking at the world'. Relations with Elliott were more complex. 'There is an old saying "Dig deep and go low, because the deeper you dig, the more you know." I went pretty low. Stephan encouraged me, played terrible mind tricks on me and kind of fucked me up mentally. It's a really well-thought-out movie . . . but tough.'

By this time Ewan was very much involved in Natural Nylon, the company which had been set up in October 1995 by actor Jude Law, producer Damon Bryant and director Richard Burns. Law came up with the name, using the word 'nylon' to represent the company's interest in working on both sides of the Atlantic, New York and London, and the word 'natural' to reflect its attitude. Law had made a name for himself in the low-budget British joyriding drama *Shopping* and then wowed American audiences, not by going to Los Angeles, but by appearing on stage on Broadway in the play *Indiscretions*. Others who became involved included Law's wife Sadie Frost, star of

Shopping and *Dracula*, Jonny Lee Miller and Ewan's old *Blue Juice*
co-star Sean Pertwee. Another participant, producer Bradley
Adams, said: 'One of the reasons for setting up the company
was that they wanted to get involved in the development
and decision-making processes that go into producing films.
McGregor is still first and foremost an actor, but this company
gives him the mechanism to develop a product that he likes.'
There were somewhat overblown comparisons in the press
to United Artists, set up by Charlie Chaplin, D.W. Griffith,
Douglas Fairbanks and Mary Pickford, when they were the four
biggest stars in cinema.

Natural Nylon showed its willingness to work with risky
material and controversial film-makers by becoming involved
with *eXistenZ*, David Cronenberg's first feature since the notorious *Crash*, starring Jude Law and Jennifer Jason Leigh. Ewan
was able to revive *Nora*, the film about the relationship between
James Joyce and Nora Barnacle, under the banner of Natural
Nylon and became involved in the planning of it. There were
proposals for biopics on the dramatist Christopher Marlowe
and the Beatles' manager, Brian Epstein, and thrillers called
Sleeping Partners and *Psychoville*, with Ewan's name attached to
the latter.

Natural Nylon's flagship project, however, was *The Hellfire
Club*, a film about the Brotherhood of the Friars of St Francis
in the eighteenth century. It might sound like a dull religious
piece, but the 'saint' Francis in question was the notorious
libertine Sir Francis Dashwood. His brotherhood worshipped
the Devil, indulged in orgies and was popularly known as the
Hellfire Club. The society met in secret and their records were
deliberately destroyed, but there is no doubt that the mem-
bership included peers and poets, many of whom were or
became pillars of the establishment. Dashwood himself was
later Chancellor of the Exchequer.

One prominent Hellfire Club member was John Wilkes,
whose newspaper, the *North Briton*, accused King George III of
lying. Wilkes was charged with treasonable libel, but acquitted.
It was subsequently alleged that his *Essay on Woman* was
obscene, he became an unlikely symbol of free speech, and

political rioters adopted the cry of 'Wilkes and Liberty'. The Brotherhood of the Friars of St Francis was just one, albeit the most notorious, of several secret societies dedicated to wine, women and devil worship at around that time. There were secret oaths and black masses, though it seems unlikely that many members took the devil worship as seriously as they did the wine and the women. The religious intention seems to have been primarily to lampoon the rituals of the Roman Catholic Church. At one meeting of the Friars or Knights of St Francis, when prayers were being offered up to Satan, Wilkes, as a joke, released a baboon into the abbey where they met. It reportedly landed on the shoulders of Lord Orford, who thought they had succeeded in summoning up the Devil. The baboon ran riot, first around the abbey and then around the town.

There was already a minor British film from 1963 called *The Hellfire Club* with Keith Michell, Adrienne Corri and Peter Cushing. But it used the brotherhood merely as a starting point for a jokey melodrama about a young nobleman who is driven out by his debauched father, Lord Netherden, and has to take work as a circus acrobat before fighting a duel with his cousin to regain his estate and his sweetheart. Natural Nylon intended a much more serious treatment of the story, with Ewan as Wilkes and Law as Dashwood. 'It's not just a costume piece,' said Law. 'It's a mirror of the present. There are so many modern connections with the Hellfires – politically, sexually and in the way the Church was maligned by them.'

The members of Natural Nylon represented the cream of new British acting talent, but it stemmed from a time when most of those involved were relative unknowns living in the Primrose Hill area of London. They were first and foremost friends. They shared common experiences, common politics and common aspirations about what they wanted from their careers as actors. None of them saw Hollywood stardom as a goal in itself. That did not mean Ewan would necessarily turn down the chance of a starring role in *Star Wars*.

His involvement in the new *Star Wars* trilogy and the financial security it provided made it easier for him to continue doing small projects. He broke into his 'holiday' to star in *Desserts*, a three-minute film, for Equity minimum pay. It was produced by Jill Robertson, who had been producer's assistant on *Trainspotting* and production supervisor on *A Life Less Ordinary*. She approached Ewan as 'a long shot'; he liked the script and said yes. It was filmed in a single day at Turnberry in Ayrshire and was directed by commercials director Ray Stark on a budget of £13,975. Ewan is the only actor in it. He walks across a cold, flat beach towards the camera, finds an eclair still in its wrapper, sniffs it and tastes the cream. Nothing happens until he bites into it and unleashes terrible forces. *Desserts* is one of those shorts that function like jokes and whose success hinges on the punchline. The sheer unexpected violence of the denouement in *Desserts* leaves the audience stunned.

Desserts was made as part of the Levi Strauss short-film scheme and, although some of Ewan's features were having trouble getting into cinemas, *Desserts* secured a national release in October 1998, along with the David Thewlis thriller *Divorcing Jack*. Despite his proclaimed intention of taking it easier, Ewan seemed busier than ever. *Desserts* was just one of three new Ewan McGregor films released in Britain in October 1998. *Nightwatch* finally turned up on video and *Velvet Goldmine* opened in cinemas to very mixed reviews. 'This might have worked if it had been played for laughs, but then The Comic Strip would have done it much better,' wrote Neil Jeffries in *Empire* magazine. It was in *Empire*'s list of the ten worst movies of 1998, and *Neon*'s list of the ten best. Commercially it made neither the UK nor the US Top Ten for even a single week, let alone the whole year. But its failure seemed to do nothing to tarnish Ewan's star and the fact that he was not away filming helped maximise media coverage.

His decision to appear in the play *Little Malcolm and His Struggle Against the Eunuchs* at the tiny Hampstead Theatre might seem even more perverse than the decision to make *Desserts*. The latter took up just one day of his time and brought him nationwide cinema exposure. *Little Malcolm* tied him up for almost six months, with rehearsals, an initial run at the Hampstead Theatre, in front of audiences of just 174 people each night, and then an additional eight weeks at the 600-seat Comedy Theatre in the West End early in 1999. *Little Malcolm* generated more publicity than any of Ewan's recent films and any recent London play, with the possible exception of *The Blue Room* with Nicole Kidman. It put Ewan on the arts pages, the features pages, the news pages and into the gossip columns. About the only pages beyond his reach were the sports pages.

Ewan had been talking about a return to the stage for years, but now he had a definite project, with his uncle, Denis Lawson, as director. David Halliwell's *Little Malcolm and His Struggle Against the Eunuchs* had been controversial when first staged more than thirty years earlier. It was Denis's choice, but Ewan welcomed the challenge of a character who is on stage for virtually the entire play and has to deliver great wodges of self-important, angry dialogue and monologue.

Malcolm Scrawdyke is Huddersfield's answer to Hitler. Expelled from art school, he forms the Party of Dynamic Erection and plans to revenge himself on those he believes have wronged him. He cooks up a half-baked plan to steal a painting, kidnap the principal, force him to destroy it with threats of sexual blackmail, and then expose him anyway. But Malcolm's aggression and contempt mask his own inadequacies, particularly sexual inadequacies. The Sixties were only just beginning to swing when the play was first staged, and the Lord Chamberlain (the theatre censor) insisted that the Party of Dynamic Erection change its name to the Party of Dynamic Insurrection. The play was praised for its comedy, though some critics had reservations about the nature of its violence and alleged misogyny.

The Hampstead production began with Ewan in bed in his spartan bedsit-studio, talking himself into getting up – except the audience could not be sure it was Ewan at first, so good was his Yorkshire accent. His face was hidden behind a scrawny beard, his body enclosed in an army greatcoat. With his blustering pomposity and his sexual awkwardness, Malcolm was both comic and tragic, pathetic and dangerous – expelling Nipple, a member of the party, for supposedly collaborating with the principal. Malcolm tells Nipple that, even if he could prove his innocence, it would be irrelevant; the mere fact that Malcolm can conceive of the offence means Nipple is guilty. The play was initially funny – Ewan's Malcolm was as much a radical student version of Captain Mainwaring as of Hitler. But the tone darkened in the second half, particularly when Malcolm and his acolytes turned on the only female in a vicious assault. Until that point Malcolm, and indeed the play itself, had been no more than a lot of talk. The play never really seemed to come to terms with its attitude towards its central character and was dated by its language, its ideas and by the very concept of student revolutionaries.

Critics still had reservations about the play, but nothing but praise for Ewan and the ensemble cast, which included Denis's step-daughter Lou Gish. 'A remarkable London stage debut' said Sheridan Morley in the *Scotsman*. 'It is a performance that proves conclusively McGregor can hold a stage,' said Michael Billington in the *Guardian*. 'Malcolm speaks in great bursts of mock-heroic, mock-lyrical eloquence, and McGregor rises to them with relish, uttering them like great demented riffs by an excited but controlled musician,' wrote John Peter of the *Sunday Times*. There was an incredible, manic energy about Ewan on stage, sometimes funny, sometimes not, as if he might explode at any moment. The bottom line on the production was that the performances were better than the material, which three decades after its original production came across like a sixth-form attempt at being shocking and controversial.

Ewan and Denis, who are both accomplished musicians, were also developing their own rock-and-roll movie, *Don't Think Twice*. 'The film is a buddy-buddy rock-and-roll road movie,' said Denis. 'It's about two members of an old rock band who are down on their luck. Their story takes them from London to the Western Isles. Once I read the screenplay I thought it would be a great idea if Ewan played the part of one of the musicians – the much younger one. When I showed Ewan the material, he got very excited about it.' Ewan said: 'We get a chance to sing and play guitar, which we do together already.'

Ewan said in a magazine interview conducted in the Groucho Club in London that he 'really can't be arsed with all this star thing'. But that was just a wee white lie; Ewan being cool. The truth is he loves it. Get him in different circumstances and you get a very different line. He says, not in an interview, but back home in Scotland, that 'It's nice to pass a news-stand and say, "That's me," and, "That's me," and ...' And that was him on the cover of the year-end, hall-of-fame issue of *Vanity Fair*, the Hollywood image of a Highland crofter in a rustic brown waistcoat, grubby brown shirt open at the chest, and McGregor kilt, with his hair gelled back, designer stubble and a cockerel nonchalantly tucked under one arm like a fixture that had been there for at least a couple of generations. 'The rest of the world gets ready for the crazy, sexy charm of Ewan McGregor,' trumpeted the front-page headline. Two months later he was on the cover again with Liam Neeson, Natalie Portman and the creature Jar Jar Binks on the set of the *Star Wars* film.

Desserts, Velvet Goldmine and *Little Malcolm* were all ultimately tasters for the main event. The countdown was well and truly under way, and the world was getting ready for the new *Star Wars* movie. It had finally been given a name – *The Phantom Menace*. Crowds queued round the block in the United States just to see a two-minute trailer, which promised new spaceship battles and new excitement. In *Screen International* Colin Brown suggested that the trailer was really the week's most successful new film, though it would not show up in the box-office charts, boosting instead the grosses of those films with which it was showing. Some people did not even wait for the main feature. So many were leaving at the end of the trailer that some cinemas decided to show the film first and the trailer second.

With two more *Star Wars* films to follow, Ewan's immediate future was mapped out. But what lies beyond *Star Wars*? 'Where will you be in ten or twenty years?' I asked him. 'I haven't thought about it at all,' he replied. 'I just hope I'll still be up there on film ... It was my dream to be up there. When the curtains open and the lights go down and its says "Ewan McGregor", it's like ...' And he draws in his breath and focuses all his passion in one single word that sums up his career and everything he feels about it: 'Ye-ess!' And he sounds a little like he has just seen Scotland get the goal in sudden-death extra-time in the World Cup final, all his emotions compressed into a single word. Ewan is right; his career is like ... Ye-ess!

And he leaves us sitting on the edge of our seats in anticipation of what might happen next, but also relishing the remarkable story and the incredible characters that have brought us this far. And now? What next? Where does he go from here? James Dean was dead by his late twenties, Sean Connery was a nonentity in Tarzan and Disney movies. Ewan is already a big star and very much alive. The one thing that we can safely predict is that he is going to get even bigger.

Filmography
(including television drama)

Ratings: * Bad, ** OK, *** Good, **** Very good,
***** Outstanding.

The filmography follows standard practice in using the year of release rather than of production.

Lipstick on Your Collar (TV) ***
UK, 1993, Channel 4, 6 hours (excluding adverts: six episodes)

Giles Thomas (Francis Francis), Ewan McGregor (Mick Hopper), Louise Germaine (Sylvia Berry), Douglas Henshall (Corporal Peter Berry), Peter Jeffrey (Lt. Col. Harry Bernwood), Clive Francis (Major Wallace Hedges), Nicholas Jones (Major Archie Carter), Nicholas Farrell (Major Johnny Church), Shane Rimmer (Colonel 'Truck' Trekker), Roy Hudd (Harold Atterbow), Maggie Steed (Aunt Vickie), Bernard Hill (Uncle Fred), Kymberley Huffman (Lisa)

Director: Renny Rye; Screenplay: Dennis Potter; Photography: Sean Van Hales; Choreography: Quinny Sacks; Producer: Dennis Potter

Ewan is a War Office clerk who fights off boredom by staging musicals in his head.

Scarlet and Black (TV) *
UK, 1993, BBC, 3 hours 45 mins (3 × 75 mins)

Ewan McGregor (Julien Sorel), Alice Krige (Madame de Renal), Rachel Weisz (Mathilde), Christopher Fulford (Napoleon), Stratford Johns (Abbé Pirard), T. P. McKenna (Marquis de la Mole), Martin Jarvis (Monsieur de Renal), Michael Attwell (Monsieur Valenod)

Director: Ben Bolt; Screenplay: Stephen Lowe; based on the novel *Le Rouge et le Noir* by Stendhal; Photography: John McGlashan; Music: Jean-Claude Petit; Producer: Rosalind Wolfes

Ewan is torn between military and Church in pursuit of power in nineteenth-century France.

Being Human ***
USA, 1994, Warner Brothers, 122 mins

Robin Williams (Hector), John Turturro (Lucinnius), Anna Galiena (Beatrice), Vincent D'Onofrio (Priest), Jonathan Hyde (Francisco), Theresa Russell (Narrator), Robert Carlyle (Celtic priest), Ewan McGregor (Alvarez)

Director: Bill Forsyth; Screenplay: Bill Forsyth; Music: Michael Gibbs; Photography: Michael Coulter; Producers: David Puttnam and Robert F. Colesberry

Ewan makes his big-screen debut with a brief appearance as a volunteer hangman in an ill-fated historical epic.

Doggin' Around (TV) **
UK, 1994, BBC, 90 mins

Elliott Gould (Joe Warren), Geraldine James (Sarah Williams), Alun Armstrong (Charlie Foster), Ewan McGregor (Tom Clayton), Liz Smith (Mrs Thompson), Anthony Etherton (Gary Powell), Ronnie Scott (himself), Neil McCaul (Pete)

Director: Desmond Davis; Screenplay: Alan Plater; Photography: Denis Lewiston; Producer: Otto Plaschkes

Ewan plays double bass in Elliott Gould's jazz band.

Kavanagh QC – Nothing But The Truth (TV) **

UK, 1995, Carlton, 101 mins

John Thaw (James Kavanagh), Geraldine James (Eleanor Harker), Alison Steadman (Eve Kendall), Ewan McGregor (David Armstrong), Anna Chancellor (Julia Piper), Elli Garnett (Sophie), Daisy Bates (Kate Kavanagh), Lisa Harrow (Lizzie Kavanagh)

Director: Colin Gregg; Screenplay: Russell Lewis; Created by Ted Childs and Susan Rogers; Photography: Nigel Walters; Music: Anne Dudley; Producer: Chris Kelly

Kavanagh is called upon to defend Ewan on a charge of rape.

Shallow Grave ****

UK, 1995, Channel 4/Figment, 92 mins

Kerry Fox (Juliet Miller), Christopher Eccleston (David Stephens), Ewan McGregor (Alex Law), Ken Stott (Det. Insp. McCall), Keith Allen (Hugo), Colin McCredie (Cameron), Peter Mullan (Andy), John Hodge (DC Mitchell)

Director: Danny Boyle; Screenplay: John Hodge; Photography: Brian Tufano; Music: Simon Boswell; Producer: Andrew Macdonald

Black comedy in which three flatmates discover a corpse and a suitcase full of money.

Blue Juice *

UK, 1995, Channel 4/Skreba, 98 mins

Sean Pertwee (JC), Catherine Zeta Jones (Chloe), Steven Mackintosh (Josh Tambini), Ewan McGregor (Dean Raymond), Peter Gunn (Terry Colcott), Heathcote Williams (Shaper), Colette Brown (Junior), Keith Allen (Mike)

Director: Carl Prechezer; Screenplay: Peter Salmi and Carl Prechezer; Photography: Richard Greatrex; Music: Simon Davison; Producers: Simon Relph and Peter Salmi

An attempt at a British surf movie, with Ewan as a London drug-dealer.

Trainspotting *****

UK, 1996, Channel 4/Figment, 93 mins

Ewan McGregor (Renton), Ewen Bremner (Spud), Jonny Lee Miller (Sick Boy), Robert Carlyle (Begbie), Kelly Macdonald (Diane), Kevin McKidd (Tommy), Peter Mullan (Swanney), James Cosmo (Mr Renton), Eileen Nicholas (Mrs Renton), Susan Vidler (Allison)

Director: Danny Boyle; Screenplay: John Hodge, based on the novel *Trainspotting* by Irvine Welsh; Photography: Brian Tufano; Producer: Andrew Macdonald

Edinburgh low-life ensures cinema high-life for Ewan and co.

Tales from the Crypt – Cold War (TV) **

USA, 1996, HBO, 21 mins (30 including commercial breaks)

Ewan McGregor (Ford), Jane Horrocks (Cammy), Colin Salmon, John Salthouse, Willie Ross, John Kassir

Director: Andy Morahan; Script: Scott Nimerfro, based on a story from the William M. Gaines comic magazine *Tales from the Crypt*; Photography: Robin Vidgeon; Music: J. Peter Robinson; Producer: Gilbert Adler

Zombie love is threatened by the appearance of a handsome vampire.

Emma ***

USA/UK, 1996, Miramax, 120 mins

Gwyneth Paltrow (Emma Woodhouse), Jeremy Northam (Mr Knightley), Toni Collette (Harriet Smith), Alan Cumming (Mr Elton), Greta Scacchi (Mrs Weston), James Cosmo (Mr Weston), Sophie Thompson (Miss Bates), Ewan McGregor (Frank Churchill)

Director: Douglas McGrath; Screenplay: Douglas McGrath, based on the novel *Emma* by Jane Austen; Photography: Ian Wilson; Music: Rachel Portman; Producers: Steven Haft and Patrick Cassavetti

Ewan is a Regency heartthrob in the film of Jane Austen's novel.

Brassed Off ***

UK/USA, 1996, Channel 4/Miramax, 107 mins

Pete Postlethwaite (Danny), Stephen Tompkinson (Phil), Tara Fitzgerald (Gloria), Ewan McGregor (Andy), Jim Carter (Harry), Ken Colley (Greasley), Peter Gunn (Simmo), Melanie Hill (Sandra)

Director: Mark Herman; Screenplay: Mark Herman; Photography: Andy Collins; Music: Trevor Jones; Producer: Steven Abbott

Miners lose their jobs, but regain self-respect through playing with the local brass band.

The Pillow Book **

Netherlands/France/UK, 1996, Kasander & Wigman/ Woodline/Alpha/Channel 4, 126 mins

Vivian Wu (Nagiko), Yoshi Oida (the publisher), Ken Ogata (the father), Hideko Yoshida (the aunt/the maid), Ewan McGregor (Jerome), Judy Ongg (the mother), Ken Mitsuishi (the husband), Yutaka Honda (Hoki)

Director: Peter Greenaway; Screenplay: Peter Greenaway; Photography: Sacha Vierny; Producer: Kees Kasander

Ewan falls for a Japanese calligrapher and lets her use his body as a canvas.

ER – The Long Way Around (TV) ***

USA, 1997, NBC, 45 mins

Julianna Margulies (Carol Hathaway), Ewan McGregor (Duncan), Abraham Benrubi, Currie Graham, Ruth Maleczech, Mason Gamble, Jan Rubes, George Clooney

Director: Christopher Chulack; Screenplay: Lydia Woodward; Created by Michael Crichton; Music: Martin Davich; Theme: James Newton Howard; Photography: Richard Thorpe; Producer: Christopher Chulack

Hospital series reinvents itself as hostage drama to accommodate Ewan.

A Life Less Ordinary ****

UK, 1997, Figment, 102 mins

Ewan McGregor (Robert), Cameron Diaz (Celine), Holly Hunter (O'Reilly), Delroy Lindo (Jackson), Ian Holm (Naville), Ian McNeice (Mayhew), Stanley Tucci (Elliot), Dan Hedaya (Gabriel)

Director: Danny Boyle; Script: John Hodge; Photography: Brian Tufano; Producer: Andrew Macdonald

Ewan is sacked from his job as a cleaner and kidnaps the boss's daughter.

Nightwatch ***

USA, 1998, Miramax, 105 mins

Ewan McGregor (Martin), Nick Nolte (Insp. Cray), Patricia Arquette (Catherine), Josh Brolin (James), Alix Koromzay (Joyce), Lauren Graham (Marie), John C. Reilly (Insp. Davis), Brad Dourif (duty doctor)

Director: Ole Bornedal; Screenplay: Ole Bornedal and Steven Soderbergh, based on the script for *Nattevagten* by Ole Bornedal; Photography: Dan Laustsen; Music: Joachim Holbek; Producer: Michael Obel

Ewan takes a job as night-watchman in a morgue and becomes chief suspect for a series of murders.

Velvet Goldmine *****

UK, 1998, Channel 4/Zenith, 123 mins

Ewan McGregor (Curt Wild), Jonathan Rhys-Meyers (Brian Slade), Toni Collette (Mandy Slade), Christian Bale (Arthur Stuart), Eddie Izzard (Jerry Divine), Emily Woof (Shannon), Michael Feast (Cecil), Micko Westmoreland (Jack Fairy)

Director: Todd Haynes; Screenplay: Todd Haynes; Story by Todd Haynes and James Lyons; Photography: Maryse Alberti; Original music: Carter Burwell; Producer: Christine Vachon

Ewan becomes a pop star in the era of glam rock.

Little Voice ***

USA/UK, 1998, Miramax/Scala

Jane Horrocks (Little Voice), Brenda Blethyn (Mari), Michael
Caine (Ray Say), Ewan McGregor (Billy), Jim Broadbent (Mr
Boo), Philip Jackson (George), Annette Badland (Sadie),
Graham Turner (LV's father)

Director: Mark Herman; Screenplay: Mark Herman, based on
the play *The Rise and Fall of Little Voice* by Jim Cartwright;
Photography: Andy Collins; Original music: John Altman;
Producer: Elizabeth Karlsen

Jane Horrocks reprises her stage role as a shy young woman
with a talent for loud impersonations.

The following films were awaiting release in the UK at the time
of going to press:

The Serpent's Kiss **

UK, Trinity Films, 110 mins

Ewan McGregor (Meneer Chrome), Greta Scacchi (Juliana), Pete
Postlethwaite (Thomas Smithers), Richard E. Grant
(Fitzmaurice), Carmen Chaplin (Thea), Donal McCann
(Physician), Charley Boorman (Secretary), Gerard McSorley
(Mr Galmoy)

Director: Philippe Rousselot; Screenplay: Tim Rose Price; Photography: Jean-François Robin; Music: Goran Bregovic; Producers: Robert Jones, John Battsek, Tim Rose Price

An offbeat thriller in which Ewan may or may not be a
seventeenth-century Dutch garden designer.

Star Wars Episode 1: The Phantom Menace

USA, Lucasfilm

Ewan McGregor (Obi-Wan Kenobi), Jake Lloyd (Anakin
Skywalker), Liam Neeson, Natalie Portman, Samuel L.
Jackson, Terence Stamp, Ian McDiarmid

Director: George Lucas; Screenplay: George Lucas; Photography: David Tattersall; Producer: Rick McCallum

Rogue Trader

UK, Granada

Ewan McGregor (Nick Leeson), Anna Friel (Lisa Leeson), Tom Wu, Nigel Lindsey, Irene Ng, Lee Ross

Director: James Dearden; Screenplay: James Dearden, based on the book *Rogue Trader* by Nick Leeson; Photography: Jean-François Robin; Producers: Paul Raphael, James Dearden and Janette Day

Ewan as Nick Leeson, the man whose dealings broke Barings Bank.

Eye of the Beholder

USA, MDP Worldwide

Ewan McGregor, Ashley Judd, kd lang, Jason Priestley, Genevieve Bujold

Director: Stephan Elliott; Screenplay: Stephan Elliott, based on the novel *The Eye of the Beholder* by Marc Behm; Photography: Guy Dufaux; Producers: Nicolas Clermont and Tony Smith

Ewan also appeared in the short films *Family Style* (1994), *Sleeping with the Fishes* (1996) and *Desserts* (1998), and he had a walk-on role in the television mini-series *Karaoke* (1996). His stage credits are *What the Butler Saw* (1993) at Salisbury Playhouse, and *Little Malcolm and His Struggle Against the Eunuchs* (1998–99) at the Hampstead Theatre and the Comedy Theatre, London. And he was heard in the BBC radio dramas *Tragic Prelude* (1992) and *The Real Thing* (1992). Further details are included in the main text.

Select Bibliography

Books

Austen, Jane: *Emma*, Penguin, London, 1966

Behm, Marc: *The Eye of the Beholder, The Queen of the Night, The Ice Maiden*, Zomba Books, London, 1983

Berney, K.A. (editor): *Contemporary Dramatists*, St James Press, Andover, England, 1993

Binns, John, and Jones, Mark: *The ER Files*, Chameleon, London, 1997

Champlin, Charles: *George Lucas: The Creative Impulse*, Virgin, London, 1992

Finler, Joel W.: *The Hollywood Story*, Mandarin, London, 1992

Groome, Francis H. (editor): *Ordnance Gazeteer of Scotland Volume II*, Grange, Edinburgh, 1882

Henderson, Diana M.: *The Scottish Regiments*, HarperCollins, London, 1993

Hodge, John: *Trainspotting & Shallow Grave*, Faber and Faber, London, 1996

Jones, Graham: *Talking Pictures: Interviews with Contemporary British Film-makers*, British Film Institute, London, 1997

Kronenberger, Louis: *The Extraordinary Mr Wilkes*, New English Library, London, 1974

Lucas, George: *Star Wars: A New Hope*, Faber and Faber, London, 1997

Mackie, J.D.: *A History of Scotland*, Penguin, London, 1964

Marshall, Michael (editor): *The Book of Comic and Dramatic Monologues*, Elm Tree Books, London, 1981

Potter, Dennis: *Lipstick on Your Collar*, Faber and Faber, London, 1993

Potter, Dennis: *Karaoke: Cold Lazarus*, Faber and Faber, London, 1996

Prebble, John: *The Lion in the North*, Penguin, London, 1981

Robertson, Patrick: *The Guinness Book of Movie Facts & Feats*, Guinness, London, 1993

Sinclair, Olga: *Gretna Green: A Romantic History*, Unwin Hyman, London, 1989

Smout, T.C.: *A Century of the Scottish People 1830–1950*, Fontana, London, 1987

Stendhal: *Scarlet and Black*, Penguin, London, 1953

Stoppard, Tom: *The Real Thing*, Faber and Faber, London, 1982

Tibballs, Geoff: *Kavanagh QC*, Carlton, London, 1996

van Gelder, Peter: *Offscreen, Onscreen*, Aurum, London, 1990

Welsh, Irvine: *Trainspotting*, Minerva, London, 1994

Articles

Bloom, Phillipa: The Anticipation is Killing Me, *Premiere*, London, March 1996

Bradberry, Grace: French Women are Difficult ... *The Times*, London, 13 October 1997

Brodie, John: Off Kilter, *Premiere*, Los Angeles, November 1997

Charity, Tom: Have You Seen This Man?, *Time Out*, London, 2 October 1996

Edwards, Gavin: Ewan McGregor Straight Up, *Details*, New York, November 1997

Eimer, David: From Cynical Yuppie to Smack Addict and Now Costume Dandy ... *Scotland on Sunday*, Edinburgh, 15 September 1996

Fowler, Rebecca: DIY Hollywood, *Sunday Times*, London, 8 May 1994

Fulton, Rick: Ewan Feud with Sean, *Daily Record*, Glasgow, 17 September 1998

Gibb, Eddie: Uncle Denis, The *Scotsman*, Edinburgh, 3 January 1998

Grant, Brigit: We Were All Shafted, *Daily Mirror*, London, 31 October 1996

Gritten, David: Something Has Survived Baby, *Los Angeles Times*, 27 July 1997

Grundy, Gareth: Hey! Hey! We're the Junkies, *Neon*, London, February 1998

Heath, Chris: The Scot Report, *Neon*, London, October 1997

Hunter, Allan: Being Human, *Sight and Sound*, London, August 1994

Lucas, George: Prequel Update: George Lucas (Q&A), *Star Wars: The Official Magazine*, London, April/May 1998

McGrath, Douglas: Raising Jane, *Premiere*, Los Angeles, September 1996

Maude, Collette: Ewan McGregor, *Premiere*, London, January 1995

Middleton, Chris: Gallic Charmer, *Radio Times*, London, 30 October 1993

Moir, Jan: Your Money or Your Life, *Harpers & Queen*, London, October 1998

Morgan, Kathleen: Friel Good Factor, *List*, Edinburgh, 6 March 1998

Morrison, Alan: Doctoring the Script, *List*, Edinburgh, 16 December 1994

Morrison, Alan: Out of the Ordinary, *List*, Edinburgh, 24 October 1997

Morrison, Margaret: Sex and Drugs ... *Daily Mail*, London, 14 January 1997

Mowe, Richard: No Lone Star, *Scotland on Sunday*, Edinburgh, 19 October 1997

Owen, Frank: Needles and Spins, *Village Voice*, New York, 30 July 1996

Patterson, Sylvie: Cock of the North, *Face*, London, November 1996

Pendreigh, Brian: Dig It, the *Scotsman*, Edinburgh, 17 August 1994

Pendreigh, Brian: Primal Screen, the *Scotsman*, Edinburgh, 8 February 1996

Pendreigh, Brian: This Boy's Life So Ordinary, the *Scotsman*, Edinburgh, 13 October 1997

Perenson, Melissa J: Institutionalizing Star Wars, *Sci-Fi Entertainment*, Reston, Virginia, February 1998

Raphael, Paul: Reel Diaries: Film Producer, *Total Film*, Bath, England, April 1998

Ross, Marion: The New Hope, *Film Review*, London, March 1998

Shelley, Jim: Charmed, I'm Sure, *Guardian*, London, 4 October 1997

Svetkey, Benjamin: It Had to Be Ewan, *Entertainment Weekly*, New York, 13 June 1997

Verity, Edward: The Odious Culture That Killed Leah, *Daily Mail*, London, 9 February 1996

Villiers, Sara: Reel Lives, *Herald*, Glasgow, 14 January 1995

Ward, Chris: Dashing New Blade, *Today*, London, 2 November 1993

Westbrook, Caroline: First Class Return, *Empire*, London, March 1996

In the course of my researches I read or consulted hundreds of books, articles and reviews. The above lists include only the most important sources of information and those that may be of particular interest to the public for further reading. One printed source which was of enormous value was the press books and production notes, issued by film companies to the media at the time of a film's release. Although these were never 'published' as such, the British Film Institute does maintain a collection, which is available for public inspection at its library in London. I am indebted also to the *Morrisonian* school magazine, to the *Strathearn Herald* over more than 30 years (and to Jenny Pendreigh for meticulously going through them), and to *Screen International* trade magazine, for box-office and production information.

Index